THE SCOTTISH
MOUNTAINEERING
CLUB JOURNAL

| Vol. XXXV | 1994 | No. 185 |

UAMHAS!

By Robert Davidson

This article won 1st Prize in the 1992 Mountaineering Council of Scotland's Mountain Article Competition, open to all MC of S members and members of associated clubs. There are cash prizes, none of which, naturally, can fully compensate for the kudos of SMCJ publication. Information from the MC of S.

AT THIS moment I am taking my ease just below the summit of Glas Leathad Mor, the greatest part of Ben Wyvis. Perhaps summit is too pointed a word since the trig point is at the highest undulation on a long, broad ridge. Broad enough to drive a four-wheel along – which has been done more than once. Leathad is a better word, being a slope or declivity. True, for it falls away at a steep, but safe, angle below my feet. Away to the right is a distinctive bump named Tom a' Choinnich with, between the tops, a bona fide bealach, formerly trafficked on a regular basis. To the left is An Cabar, the most usual route of ascent and my way up today. An Cabar means 'the antler' and if you make your approach from Strath Bran just a little imagination will pick out the downturned headgear of a battling stag. It also means 'roof timber' but I choose to take the romantic view.

It must be said at the outset that I love this mountain, but, boy, this is not true of everyone! On my way up I met a fit-looking English chap on his way down. 'Nice day,' said I.

'Certainly is,' he replied. 'Pity you can't say the same about the hill.' Seeing me prickle he added, 'Well, it is pretty dull, you have to admit.' For the next 10 minutes of descent he had my hot, resentful gaze on the back of his head. Balding, I happily recall.

People come up here for all kinds of reasons, but mainly so they can put a tick on their Munro list. Then, great, they won't have to come back. That 'great', is theirs incidentally. It's not that I'm glad to see their backs disappearing down An Cabar for good. No, sir. The idea is going around that this is a boring hill.

Excuse me while I beat my forehead with my palm. That's better! People can be dull and so can their words. Any politician's words might be boring, so might these, the collected works of Robert Ludlum could be fatally so, but not a hill or loch. Vocabulary like this implies that the hill can in some way be consumed. Yet it was here when our ancestors were grubbing for roots around where Kenya is now, and will still be standing when we are reduced to little piles of irradiated carbon.

Sadly, this concept has been put forward in that wonderfully entertaining body of work, Scottish hill literature, and by its most venerated contributor. Stand up W.H. Murray! Was it you who wrote: 'This is one of the dullest of all Scottish mountains' . . . ? Oh, yes it was! However, since you also gave us *Undiscovered Scotland* , justice must be tempered with mercy. Go, memorise the first two chapters of the *Scarlatti Inheritance,* and sin no more.

Another time I traversed over An Cabar to Dingwall, taking in the summit on the way. It was misty October and all was grey. I ate my frozen piece up here by the cairn and headed back towards Sron na Feola, congratulating myself on discovering a new form of madness. Suddenly, a ghostly figure materialised before me. It was wearing shorts and a vest and had a sweat band round its forehead: 'Is it much further, mate?' I continued feeling really quite sane. This question: 'Is it much further?' is often asked up here in the mist. One winter Tony and I made this trip. A big works' outing was changing in the car park and among them was an old friend with his wife and daughter. Well, Tony is as fit as all who get out so, with me trailing in his wake, he soon pulled clear of the bunch.

Up on top we fought our way through a chilling wind to here. After a few disdainful comments (Like the view? Nice shade of grey.) we headed back. About halfway along we met my friend and his family leaning into this Arctic gale. The little girl was in the middle. She had ear muffs on under her beret and wore a nice blouson jacket. Wind-blown rain had so saturated her clothes we could see the blue of her tights through her white jeans. She did not utter a complaining word. I loved her. Then came the question: 'Is it much further?' We got ourselves in front of them and said, no, it was not much further. Groups of two and three were walking past, looking straight ahead. My friend has a tremendously competitive nature and others were getting to the cairn. His face worked as he struggled internally. Eventually, he said: 'I think we had better go down.' There was something of reluctance in his manner. He looked at me and said: 'It's the wee one.' It was important that his reason for going down was understood. It was the wee one, not him. Something twisted in my gut.

As usual Tony was master of the situation. He got his face close to the wee girl. 'Cold, Miss?' She nodded and in a moment was in a Gore-Tex jacket that reached to her ankles and a pair of gloves that hung down past her knees. A toorie bonnet and a bar of chocolate finished the business and before too long, going with the wind, we were in the lee of the hill and below the cloud. All was well.

Back up here, though, the great thing is natural beauty. I mean landscape beauty. This thing produced by the hills and the water and the way the light plays on them that is not simply looked upon but reached out for. This thing that induces silence. Nor does it only come in through the eyes – blind Sydney Scroggie of the Words is proof of that. It is encompassing, the right environment for the human heart and known when experienced.

This is the way it is today and all of life seems to be in just sitting here with a sandwich and a cup of tea. Over there is Torridon. Liathach! An Teallach is a bit closer and to the right and that is where most folks' eyes linger, but straight ahead are the Fannichs and they are what draw me. Oh, the good days I've had over there. And look, out at the Torridon end, that patch of blue poking round An Coileachan is the neb of Loch Fannich. Nice!

The first time I got this view I was with my dog. Finn used to sit on the edge of the hill and look at the view. Some people choose not to believe that but it's true. He did it again that day when we got to Tom a' Choinnich and we enjoyed a tin of orange together looking down onto Loch nan Druidean. I didn't know it then but there is a lot of heartache in that view.

Away back when the glens were still well populated the people upped and drove the sheep that were to displace them out of the Straths. As they moved south others joined them, driving the growing white wave down through Sutherland and Ross to Loch Morie – just over the next hill after Tom a' Choinnich. Here there was good grazing so they stayed a while. This was in what is known as the Year of the Sheep.

Sometimes I wonder if that was when the hill got its name. Wyvis is from Uamhas (that is oo-ah-vas), the Gaelic word for fear. You see, three companies of the 42nd Regiment had been force-marched from Fort George and were resting not far away. Along with them was a goodly representation of the local gentry and 20 or so urban collaborators from my home town. Fortunately, the drovers got wind of this and scattered, so when the soldiers advanced up Strath Ruisdale all they found were smoking embers and thousands of milling, bleating sheep. I say, fortunately, because there is no doubt the drovers would have been eviscerated had they not fled. The Black Watch are no wimps. They . . .

A roaring noise of incredible volume has broken into these thoughts. I am in no doubt as to what it is and I know that to see it I must look well ahead of the sound. Over there! Above Loch Luichart, less than a 100m up is a tiny black dart going like a bat out of hell for Strath Bran. They come in pairs, so where is his partner? Wow! This one has veered round An Cabar, wobbling at the extremity of his turn. He is just below me, well ahead of his own sound. I can see into the cockpit, see the pilot move in his seat and, look, poking out below the wings – is this one armed? In an instant he is gone, his engine noise follows, and I find I am on my feet with my sandwich pulped between my fingers.

Sit down, man. Breath deep or something. I take off my boots and sit with them wedged behind me to prop up my bad back. That's better. What can't be cured must be endured.

To speak of the military-industrial complex is no longer quite the thing. People look sideways at you. Ah-ha! One of those. As a matter of fact, I too think, it is something of an outdated term. The military makes its presence felt clearly enough but it can be difficult to identify much in the way of industry in these empty glens. It was the Northmen who first depredated the great forests. Iron smelters and ship building did for the rest. Sheep displaced the people who worked the land and the land has paid for it. Industrial tourism is everywhere, though.

The great thing to realise is that all this takes from the land without giving back. Accept that as a system and you accept its morality. Do that, and you clear the names of some real monsters – Cumberland, Sellar, Brocket. Right now, Nirex is straining to get in.

Maybe I shouldn't get so excited. After all, this is still a glorious view. Everyone says so and everyone is correct. All of it so beautiful and, compared to wherever they come from, so empty. In lay-bys and picnic spots all over the Highlands the couples, they are usually couples, look into each other's eyes and on all their lips forms the same question: 'How can we make money out of this? Buy just a little place – do bed and breakfast. Buy a bigger place – farm sheep.'

Outbidding the locals is no problem. Now more than ever before they ask: 'How can we fleece other tourists and fatten up our account in the Leeds?'

This is bartering the gift. Worse, dressing it up and selling it off as dross. The Outdoors? Plant it with ski-tows, holiday cabins! Gaelic culture? Tartan drawers in a can! What it needs, of course, is development. That would improve things. So far though, the process seems mighty like destruction. As is now well known, God made the Highlands sylvan. Improvers have developed it into a wet desert.

Here cometh the message. Hearken unto the words of Jeremiah: If the development of appreciation is not put before all others then all that is natural and native to the Highlands; all that grows out of the land including its humanity and lifestyles; all that stands tall and straight and strides out to take its place in the world, will surely die.

Yet there is something we can take with us when we leave. You know, one of the hardest things to accept when we try to put our feelings into words is that just about all we are capable of has certainly been articulated before, and better.

Not long ago some people got together on the Dingwall side of the hill to erect a monument to the writer Neil Gunn. It is a standing stone, some carvings, a few trees by a small loch. More than anything else, though, it is the wild place itself that points the way into Gunn's work. On opening day they ran buses up, a piper played and everyone got to walk around. It is a participatory sort of place. Some words of Gunn's went through my head and when I got home I took out the right book, half by chance, and memorised them. Right now I am going to recite them out loud. The heat of the sun is on my neck and I can feel the tufty grass under my thighs. No one is coming so here goes . . . yet I remain convinced that at the core of every normal man and woman there lingers these days a desire for peace and renewal, however fugitively and whether actually indulged or not.

It's the word renewal that goes home. We are like the land in this respect, only so much can be taken out without something going back. Or life shrivels from within.

One time I came up here with a big bunch. There must have been about 60 people. The idea was to watch the sun go down on the shortest night of the year. Truthfully, this was not such a great idea. People who had never been on a hill before set out at 11p.m. in overcoats and town shoes. Of course, the party was soon strung out and some of us had to drop back. There were plenty of rest stops, and during one, about three-quarters up An Cabar, a certain quality in the air made itself felt. It was still. Distant voices become unusually distinct. Vision becomes clearer too and when a small cloud came creeping round Tom a' Choinnich at a level well below us the night took on a sort of fey aspect.

By the time we got to the top, cloud had gathered all around, and was closing up below. Soon we were in the middle of a cloud sea and the sun was dropping down onto the horizon like a big, golden ball, more or less to the north. Mountains jutted up like rocky islands in a placid ocean – Ben Hope, Foinavon, Suilven, the Fannichs. Away to the south the Cairngorms were an undiscovered continent.

People said little, all gathering near the cairn as the sun first touched then dipped below the horizon. The blue of the sky deepened slightly. It got no darker. When it bounced up again the crowd gave a self-conscious cheer. Everyone broke open their food and a flask of spirits was passed round. We were up for eight transcendental hours.

I look at my watch and see that if I don't move soon I'll be up for that sort of time again. Two hours too many for this great boring lump! Pulling the boot support from the small of my back induces the usual stab of pain at that damaged disc. Ah, it's worth it. Boots on and rucksack hauled up I tap the triangulation pillar for luck. That reminds me, these things aren't used any more. It's time they were gone.

Along to Tom a' Choinnich I think, then down by the Allt na Bana-Morair for a change. Every so often we need a change.

COIRE LAGGAN

From Black Cuillin, lost, we stumbled
In black air down into Coire Laggan
And gasped: 'Thank Christ'
As gabbro gave way to turf.

No stars, no wind
Gradient was all our guide
Till an abrupt edge;
Brown grass bowing before blackness.

I crawled forward, blinded
Thighs ploughing peat
And breathed on the abyss.

Trembling under my breath
Black water wrinkled
Six inches beneath.

Jack Hastie.

THE MUNROS MY WAY

By W. P. Maxwell

THERE USED to be a 'post' box (a biscuit tin) under the cairn on Carn Liath (Beinn a' Ghlo) – I mean 50 years ago, when I was a boy. The idea was to leave a post card stamped and addressed to oneself, and the next climber up would write on it a suitable message, and post it on. This is my abiding memory of climbing – what I didn't know then, aged nine – was my first Munro. No question of cars, or even bikes, in those days, just a long, dusty walk up Glen Fender from our house at Bridge of Tilt. Later in the War came the ascent of the two other Munros in the group. Memories of these happy days returned recently when I revisited the area to climb Carn Chlamain and Beinn Dearg. Beautiful Perthshire, indeed, and although one may castigate the builders of the new A9 in some respects, one cannot but compliment them on the views of the Tilt hills which the road opens up.

As I grew up, I went on hill walking expeditions frequently, and did some modest work on rock and snow, without considering the possibility, or the need, to climb all the Munros listed in my first copy of the Tables (1929 edition). In fact, I tended to return to the same hills time and again, rather than to seek out new peaks. So favourite stomping grounds from an Edinburgh base were Ben Vorlich and Stuc a' Chroin, Ben More and Stobinian and Ben Lawers.

Holidays with my parents, prior to National Service and university, took me farther afield. The first of these was to Skye – a memorable rail journey to Kyle (the family car was still up on blocks after the end of the War) and then the tremendous experience of the sail to Portree on the Loch Nevis, a seemingly huge ship. We saw nothing of the island for 19 of the 20 days of our holiday, so bad was the weather. However, on the other day, the skies cleared with dramatic speed, and I was able to see the Cuillin in all their sublime beauty. I remember vividly our cycle run from Portree to the west coast at Bracadale, then down to Sligachan where we marvelled at the well-known view that brought Norman Collie back to spend his last days near the mountains he knew so well.

My first Cuillin summit was Bruach na Frithe – not in boots – but in a pair of old golf shoes. You can imagine what the gabbro did to these. However, the bonus was that their fate induced my parents to come up with the necessary cash for me to buy my first pair of nailed boots – clinkers, tricounis and all.

I shall never forget that first prospect of the Cuillin Ridge, a landscape that I still find as thrilling now as I did then. The unique abrasiveness of the rock, the pinnacles and aretes combine to fascinate all who come to grips with the ridge and its spectacular coires. Successive visits enabled me to climb Sgurr nan Gillean, first by the Tourist Route, and later by the Pinnacle Ridge; Sgurr na Banachdich, on a broiling day, and Sgurr Dearg, but not the Inaccessible Pinnacle. Some of my most vivid memories of these early days are of the extraordinary effects produced by mist boiling up out of the coires and parting to reveal sensational views of Coruisk, or the Red Hills, or the mainland. Above all, I think, it is the proximity to the sea which adds much to the beauty of the Cuillin and indeed all of the mountains near the West Coast. I never find here the dullness of panorama that can be experienced farther east.

This leads me happily to the Cairngorms which I began to explore when I moved to Aberdeen in 1969. Previously, I had climbed Cairn Gorm, walking from Glenmore Lodge. It was quite a long trek, and, if wishing to walk across to Macdhui, as well, one had to leave very early in the morning. How things have changed today when one can motor to 2500ft and begin walking with more than half the work done. Truly, the wilderness is shrinking.

The impact of the Cairngorms stems from their vastness and their superb northern coires. It lies in the magical setting of the lochans, and the springs of Dee on the Braeriach plateau. My base in Aberdeen enabled me to climb all the main group, and all the others neighbouring it. A great thrill was my first outing with the Cairngorm Club. Our route took us over Cairn Gorm, down the stiff descent of Coire Raibert to Loch Avon, past the Shelter Stone, up over Beinn Mheadhoin, Derry Cairngorm and down to Derry Lodge where we halted briefly before walking the last tedious miles to the bus at the Linn of Dee. This was a high-level walk of a kind I hadn't previously experienced, but as I discovered, typical of what can be done in this terrain. The round of Loch Muick, the Braeriach-Cairn Toul walk, or the cirque of Glen Geusachan all illustrate the spacious beauty and contrasting dangers of plateau walking in bad weather when navigation, and indeed survival, can be major problems.

Somewhere in the 1980s a change occurred in my thinking about the Munros. What I mean is that, I actually began to think of mountains as Munros which is probably a dangerous, even silly thing to do. Why this happened isn't entirely clear, but, reading Hamish Brown and Martin Moran had something to do with it. And then someone, friend or foe, presented me with a copy of the SMC publication, *The Munros*. At this point in 1986 I had climbed about 100 on the list – beyond the point of no return as Hamish puts it, and he's certainly proved right in my case. Better, or worse still, from the same donor came, soon afterwards, the Munro map AND coloured pins! Thus was I persuaded as I viewed the map at breakfast each morning. Outings, with colleagues and friends were organised on the basis of which new area next. These often involved lengthy journeys since I was based in Aberdeenshire, but somehow this didn't seem to matter because my great quest was taking me to the hills and glens I had never previously visited. Especially enjoyable was ridge walking in the Glens – Shiel, Affric and Strathfarrar. Yes, it was nice to be able to say that one had 'done X Munros' in a day, but of course, number has little to do with the quality of experience. The most memorable days are those when you have given your all physically, or when bad weather has suddenly relented to allow stunning views, or when the company of your fellows has been specially felicitous.

Sometimes, it may be a combination of all of these, as in the case of a boat trip up Loch Mullardoch to attack Beinn Fhionnlaidh and its higher neighbours, or of my first experience on a mountain bike – indeed on any bike in the previous 25 years – in Glen Affric to Alltbeithe so that the round of Sgurr nan Ceathreamhnan could be accomplished. On this latter occasion, my companion was a 1973 Munroist, who had had recent heart bypass surgery. The day, highly strenuous for me, must have been almost intolerable for him. However, he seemed to have suffered no lasting damage, and was able to stroll up Am Faochogach the following day.

Slowly, but surely, as the 1980s progressed, my knowledge of the hills west of the Great Glen increased. Old friends kept appearing on distant horizons as new summits were reached. Characteristic outlines drew the eye again and again. How unmistakable they are – Bidean Choire Sheasgaich, Mullach Fraoch-choire, Sgurr na Ciche to name but three. To get to them dominated holiday planning. Knoydart, most inaccessible of all, became a top priority. So it was we went to Doune, where the Robinsons are happily ensconced, opposite Mallaig on Loch Nevis. During a moist, midge week in August, we climbed the three Munros and, poor though the weather was, we experienced something of the majestic quality of Knoydart topography. One of the pleasures of having completed the Munros will be to return freely to very special places like this. If you take the Robinsons' beautiful chalet, which sleeps 12, you will not be disappointed – stunning views of Skye of course, magnificent cuisine from your hostess and the company of your friends. What more can you ask for?

However, the view of the Cuillin did remind me that I had yet to complete the Munros there, not least the Inaccessible Pinnacle. This, the following year, was certainly one of the greatest thrills of my life. I hadn't had a rope on for 25 years, so my son dictated some practice on the Aberdeenshire coastal crags. This done, and after two attempts aborted due to bad weather, we finally got a good day for the round of Coire Lagan. How it lived up to our expectations. There can be few views so dramatic as those from the Pinnacle or Sgurr Alasdair. The scrambling involved isn't particularly demanding, even for someone who can be described as of high middle age, and the holds on the Pinnacle are generous. Nevertheless, there is the exposure.

We were fortunate that day to have it to ourselves. How different when I returned to the Cuillin this year to climb Sgurr Dubh Mhor on a gloriously hot day in late May. Round Loch Coire Ghrunnda on every visible crag there were people. Between Sgurr Dubh na Da Bheinn and Sgurr Dubh Mhor there were some two dozen of us. It was literally the case that we had to queue to reach the acute top of the latter. At the Thearlaich-Dubh gap, there were delays of 45 minutes for those waiting to cross. There is much to rejoice in this growing popularity of the outdoors, but as I've moved closer to the magic 277, I've wondered more and more about the problems caused by the pressure of numbers on the hills.

How is sufficient funding to be found to counter the problem of erosion? Will future generations of Munroists have to pay a levy for the privilege of walking the hills – an unthinkable thought, or, is it? How are the increasingly large numbers of anti-social walkers to be dealt with? We can't cope effectively with litter louts in our towns, how much more difficult to deal with them on the hills. And then there are the vandals who desecrate bothies, and cause damage to other property. Perhaps, like me, you read of and were appalled by the case where a bridge (specially built by the Affric landowner for stalkers) was dismantled for firewood by some walkers staying overnight at Alltbeithe. Small wonder indeed that the proprietor, a very reasonable man whom I've met, thought seriously about burning down the youth hostel to save himself further inconvenience and financial loss.

Another problem, and a growing one, is how to cope with the intrusive mountain bike. It can be a valuable asset if used sensibly as I discovered when in Glenfinnan, but certain estates, such as Letterewe and Fisherfield, feel forced to ban them altogether. I am sure this is the correct decision here, otherwise this area, like Knoydart, one of the last wildernesses in Scotland, will lose much of its remoteness. My overnight expedition to climb the six Munros would have been much less memorable if I hadn't walked every last inch of the way. This 'epic' was made possible by my recent retirement, enabling me to make the most of any 'guaranteed' fair weather. Sleeping out overnight without camping gear demanded the most optimistic forecast that Ian McAskill could manage, and for once he got it right. I left Kernsary at 14.15, stood on the summit of Ruadh Stac Mor at 21.00, and saw the sunset from A' Mhaighdean at 22.00. Then a quick descent to the Beinn Tarsuinn col where I bivvied at a large boulder. It was a perfect June night – no rain or wind and no darkness, only the most ethereal, roseate glow over An Teallach as I dozed amid many grazing deer.

By 04.00, I was ready to move, semi-fortified by a flaskful of tepid sausages and beans. At 06.00, I was at the summit of Tarsuinn where the temperature was already climbing too high for comfort. Along the ridge to Beinn a' Chlaidheimh, thirst became an increasing hazard. Only in the shade of the huge cairn on Sgurr Ban, where I halted for half-an-hour, did

I gain respite from the remorseless sun, and only after the long descent to the Abhainn Nid did I reach water. Till then every watercourse had been dry. Even this stream, often uncrossable, was scarcely flowing, but there was enough water to quench thirst and bathe very tired feet. I was thus sufficiently refreshed to make the final push past Shenavall and down to Corrie Halloch by 16.00. Truly, one of the great days in my life on the hills – breath-taking scenery, new perspectives, solitude, colour, and an immense sense of achievement. The six Munros were almost incidental.

Retirement enabled me to plan flexibly for the 'conquest' of the final 50 Munros. Somehow, I felt that I should accomplish this in 1993 since, without any apparent effort, I had reached the age of 60. So, from March onwards, I had been working my way from north to south over some of the finest peaks in Scotland – such as Sgurr Fiona, Slioch, Beinn Sgritheall. I stayed for a week at Cluanie, a weekend at Fort William, and a few days at Fersit for Loch Ossian. By this stage, I had decided that my final Munro would be Meall nan Tarmachan because its accessibility would enable friends to gather easily for a modest celebration. This decision made and invitations distributed I found myself facing self-imposed deadlines to get into areas such as Glen Etive and Glenfinnan before stalking began. Typical summer weather didn't help at all, and I have been disappointed more than once, especially on Buachaille Etive Mor and Aonach Eagach where I had prayed for warm dry rock.

I look forward to returning to these memorable places (let's face it, many Munros are distinctly unmemorable). I shall go back to summits like Sgurr na Ciche which was mist enshrouded to my great disappointment. What I certainly won't do is work my way through the Tables again. It is still a flawed list – if An Teallach deserved a second Munro, (as it surely did), why not Beinn Eighe? Can it be right to include Beinn Tulaichean but not Beinn Dearg (Torridon) or Beinn Dearg Mor (Fisherfield) and so on?

I am pleased to have done the Munros once, albeit that it's taken 50 years. I've learned much, including a good deal about myself. I've met interesting people, and made lasting friendships. I've experienced the delights of life in tents, bivouacs, bunk houses and bothies (ah, the characteristic odour of drying socks at Culra.) and I've seen nature at first hand in all its infinite variety.

I've witnessed the revolution technology has wrought on equipment. Rubber-soled boots, Yeti gaiters, cagoules alleged to be waterproof and condensation defiant, crampons – all of these are a far cry from golf shoes on Bruach na Frithe. And I am quite bewildered by the array of hardware which today's rock climber carries. However, I have to admit that my suspicion of the benefits of modern technology marks me out as rather old-fashioned. Perhaps, if I'd been wearing crampons in Gardyloo Gully in April, 1949, I wouldn't have fallen about 1000ft as I did – but that's another story.

CASTLES IN THE AIR

By Graham E. Little

A CRY FROM the gully above jerks my attention. A body is accelerating down the hard névé – out of control. I stare, mesmerised, as it ricochets hopelessly towards me. It is Patricia.

Instinctively I crampon a few steps towards the line of fall as the rag doll-like form shoots out of the narrow confines of the gully. With just one chance, my free hand snatches at her blurred harness, the other axe swinging into the hard snow.

The wrench spins me around. We are falling together. Frantically I brake with one extended arm but the axe bounces out. We are sliding towards the steep bare rock slabs at the base of the snow field. Digging in crampon points, I grind the axe adze back into the crystal surface. We are slowing. I watch with fascination as axe-gouged spurts of snow glint in the sunlight. We stop; all is silent, my arm feels dislocated, the snow is red with blood.

It was Saturday, March 20, 1971. Patricia was caught up in my passion for the mountains. As we strolled across the frozen bogs of the Allt a' Mhuilinn, I was pleased that she was with me, yet frustrated that we must tackle an easy route when conditions looked so promising.

Ben Nevis was my other lover, not so warm, not so tender, yet that day displaying her magnificence in the crisp air; dark ribs, walls and buttresses sharply defined by a skeletal network of snow gullies, ribbons and patches. I reeled off a litany of names, evoking the very essence of Scottish winter climbing.

Although Patricia had only tackled a couple of winter routes before, I convinced myself that she could handle The Castle. Avoiding the bare slabs on the right, we cramponed up the steepening snow fan that fell from the twin chutes of the North and South Castle Gullies. Between them lay the dark triangular buttress of The Castle. Although the snow and ice that draped and dribbled over the crag was in perfect condition, the early onset of Spring had left much rock bare; the snow bank below The Castle receding to reveal an ice glazed overhanging wall. It looked too hard.

As I unpacked our gear I hatched a selfish plan. While I soloed The

Castle, Patricia could solo South Castle Gully, then we could rendezvous on the plateau. She was apprehensive but I assured her that the gully was only Grade I – a straight-forward snow slope. 'You can manage it,' I reassured her. She smiled and I felt confident.

She watched my urgent muscling over the overhang, then started her own climb. I stopped for a moment to warm my hands and admired her long dark hair tied back with a turquoise silk scarf. I regretted that I hadn't been able to borrow a helmet for her.

After the overhang, the slabby rocks of The Castle were masked with a thin blanket of old hard snow. I ran up them with a freedom that only the solo climber could know. As The Castle steepened, I concentrated on every move: each crampon kick, every front point nick, each clumsy rock hold glazed black with ice, mittened hands making a transient union; the body's tension and balance completely attuned to that primitive dance simply called climbing.

A short wall stopped me. Ice dribbled down it like wax from a candle. Pinching a brittle flow, crampon points scratching a shallow edge, I teetered between safe ground and commitment. This state of limbo was momentary as I crossed the barrier and climbed on via grooves, corners and chimneys through the upper ramparts.

Cutting through a curl of crusted snow, I pulled out on to the plateau expecting the welcome of a smile but I was alone. It was a windless day and the silence was immense. I walked to the top of South Castle Gully and sat waiting and thinking. Time was gauged only by my watch. Contemplation soon gave way to impatience. How could she take so long over an easy snow gully? Impatience was replaced by concern. I started to reverse down the gully.

After about 200ft of descent I encountered a short, steep ice pitch. This shouldn't be here said my inner voice. Patricia's crampon marks were visible below but it was obvious that she hadn't climbed the pitch. I cursed loudly.

With some difficulty, I step cut down the ice bulge then carried on down the narrow gully. Nearing its mouth, I called her name, my voice echoing on the frosted Castle walls yet finding no reply. I traversed to our starting ledge at the foot of The Castle, dumped my sac, helmet and jacket and tried to think clearly. There could be only two options; either she was tackling North Castle Gully or she had carried on down.

Taking only my axe, I crossed to the mouth of North Castle Gully. It was empty but there were crampon marks. Reasoning that by then she must have reached the top, I turned to return to the sac.

A cry from the gully above jerks my attention . . .

Patricia's body is crumpled and still. Blood pours from a gaping head wound. I experience a moment of hopeless despair and remorse. I am responsible for this! I am lying next to her feeling her body heat yet I am also detached, a curious stranger observing these dramatic series of events.

On my first attempt to stand we slip a little further. With a strength born of necessity I ram my ice axe shaft into the compacted surface then clip her harness into its wrist loop. She moves one arm and groans. I crouch over her stunned by the seriousness of our situation. Blood still wells from the great gash in her scalp, plastering dark hair to her pale face. 'I'm sorry', I fatuously declare. She stares at me blankly as one accosted by a stranger. 'Where am I?' her disembodied voice enquires. 'I must go and get the gear', I explain desperately trying to control my shivering. She fails to understand, her vacant expression showing neither fear, pain nor comprehension.

As I crampon cautiously up the snowfield, a pall of guilt envelops me. I have sacrificed a special friend and lover upon the altar of my own ego. It is unforgivable.

Collecting my gear and Patricia's lost axe, I descend to the motionless figure, stranded in the centre of this great snow shield. Tiny moving figures are visible on the path far below but whistle-blowing and shouting fails to attract their attention. We are on our own.

As I bandage her head (thanking providence that I have a First Aid kit with me) it becomes clear that I must not leave her until she is on safe ground. I wipe the blood from her eyes, tears blur mine.

Using an axe belay, I commence a series of lowers; descending to her at the end of each to move her to a secure stance at the start of the next lower. In this manner we make slow, methodical progress, avoiding the rock slabs and eventually reaching flat ground below the crag.

It is late afternoon. Making her as comfortable as possible, I run, heart thumping, to the CIC Hut. I blurt out my story to the first person that I meet. Using the emergency telephone they contact the mountain rescue in Fort William and the well-rehearsed rescue procedure is under way.

Returning to Patricia, with some hut residents carrying the stretcher, I am completely numb; neither feeling tired nor energetic, neither depressed nor elated, just numb. She is as I left her, half sitting, insulated from the cold ground by my jacket and rucksack.

We spoke but I cannot remember of what. She lapsed into occasional sleep, induced by the motion of the stretcher. Our numbers swelled as the rescue team joined us, rendering my help completely superfluous. I again become detached from the course of events.

'And what climbing experience did Miss . . . have', the business-like Police Constable asks me. I am too tired to lie and answer: 'Not much.' He frowns and scribbles on a form. 'Now tell me, in your own words (as if there were any other), just how this accident happened.' It has taken me 21 years to remember.

DARKNESS AND LIGHT

By I.H.M. Smart

This note describes a solo flight from Riverside Airfield, Dundee, made late on a sombre winter's afternoon. Flying provides the same sort of controlled excitement as exposed climbing but without the physical effort: it is ideal exercise for a brain trapped in an ageing body, a sort of armchair exposure to the E-numbers; it generates the same creative tension as the mind tries to balance the aesthetics of the ambient situation against the gravitational imperatives of the real world.

THIS IS the story of a flight over Beinn a' Ghlo late on a still, February day. The sky was overcast with layers of blues, greys and gunmetals leading into the cave of the advancing night. The snows of the Grampians, backlit in the dim light, glowed above the dark glens. Gloom and mystery reigned over familiar country. Heading into desolation and winter darkness grips you with apprehension and exhilaration. Maybe this desire to put yourself to the test, to explore the unknown and risk passing the point of no return is keyed into the nervous system. Back in the Palaeolithic it was probably a daily necessity, a *sine qua non* for survival and the bane of your existence. In these luxurious times frolicking about under the paw of the unknown is a form of play, a toy metaphor for the bored mind to peep behind to send a tonic shiver down the spine. Maybe in the somewhat over-civilised situation I am describing, the psyche saw it as a metaphor for death, a sort of training run, a reconnaissance into territory from which this time you could return if you found it more than you could handle. North is a metaphorically safe direction to explore because, as everyone knows, come summer the darkness will turn into brilliant continuous daylight, everything will be young again and spring will return to the step. Be such speculation as it may, the little plane with its navigation lights twinkling flew into the intimidating gloom. I circled Beinn a' Ghlo about half-a-grand above the soft glow of the snow, acutely aware of being alive and in a state of high exhilaration in the closing mouth of the winter night.

Stylistically, the story should end on this eirenic note of contemplation of the final things but real life doesn't seem to be much interested in style which is a grammatical conceit, a sort of retrospective tense applied in the reflective mood. In the real life aspect of this story there was a lot more hard reality to be handled before a safe touch down allowed the luxury of literary style to emerge.

I came back the long way round using Broughty Castle as a landmark. Over the Tay the setting sun had broken through a complicated cloud system. We have all seen memorable winter sunsets; this one was as complex and colourful as they come, doubled in the reflections of the

mirror-smooth river and enhanced by the spectacular glooms that sur-
rounded it; like an impressionist painting it was full of bits of light and dark;
you were aware that there were complementary colours resonating in the
shadows. An imaginative man would not have been surprised to crash
suddenly into a giant Monet hung on the wall of an art gallery. Blessed with
a phlegmatic, unexcitable disposition, however, no such thoughts went
through my mind; I boringly lined up the plane on long finals for a straight-
in approach to runway two eight zero, carried out my down-wind checks
(brakes off, under-carriage down, pitch fine, carburettor heat on, engine
dials reading okay and seat belt tight), lowered 20° of flap, trimmed for an
approach speed of 65 knots and made a passable landing with knuckles
maybe slightly white on the control column.

Tom Patey on the Stac of Handa traverse. Photo: Chris Bonington.

STAC OF HANDA: FIRST CROSSING

By W.H. Murray

CONTINUING MY shredding of old files, I have found another exchange of letters with Tom Patey. In July, 1967, Tom (aided by Chris Bonington and Ian McNaught-Davies) had made the second crossing by rope to the top of the Great Stac of Handa. He wrote to me early in 1968, saying that he'd heard that Donald MacDonald of Lewis, whose father had made the first crossing in the 1870s, was alive, had recently visited Handa to view the scene of his father's famous exploit, and now lived at Dunoon (having been headmaster of the grammar school). Would I please visit Donald and ask if he remembered details of the first crossing? Tom still felt shaken by his own 120ft traverse across the 350ft-deep gulf. The big sag in the rope had given him a tough fight to get any footing on the Stac. He could scarcely believe that the first crossing had been made without aids, for he could not have done that himself. So what aids had been used?

My visit to MacDonald was fruitful, and my report to Tom is of interest to climbers on two counts. First, it discloses a double error in our Club's guidebook, *The Islands of Scotland* (1989), which ascribes the crossing to 'inhabitants of Handa' thus ignoring that Handa had been cleared in 1848, and also misquoting Harvie Brown's *Fauna of the North-West Highlands* (1904), which, itself erroneous throughout on the Handa passage, gave the credit to 'two men and a boy from Uist, at the request of the late Mr Evander McIver . . .' In fact, it was done by three men of Ness in Lewis on their own initiative. Second, and more importantly, it revealed a more advanced state of climbing ability in the Outer Hebrides than our Club's members had realised. Even Patey, comparing his own hair-raising traverse with that of last century, wrote (SMCJ, XXIX, p. 319): 'It is even more certain that no mountaineering amateur of that era would have committed himself to such an undertaking.'

He might be right. But, his words draw notice to a moral ripe for plucking – and for slow digestion. Climbers of every period share a common frailty (I too being guilty in past days): we imagine that our fellows of an earlier age could not have been as bold and skilful as we. From one century to the next, our self-flattering hearts offer up that much-beloved toast: 'Here's tae us! Wha's like us? Nary a one and they're a' deid.'

> Loch Goil,
> 26 March, 1968

Dear Tom,

I have at last seen Donald MacDonald. I called on him yesterday at Dunoon. His wife died three years ago, just after his visit to Handa, and he now lives alone. One son is a doctor in Fife, and another I forget where. Donald in his mid-80s, is fresh complexioned and fit, with all his faculties

Mark Garthwaite on the first winter ascent of 'Terminator', Creag Tharsuinn. Photo: George Szuca.

except for a slight deafness. He's not frail-looking like Tom Longstaff at the end, and is equally alert in mind. He remembers the whole story of his father's crossing to the Great Stac, which had been told to him many times by his father and friends. He can't remember the month, which would be prior to September. The year was 1876, when his father was 26.

His father's name was Donald MacDonald, fisherman and crofter at Ness near the Butt of Lewis, of mixed Norse and Gaelic stock – like all the other families around, fair-haired and blue-eyed. Donald, the son, still has strong impressions of how hard his father and all these men worked, out on the sea in all weather, line fishing, yet still managing to wring a good product from the croft: enough to put sons through universities before the welfare state had been thought of. He remarked that the mainlanders' idea of the islesmen as idlers is quite wrong, the reverse of truth, and that few mainland farmers or crofters could begin to cope with the work these men did. But they might appear idle if seen after a voyage, when they'd stand around for a brief spell with hands in their pockets relaxing. Their one outdoor recreation was rock climbing.

His father in his twenties and thirties was in constant practice on rock, very strong in the arm, and supremely confident in his physical fitness. He and the other men of Ness learned their rock climbing initially in hunting the birds on the sea cliffs of Ness, and nearly 50 miles north on Sula Sgeir and North Rona, which islands they never referred to by name, but always (in Gaelic) as 'The Lands Out Yonder'. This kind of naming seems to be a typically Norse idiom, just as they originally referred to the Scottish Western Isles as Havbredey, which meant in Norse 'The Isles on the Edge of the Sea'. Hence the word Ebudae picked up in Lewis by the Roman navigators of AD 129 and rendered thus in Latin by Ptolemy.

Donald, the son, says that the men of Ness did not merely cull seabirds for the pot. They liked birds in the same way as modern birdwatchers. They observed and studied them and could tell you as much about the life of seabirds in detail as any amateur ornithologist today. Hunting the birds for food was another matter, which of course had led to their rock-work: but they did also have a genuine love of birds for their own sake, as they did too of rock. His father would often be working out on the croft – and when the main work was done would suddenly 'disappear' – he'd be off to the sea cliffs just to enjoy the climbing. All his spare time went to the rocks. The best cliffs near Ness were those down the east coast to Tolsta. On the west coast, from the Butt to Europie, the cliffs were lower.

The men spent much more time than they do today in culling the birds from The Lands Out Yonder. Now they spend only a day or two. Last century they'd spend at least a fortnight every September, taking the gugas (young gannets) as they 'ripened', salting them in the barrel as they took them, so that they were nearly all cured by the time the boats returned to Ness. They tasted, said Donald, not unlike good kippers. The birds were exported world-wide. The young men rejoiced in these expeditions, hard living but a wonderful change from the croft-work and deep-sea fishing. They went wild with delight and would naturally throw off some feats of daring that would make your hair curl. One of these was the Handa epic.

This was organised, not by Donald MacDonald, but by his neighbour Malcolm McDonald (no relation). Malcolm, then in his fifties, was a natural leader, full of resource and bright ideas. He planned the visit to the Great Stac of Handa and decided how it would be done. Donald was the man chosen (or maybe the volunteer) to make the first crossing. He had the needed nerve and strength. The Stac had already been reconnoitred with a full intention of climbing it from the sea upward. But no line had seemed practicable. The idea of nailing rocks had been thought of and been not acceptable. Their method of crossing was in general outline the same as yours. A long rope – five or six hundred feet – was carried end-outwards to the farther points of Handa until its centre crossed the top of the Stac. The ends were then secured to stakes. It could be they used the same boulder as you at the north-east end. Donald then crossed from the west side hand over fist, bare feet curled round the rope. He used no waist-loop or foot-loop or safety line at the waist. He carried nothing at all. The fixed rope was a thick fishing-rope normally used for securing the deep-sea fishing lines to buoys – he gave it a Gaelic name that I can't remember.

There was a tremendous sag in the middle and worse under the Stac. Donald had a hard job at that last bit. This was the only time when he thought he might fail. It was made especially difficult because he was unable to make his landing where he had hoped. There was a point where the Stac sloped abruptly down toward the gulf, and the rope had slipped while he was crossing until it hung over this sloping ground, where the steep, loose rock gave no firm hold for the foot when he tried to make lodgement. He was now fighting for his life and tapped the reserve of strength needed to pull himself up. When he was rested, Malcolm threw him a line, by which he pulled across two stakes, a block-and-tackle, a breeches-buoy, and baskets. Donald fixed the stakes, attached the tackle, and his two companions crossed by breeches-buoy. They culled the sea cliff birds and filled the baskets. All were then able to return to Handa by breeches-buoy, leaving the stakes behind on the Stac, where they were seen during the next 70 years.

This ploy became one of the wonders of Ness for many a year, but no one thought that the islemens' high-spirited play would interest mainlanders.

So that's the story. There are lots of details one would like to know more about. For example, how did Donald hammer in his stakes? And what was the thickness of the fixed rope? Given a very thick and taut rope, crossing hand over fist is not in itself difficult for a skilled man, as we both know. In western Nepal, hillmen habitually use this method for crossing rivers much wider than the Handa gulf. But, their grass ropes are one-and-a-half inches in diameter, stretched so tight that little sag comes in the middle, and lead to easy landings. The rivers may be killers if one falls in, but with nothing like that fearsome drop at Handa.

Eight years later, Malcolm McDonald, the prime mover, quarrelled with his Presbyterian minister at Ness. Rather than submit to his rule of the parish, Malcolm chose self-exile to North Rona. A fellow crofter, McKay, went with him. The island had lain uninhabited for 44 years. They arrived early in the summer of 1884 and occupied a ruined house. Their friends at Ness, feeling uneasy about them after a stormy winter, sent out a boat in April 1885, when Malcolm and his friend were found indoors, dead of exposure.

I hope to see you at Easter.

Yours,
Bill Murray.

THE BUACHAILLE UNDER SNOW   JOHN MITCHELL 1984.

ILLUSTRATIONS IN THE EARLY JOURNALS

By John Mitchell

THE SCOTTISH Mountaineering Club has, from its earliest days, been concerned with the artistic expression of natural beauty through words, photographs and drawings.

'The glory of the hills then, gentlemen, the beauty of natural scenery, must be our motto.' So spoke Professor Ramsay, the first President, addressing members at the AGM on December 12, 1889.

When it was proposed, also in 1889, to produce a Club Journal, A.E. Maylard, an original member and the first Honorary Secretary, hoped that it would have articles on 'art, literature, and science'.

It was decided at the Sixth AGM to produce a 'well-illustrated, attractive and interesting' climber's guide to Scotland.

These examples surely underline the SMC's artistic concerns. This article is intended to show that these were amply fulfilled within the first 10 volumes of the Journal.

I suppose it was natural that the SMC, with its roots in Glasgow – that city provided the largest group of original members – should reflect the artistic aspirations of a wealthy city that had built magnificent town houses and offices in the 19th century. A city which had opened the Kelvingrove Galleries and Museum, had supported the work of the Glasgow Boys and would lay the seeds of the modern movement in the work of C.R. Mackintosh.

Remember too, that the membership of the SMC was drawn from a well-educated class, many of whom would have the means, and some the interest, to support the arts – and indeed would have the opportunity to go mountaineering.

In looking at the early Journals the most obvious and impressive illustrations are photographs. Such was the interest that on February 15, 1893, members gave an exhibition of lantern slides in the Windsor Hotel, Glasgow. Sixty members and friends viewed 180 slides. This event was reported in the Journal of May, 1893, after which J. Rennie invited members to present duplicates of their slides to the Club. As a result the Club's photographic archives were boosted when W. Lamond Howie, Howard Priestman, J. Rennie, W. Douglas, and Cameron Swan presented copies of their work. They were given a generous vote of thanks at the Fifth AGM, 'for their kindness in presenting the Club with sets of very beautiful photographs taken by themselves'.

Mountain photography, although popular in their period, was considerably different from that in ours. There were no lightweight, miniature, auto-focus cameras that allow you to take a photograph – with one hand –

of your partner as he falls past you, while holding the rope with the other. Or, if in winter, when sitting on it. Cameras were bigger, therefore heavier, however, they gave large negatives – sometimes 7" x 5", which goes some way to explaining the quality of these early illustrations.

W. Lamond Howie was an interesting man. He was a pharmacist and a member of the Chemical Society. Joining the SMC in 1892, he contributed an article on mountain photography to the Journal (Vol. II pp. 249-253), which not only described how he had made his own telephoto lens (lighter than commercially made ones) from old opera glasses, but went on to give advice on photographic composition and aesthetics, recommending the use of a wide-angle lens to give scale.

On one occasion he went to the top of Ben Nevis wading across the River Nevis en route, carrying a 5ft-long wooden tripod, a smaller metal one, a heavy half-plate mahogany camera, six slides, 12 glass plates and a spare box of another 12, two lenses and a changing bag. And that was just his photographic equipment.

A good example of his work can be seen (Vol. III, facing p. 316). 'Ben Nevis from Carn Mor Dearg.' This is a composite 145° panoramic view using three photographs. You will be pleased to note that mounted copies could be obtained from Messrs. Stott priced at one guinea.

This photograph is also reproduced (Vol. VII, p.166), where it can easily be compared with a similar work by William Inglis Clark on p. 146. A print of Inglis Clark's photograph hangs over the fireplace at Black Rock Cottage.

William Douglas, for 18 years Journal editor, also produced exciting work, including an atmospheric study of the 'Pinnacle of Sgurr Dearg from the N.E.' (Vol. IV p. 201) which brings out the 'colour' and texture of the rock, with figures in the top to give scale, while the mist swirls behind and below the pinnacle. I've seen few better photographs of the Inaccessible Pinnacle than this.

When A.E. Maylard became President in 1901, he and his wife held a reception for members on the afternoon of the Annual Dinner. Chamber music was provided by Coles' Piano and String Quartet, but more relevantly, around 1000 mountain photographs were on show along with drawings and other mountaineering-related material. This display included works by Naismith, Gilbert Thomson, Lamond Howie, and the Keswick photographer, Abraham. Lamond Howie's panoramic picture of Ben Nevis was considered to be 'the finest photographic representation of Scottish mountain scenery'.

William Inglis Clark, who joined the Club in 1895, became a prolific contributor to the Journal. Volume X contains his article on colour photography, (pp. 294-306), illustrated with four superb examples of his work, in particular 'In the Forest, Inveroran' (p. 304). Looking at them it is difficult to believe they were made in 1909. Inglis Clark recommended the use of Lumiere's autochrome plates which had just come on to the market. Their advantage was that you only needed one plate and exposure rather than three as before – one each for red, green and blue. An obvious benefit was that cloud images were much sharper because they moved less in the course of one exposure rather than three. Inglis Clark volunteered to help any member who was interested in turning to colour work.

Drawings vary in kind – diagrammatic, humorous, and expressive. The diagrammatic drawings range from sometimes rather wooden copies of photographs to crag diagrams that are familiar to us in modern guide books. 'Bhastair and Sgurr nan Gillean' (Vol. II, p. 214), is a line drawing by R. Dawson from a photograph by Harold Priestman, strongly lit from the left side of the picture to give an almost three-dimensional effect.

'Two Peelers', (Vol. IV, p. 140), is a lively and humorous pen and ink sketch of the kind often found in Victorian and Edwardian autograph books. The humour lies in the contrast between the hapless boulderer and the stout policeman attracted to the scene by the 'private' notice on the

Two Peelers

rock, past which the climber is progressing in a determinedly downward direction. This sketch also appeared on the back of the menu card for the Sixth Annual Dinner. Unfortunately, it is unsigned but I believe it may be by F.C. (see below) because of the handling of the hatched shading, and the freedom of line.

Another good example of this genre is 'Oh, my big hobnailers' by F.C. in (Vol. II, p. 204) – reproduced in *A Century of Scottish Mountaineering* (p. 12). F.C. was almost certainly Fraser Campbell, an original member,

"Oh! my big hob. nailers a reminiscence - 13/12/92   F.C.

who also illustrated the front cover of menu cards for the Fourth and Fifth Annual Dinners. His sketch for the Fourth (1892) shows Sir Hugh Munro and three other members on top of Ben Cruachan. He produced several drawings of boulderers (Vol. IV, p. 55; Vol. X, p. 110).

Sometimes the humour is unintentional but lies in our more disrespectful modern taste, as in a diagram by J. Rennie demonstrating a method of determining the angle of a snow gully (Vol. II, p. 92). See also *A Century of Mountaineering*, (p. 215). Never let it be said that the pioneers ignored the more scientific and educational nature of their mountaineering.

There are some excellent expressive drawings too. By this I mean drawings that attempt to show more than just a naturalistic impression of a scene, drawings that interpret nature using line, tone and sometimes distortion to create interest and atmosphere. Indeed it was seeing two of these that sparked off my interest in this subject. These two illustrate an article by A.E. Maylard on Ben Lomond (Vol. III, and face pp. 146 and 147).

Ben Lomond from the head of Glen Dubh.

Maylard, it will be remembered, wanted a serious agenda for the Journal. In all he contributed more than 20 articles, this being one of his earliest. The drawings, both titled 'Ben Lomond from the head of Glen Dubh' are done in pen and ink, using a lively technique to suggest light and form. The second uses a long-rising left-to-right diagonal in the foreground to give scale. The artist has distorted the height of the mountain to increase the dramatic impact of the scene. This is a legitimate tactic often used by artists, like Turner, for example, in his imaginative evocation of Loch Coruisk in the National Gallery of Scotland.

Although there are some crudities in the drawings, as in the trees in the first one, they are still interesting and of a different order than those previously mentioned. They are unsigned, are they perhaps by Maylard himself? However, I have found no similar drawings illustrating his articles.

One artist whose work appears often in the early Journals is Fred W. Jackson. Jackson, who lived near Manchester, joined the SMC in 1893. He climbed in Skye with Naismith in July of that year. Indeed it was Naismith who proposed him for membership. His method was to make sketches on the spot and to use these, sometimes backed up with photographs, to produce his final works. There is a good example of his technique illustrating his own article on Y Tryfaen (Vol. IV, p. 319). It is a fine dramatic contrast in light and dark showing the Cave Pitch, and is based on a photograph by J.B. Pettigrew.

Almost from the beginning the Journal exploited all methods of pictorial technique and approach, blending seriousness and humour, information and entertainment. What is surprising is not that this should have been the case, but that I should have been surprised to find it so.

The SMC holds a treasure trove of early mountain photography and other illustrations. It seems a pity that these should be seen so rarely, and only then in specialist publications. Perhaps the possibility of an exhibition could be explored. Such a project might attract sponsorship from the Scottish Arts Council or support from the National Library of Scotland. The work of these pioneers deserves to be seen again, and by a wider audience.

The quality of the photographic and drawn work in the early Journals surely justified and fulfilled the hopes of Ramsay, Maylard and the other visionaries of the Scottish Mountaineering Club.

EXTERNAL INFLUENCES ON MOUNTAIN SAFETY – WEATHER OR NOT

By Brian Hill

I HAD OFTEN considered plotting the information given in the SMC Journals' Scottish Mountain Accident reports. Every new issue added another data point to what was becoming a lengthy time-series. Why were some years worse than others? Could these years be correlated with some other factor that could influence a climber's safety? The publication of the graphs in last year's Journal, displaying the trends of mountain rescue callouts from 1964 to 1992 encouraged me, at last, to have a detailed look at the accidents as reported in the journals.

Methodology:

As suggested in the graph published last year, there are a number of possible ways of looking at the data – total mountain rescue callouts or callouts involving fatalities or non-fatalities. The tables, often published, give additional break-downs summarising the total casualties which include those with injuries, hypothermia and illness, and incidents which include accidents with casualties, those cragfast, separated, lost and benighted. Initially, I looked at the casualties list although each time-series is broadly similar to any other; a dip or rise in one being generally reflected in the others with only minor differences here and there. For example, a year with a high number of fatalities is also likely to be a year with a large number of callouts and casualties, though the numbers involved in each may be substantially different.

From the SMC Journals in my possession I was able to plot the annual total number of casualties from 1962 to 1992 with the years 1963 and 1966 missing. To compensate for the long-term increase in the number of casualties, a trend curve was fitted to the data and the difference from the mean, or anomaly, for each year calculated. Years with few casualties then have a negative number and years with higher than average a positive number. This allows for easy comparison with other data sets.

Solar Cycles:

I have long been interested in solar-terrestrial relationships, particularly those related to the solar cycle, an 11-year period of activity in which the number of sunspots increase and decrease. Sunspots occur in pairs as in the poles of a magnet. The leading polarity as they traverse round the sun reverses every 11-year cycle so that frequent mention is made of a 22-year magnetic cycle. Years of high number of sunspots are characterised by an increased number of solar flares from the surface of the sun and increased radiation of which the most obvious effect to us is more frequently observed aurora. Intense flares are also responsible for black-outs by causing power surges through electrical transmission lines, and are also a frequent disrupter of radio communications, navigational compasses, and homing pigeons (even as I am writing this, two of our Anik series communication satellites suddenly developed problems within minutes of each other, supposedly caused by some cosmic outburst). Less well known is the effect on the terrestrial atmosphere, an unexpected result being the premature demise of a number of orbital satellites. These had been launched into orbit to skim just above our atmosphere free from air friction. However, during the periods of high solar activity, the atmosphere expanded to envelop the lower satellites and the increased drag took its toll.

Solar cycle relationships have been proposed ever since the cycles were first detected and are still vigorously argued and contested. There are correlations with crop yields, precipitation amounts, droughts, river and lake levels, frequency of hurricanes, power black-outs due to lightning strikes, the incidence of polar bears off Greenland, and storm tracks to name just a few. Most are directly related to the climate, thus crop yields are dependent on sufficient moisture, and the incidence of polar bears dependent on sea ice coverage to distribute them to the hunters. The two main objections to the solar-climate relationships are the inability to prove a physical mechanism whereby small changes in solar output cause significant changes in climate, and, particularly, that nearly all the proposed relationships which appear to hold true for a number of cycles, fail to hold true for a longer period of time and may even reverse. There are

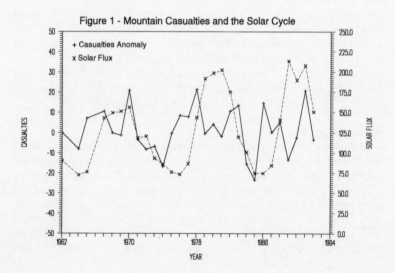

Figure 1 - Mountain Casualties and the Solar Cycle

many counter arguments, of course, involving significant climate shifts, but it is not intended to get into an elaborate discussion, only to point out that many consider such relationships to be mere quirks of chance while on the other hand there is such an abundance of proposed connections, many often inter-related that it is difficult to dismiss them all out of hand. At the turn of the 18th century solar activity was at an all-time low with few sunspots observed for several consecutive cycles. On Earth, this was the time of the Little Ice Age when colder than normal temperatures were experienced and many glaciers re-advanced. It is difficult to accept this as just coincidence. For any comparison, however, the main difficulty is in constructing long enough data sets with consistent data, as observation techniques often change with time so that when when comparisons with the 11-year solar cycle are attempted a minimum of 30 years of data is barely sufficient.

My own interest with solar climate relationships has been in establishing a correlation with the sea ice extent off the east coast of Newfoundland for the past 70 years and researching ice data back to 1800 which I hope will lengthen considerably the correlation. So having the time-series for solar activity readily accessible I plotted it against the anomaly of Scottish mountain accidents, as described above, in Fig. 1. Visually, there was a broad similarity between the two curves, particularly in years of maxima and minima. In the graph, the solar activity is measured as solar flux, the modern method of describing solar activity as opposed to the older visual method of actually counting the spots. The radiation is detected by a radiometer on the 10.5cm wavelength and is measured in watts per square metre. This is not meant to imply that in years of increased solar activity, the unfortunate climber becomes over irradiated, like a forgotten wiener in the microwave oven, and eventually succumbs. As we all know, weather plays an important part in safety on the hills and it would not be unrealistic to argue that many accidents or incidents were due in large to vagaries of the weather. A quick glance at the accidents reports in the Journal will reveal a number of instances where the party was ill-prepared to meet unexpected changes in the weather. Late returns, benightments, and hypothermia cases are the more obvious ones, but any sudden change in the weather can catch even the experienced parties at odds – avalanches in sudden thawing conditions, a sudden shower on a hard VS move, rapidly lowering and freezing temperatures hardening wet snow or wet ground to iron hard ice, a sudden gust of wind in an exposed situation. We can all think of several incidents.

Storm Tracks:

It seemed reasonable to assume that the implied connection between solar activity and incidents was the weather. I was aware of some work that had been done in relation to storm (cyclone) tracks, the author, B. Tinsley, demonstrating that the average track of winter (January to February) storms in the north-eastern Atlantic were pushed further south during years of high activity. Estimating the latitudes from their publications, Fig. 2 displays those numbers with those of the casualties anomaly. For the first 20 years there appeared to be a higher number of casualties with decreasing latitude, as one might expect, so for easy visual comparison of the two data sets I displayed the latitude as a negative number in order to put the two curves in phase. This indicated that the years in which the average position of the storm track came closer towards Scotland (the north coast being about 58.5°N) then the higher the mountain casualty rate. It all made sense. In years of high sunspot activity, the increased solar flux expanded the atmosphere thereby altering atmospheric circulation and pushing the average storm track in the north-east Atlantic closer to the Highlands, thus bringing more cloudy conditions, heavy precipitation, strong and rapidly-

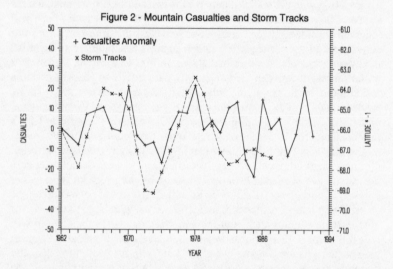

Figure 2 - Mountain Casualties and Storm Tracks

shifting winds, and large fluctuating temperatures from the effects of the passing warm and cold fronts – the combined effects of which only the sturdiest and hardiest climber could endure. Except, after about 1982 the correlation didn't appear to be so good anymore, and after 1989 I didn't have any storm data and the storm data I had for the previous years was for January and February only and I was comparing it with annual casualties. That latter point may indeed be a minor one as winter casualties tend not to differ greatly percentage wise of the annual total from year to year. Still if you are going to compare apples . . .

In seeking advice from a colleague he warned against trying to average storm-track data for the whole year. Tracks can vary greatly from season to season, by the time they are averaged every year could result in the same. He also cautioned that there could be 100 people like me trying to find weather correlations from the Amazon to the Arctic and the fact that I appeared to have found one was no more than chance alone, and he suggested that I try more specific correlations with the accidents such as temperature or precipitation.

Rather than taking the whole year, I decided on looking at the winter months January to April inclusive though that window as it turned out may, in fact, be too large as well. Though March and April are not really winter months I decided to include them as they are still winter climbing months, but I included all incidents occurring in those months whether they were winter climbing related or not. Since not all Journals included a seasonal breakdown of accident statistics I went through all Journal entries. I also decided to change tactics slightly and report the number of separate winter incidents rather then the number of casualties. In the long run this probably should not make any difference – the more the incidents, the more the casualties, but by including benightments and late arrivals a truer picture of difficulties in the hills can be drawn.

Consistent data was still a problem. Some of the early Journals in the period had no extensive accident reports and many in the early 1970s reported only some selected incidents. The earlier ones also ignored

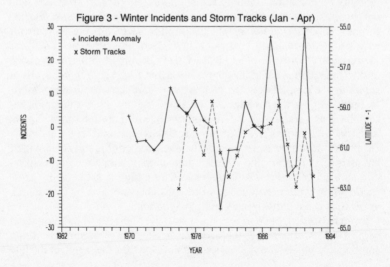

callouts for those benighted or unduly delayed. I have to admit I only made use of what was readily available to me. It is possible that mountain rescue authorities have more complete information. Again, I only made use of meteorological information and storm-track data that was readily available here in St. John's, Newfoundland, the former being from 1970 and the latter 1976. The latitude of storm tracks crossing 5°W longitude was estimated from the charts as presented in the Mariner's Weather Log between 50°N and 70°N from January to April for each year. The average for the four-month period for each year was plotted against the incident anomaly for the same period, Fig. 3, with somewhat ambiguous results. Again, it appears that the nearer the average storm-track latitude is to Scotland then the higher the incident rate with the converse being true, but there is still a large amount of scatter. This method of comparison is perhaps simplistic and a more sophisticated analysis would probably be of merit. As an example, if for the given period storm tracks were limited to exactly 50°N and 66°N then the average would indicate a latitude of 58°, right over the Northern Highlands where, in fact, no storm occurred at all. Nor does this approach take into account the duration of the system. A stalled low-pressure system hanging over the Highlands for days is essentially ignored since it is only counted once as it crosses 5°W.

Conclusions:

Meteorological data for a number of different stations throughout the UK from 1970 were available through the publications of the National Oceanic and Atmospheric Administration and those from Stornoway and Aberdeen were chosen as suitably bracketing the Highland area. The monthly precipitation amounts, temperatures, atmospheric pressure, and the percentage of normal sunshine hours, for the four months was selected for the combined stations and the mean and consequently the anomaly for each parameter for each year calculated. Each anomaly time-series was then compared with that of incidents. There were broad similarities in each of the comparisons but still a degree of scatter. Fig. 4 shows the results of summing the anomalies of temperature, precipitation and sunshine hours. In order to give each parameter an equal weight each value was re-calculated as a fraction of the maximum value of that time series. Again, for easy visual comparison, a negative scale has been used for the anomaly. Despite some scatter there appears that the number of incidents in winter has an inverse relationship with a combination of temperature, precipitation and sunshine. For example, years with a high number of incidents occurring in winter months are in months characterised by cloudiness, lower than usual temperatures and precipitation.

It can be argued, of course, that if a sufficient number of meterological parameters are examined, then sooner or later, by chance alone, some combination will be found that 'looks good'. On the other hand, of the few

Figure 4 - Comparison of Winter Incidents Anomaly
and Weather Anomaly

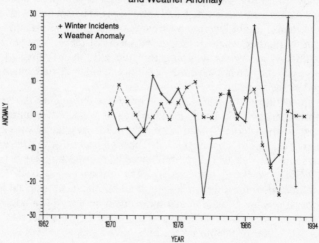

meteorological parameters available these three are ones that have a direct influence on a person's physical comfort. The one parameter omitted is atmospheric pressure but that does not have a direct influence on the physical well being unless one is susceptible to migraines, arthritis or rheumatism. It would also be interesting to include wind speed but that was not available.

The results so far, however, even if arrived at by chance, are interesting and not illogical. I had initially perceived that precipitation might have been a major factor in relation to incidents, but the results do not indicate that. The logical argument is then that when heavier than usual precipitation occurs, people generally stay off the hills. That most incidents occur in cloudy, colder conditions is also perhaps an understatement since that is probably the most frequent condition on the hills but the reverse of this is that there are less incidents when the weather is sunnier and warmer and when more people would be expected to be on the mountains. However, the present study was still unable to take sudden weather changes into account.

The data appear to support the hypothesis that weather has an influence on accidents on the mountains. Whether this correlation has been arrived at by chance I leave to the statisticians to argue. It would be interesting to compare the fluctuations of mountain accidents or incidents with those of another sport or activity directly exposed to the whims of nature such as yachting or boating, or even motorway driving. Such associations would reduce the probability of the correlation occurring by chance. A more detailed study of incidents with a particular weather pattern, like the proximity or approach of a low-pressure system might help demonstrate a closer relationship. The passage of such a system also implies rapidly-changing weather conditions which add extra perils. If a firm link could be established then it might increase awareness of the potential hazards of climbing in borderline weather. Organised meets of clubs, schools and other institutions are prone to going into the hills in less than ideal conditions since they do not have the flexibility in changing the venue to accommodate the weather.

Fig. 5 shows the daily distribution of incidents throughout the year totalled from 1968 to 1992. That one of the highest peaks occurs immediately after Christmas perhaps demonstrates the need to test the new ice axe or new pair of crampons, no matter what. The high peaks towards the end of February and May are also likely influenced by the mid-term break and Victoria holiday weekend respectively. The lowest period is in late autumn, a time when the hills are devoid of all but the most dedicated.

The correlations undertaken above have made no attempt to address social and economic influences. Even accepting that there is a 'flat rate' of 0.01%, or whatever, of people on the hills have incidents, there is still bound to be some year-to-year variation due to the number of people who can or cannot afford to go to the hills or who can or cannot buy adequate equipment. What about social interest? Was there a sudden rise in climbing

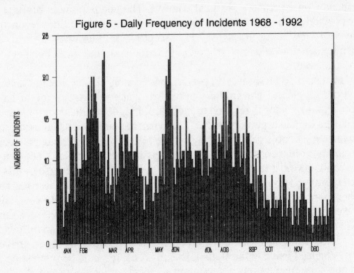

Figure 5 - Daily Frequency of Incidents 1968 - 1992

popularity after a particular television or movie spectacular which encouraged a surge of novices or tourists to take to the hills? If the rise in accidents in the hills continues at the present rate then we can expect about 320 incidents in 1993 with about 220 casualties. Winter incidents should be about 100. The weather anomaly for January to April was very close to zero and solar activity was about halfway down from the maximum, so all things being equal the actual figures should be very close to those above. (I have the weather data but do not have accident reports so it will be interesting to see!)

There is a strong logical argument for a weather influence on mountain incidents and it would appear that some degree of correlation can be made, though an accident of numbers cannot be ruled out. But why chance it? Next time your ex-spouse gives you an ice axe for Xmas, and sunspot activity is on the rise, and the forecast calls for lower-than-seasonable temperatures and cloudiness, take my advice – stay at home!

References:
Scottish Mountaineering Club Journals, (1966, 1969-1993).
Hill, Brian T. & S.J. Jones. (1990). The Newfoundland Ice Extent and the Solar Cycle from 1860 to 1988. *Journal of Geophysical Research,* Vol.95, No. C4, pp 5385-5394.
John, J. Ivor. (1989) Storm Tracks and Atmospheric Circulation Indices over the North-east Atlantic and North-west Europe in Relationship to the Solar Cycle and the QBO. Proceedings from the Workshop on Mechanisms for Tropospheric Effects of Solar Variability and the Quasi-Biennial Oscillation, NCAR, Boulder, Colorado.
Mariner's Weather Log (1970-1993). National Oceanic and Atmospheric Administration.
Monthly Climatic Data for the World, (1976-1993). National Oceanic and Atmospheric Administration.

Note: The tables containing the raw data are available through the Editor.

IMPRINTED ON THE NOSE

By Philip Gribbon

MY PARTNER and I went to climb on the unseen flank of the classic Cioch Nose in Applecross, where an irregular histogram of buttresses marched upwards on the rise and fall of the ridge. Such unfrequented rock held for us the wonderful air of mountain exploration.

We stood and looked at the new guide. Yes, we had to agree the vague gash must be the obvious 5m difficult chimney. About 30ft up, teetering on a steep slab, and faced by a mantelshelf on to a pelmet of fringing fronds I began to wonder. Where was the next traverse? Slimy ledges fading into space were not ready candidates. What about the shallow grassy scoop? A thrashing struggle up a curtain of woodrush leaves and over crumbling chokes hardly qualified, but it did lead to a well-used deer track traversing out under the upper section of our buttress.

Small snowflakes began to float out of grey clouds. We could just make out the totem, a curious pinnacle silhouetted against the sky and which gave a name to our route. We read: 'Surmount a small rocky nose.' Aye, there was the rub.

A nose? What about this short but abrupt wall wrapped round the edge of the buttress? Was this the nose? Unrelenting sandstone, massively jointed and blind cracked, stuck between ledges of vegetation. I got into a sentry box, clinging and leaning out. To the right, an uncompromising purple hippo-hide bulging flank capped with a moss mane; to the left a hanging inverted flake, tacked under the higher bedrock and towards it with some improbability a new scrabbling crampon scratched question mark. Where no man had gone before we would follow. It was an invitation to disaster, the most unhelpful of markings.

I descended and moved under the flake. Our route seemed to be overstretching its difficulties. Just a tentative attempt, once, twice. C'mon, a bit more motivation. Hooking my fingertips behind the flake I embraced its fin-like shield, legs wide, my arms all tension, and began shuffling awkwardly upwards. This is crazy!

Suddenly, there was a sharp crack and with a clean break a shaped block as long as my arm and as thick as my thigh came away. I landed in the bilberries on the ledge and then the overwhelming forces came at me. My ribcage was being stamped on by an elephant. Involuntarily, I heard my primitive sounds unlike any of those I have ever heard before. A gushing exhalation of air, a twisted groaning cry of suffering, not a breath left inside me, my heartbeat in a spasm, squirming like a worm, trying to escape martyrdom, on my knees, waiting for Time to begin again.

I lay panting, feeling more in control of my destiny, gathering specks of sense out of my surroundings. Some minor stones were still clattering down the hillside, while my battered block lay beside me like a pet dog with its master.

'I'm alright,' I shouted down to my second.

'Are you?', came the reply.

Get back to normality, recover some *sang froid*, get on with the climb. All quite irrational. It would have been easy to retreat and escape.

'Surmount the nose ' . . . before it became impossible. 'Don't hesitate' . . . go for it. Feet out on the hippo's flank, fingers embedded in the mane, struggling right to grasp frantically for the edge. It was sufficiently incut to hold, now pull and push, get an arm linked under a block, struggle, thrutch and roll exhaustedly on to the ledge above . . . the nose.

We tried the next crack. It didn't make sense with the guide book. It was getting harder. There were more crampon marks. Let's go home while we're winning. It's the means not the end that matters. My back hurt. You could say already I had the imprint of a memorable day.

. . . with a clean break . . .

SCALING THE HEIGHTS

By Helen E. Ross

HEIGHTS and slopes are not always what they seem. From the top of a mountain the facing mountain appears much higher and steeper than it is, and a flat bealach between the two appears to slope upwards. If there are skiers descending the lower slope of one's own mountain they may appear to be skiing uphill. If the sea is visible, the horizon will appear unexpectedly high and the water will slope up to it. On descending to the bealach the ground becomes level and the facing mountain appears less formidable; however, apparent heights may still be slightly raised, and slopes continue to appear too steep from a distance.

Phenomena of this sort are well known, but their explanation remains controversial. The main types of explanation involve mistakes about eye level, slope, distance, perspective or angular size. I shall argue that slope illusions are best explained by the effects of perspective, while raised apparent heights are caused both by perspective and by the enlargement of the apparent angular size of distant objects viewed horizontally.

Mistaken eye level:

Knowledge of the true slope of the visual scene depends on knowledge of the angle of the eyes with respect to the gravitational vertical, and knowledge of the angle between the line of sight and the slope. Several authors have suggested that the direction of gaze of one's eyes is normally felt to be higher than it is, resulting in the overestimation of the height of all points and the overestimation of slope (Fig. 1).

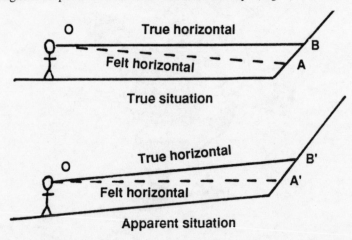

Fig. 1 Mistaken eye level. The gaze level OA is felt to be horizontal (OA'), and the true horizontal OB feels raised (OB'). Slopes are apparently steepened.

This theory supposes that the error lies in the calculation of eye, head or body position rather than in visual processing. The theory is partially supported by experiments conducted in the dark on judgments of eye level and of the apparent height of lights. However, mistakes about the height of mountains occur in broad daylight, even when the viewer surveys the scene with head erect and level gaze. The main source of the error must therefore lie in the interpretation of the visual scene.

Mistaken slope:

A common visual theory is that the descending slope of the viewer's mountain is taken to be less steep than it is: if the angle between the two mountains is correctly perceived, the opposite slope must appear steeper and truly horizontal points must appear to be above eye level (Fig. 2).

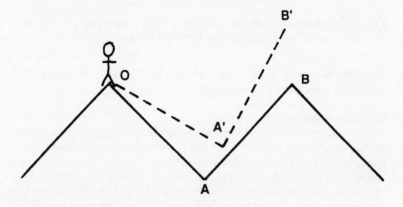

Fig. 2 Mistaken descending slope. OA is perceived as flattened to OA', and AB as steepened to A'B'. All points in the visual scene are raised in height.

However, this cannot be the whole explanation because the effect occurs when looking from a precipitous cliff over an empty gulf, or when looking over level ground, or when looking up to a coire headwall. It could be argued that the slope opposite is always drawn towards the vertical, regardless of the visual presence of a descending slope (Fig. 3). That could also raise apparent heights, but only if the slope is changed by apparently bringing the top nearer rather than by displacing the base backwards.

These slope theories fail to explain why descending slopes should be drawn towards the horizontal, or ascending slopes to the vertical. The slope errors are sometimes said to be an example of 'normalisation' towards a rectangular framework – but it is unclear why facing slopes of less than 45° should be normalised to the vertical rather than to the horizontal. An

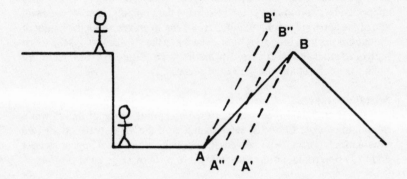

Fig. 3 Mistaken facing slope. AB is perceived as steepened to AB' or A"B" or A'B. Only the former raises all points.

unexplained error of slope perception should preferably not be used to explain an error of height perception.

Mistaken distance:
A better class of theory attempts to explain both slope and height errors by misperception of distance. Such theories are based on the view that the image in the eye is projected back in a geometrical manner on to a supposed surface at a certain distance, and mistakes of distance must necessarily cause mistakes of size and slope. This view dates back to the Arab scientist, Alhazen, in about 1000 AD, and has remained the dominant theory of spatial perception to this day. However, antiquity and respectability do not make it correct.

The theory accounts well for the appearance of surfaces below eye level, if it is assumed that apparent distances are progressively foreshortened (Fig. 4). The decreased apparent distance flattens descending slopes, causes horizontal ground to slope upwards, steepens facing slopes, and raises the apparent height of all points.

Unfortunately, the explanation will not work for the apparent height of objects at, or above, eye level. Those at eye level must remain at eye level regardless of apparent distance; while those above eye level should appear too low and too near, or too high and too far. Thus a more general raising of height demands that lower objects appear too near and higher objects too far (Fig. 5). This would have the effect of flattening the apparent slope of a facing mountain – which is the opposite of what is perceived.

The theory can only be rescued by returning to Fig. 4 and assuming that perception is dominated by the lower part of the visual scene. While this may be generally true, some interesting misperceptions also occur in the upper part of the visual scene (e.g. Fig. 7). It is therefore better to consider theories that encompass the whole of the visual scene.

Mistaken perspective:

Photographs of the visual scene show that many slope illusions are present in the visual image: the illusions are caused by failure to compensate sufficiently for perspective effects. Thus when looking along a rectangular

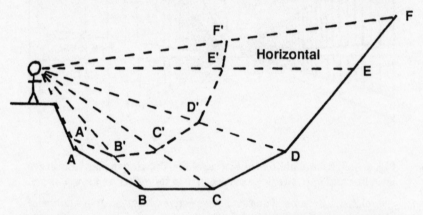

Fig. 4 Errors of foreshortened distance. All points below eye level are apparently raised, those at eye level remain unchanged (E to E') and those above eye level are lowered (F to F'). Descending slopes are flattened (AB to A'B') and all horizontal and facing slopes are steepened.

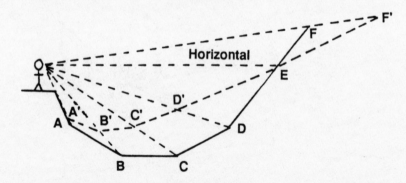

Fig. 5 Mixed distance errors. Points below eye level appear too near and too high, and those above eye level too far and too high. True eye level (E) remains unchanged. The facing slope appears flattened (CDEF to C'D'EF').

and level corridor, the image is one of converging spokes (Fig. 6). The lines below eye level slope upwards, those at eye level remain horizontal, and those above eye level slope downwards.

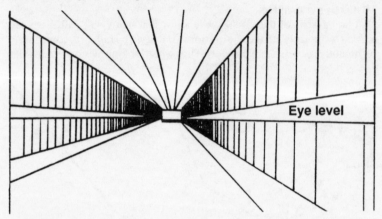

Fig. 6 Sketch from photograph of corridor, showing the horizontal eye level line and opposite slope perspective in the upper and lower scene.

It might be argued that mistaken perspective is equivalent to a failure of distance perception. This is not so, because even with excellent distance perception the apparent slope of the architecture is visible in real life. In a built-up environment we are rarely misled about the true horizontal and vertical, but in hilly country with few unambiguous cues we make frequent mistakes.

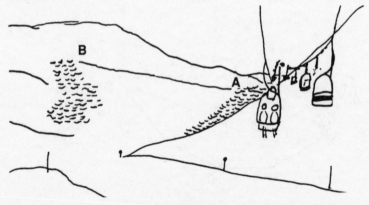

Fig. 7 Sketch from photograph looking up from the Féma chairlift, Val Cenis, France. Skiers alight near the top of the mogul field at A, and may ski *downhill* to the other mogul field at B. The path appears to slope upwards from A to B owing to perspective.

The ambiguity is illustrated in the accompanying sketch of a ski area, which shows a path running apparently uphill from right to left (Fig. 7). In reality skiers ski down that path, and the false apparent slope is caused by the fact that the right side is farther away than the left and that the scene is viewed from below. The true slope is not revealed until one is nearly level with the scene.

Perspective also contributes to the raised apparent height of other mountains, and of the sea horizon, when viewed from a height. The raised viewpoint makes the line of sight more perpendicular to a facing slope (unless the slope is very steep), and thus enlarges the image in the upper part of the visual scene compared with the same scene viewed at ground level (Fig. 8). Viewed from ground level, a mountain may subtend a smaller visual angle than a tree; but viewed from a height it will both tower above the tree and subtend a larger angle than from the ground.

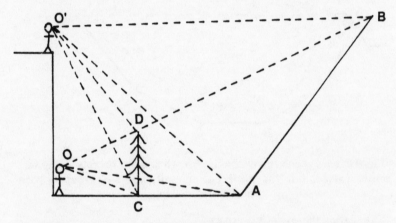

Fig. 8 Perspective and viewing height. Viewed from the ground, the slope AB subtends the angle AOB, which is slightly smaller than that of the tree (angle COD). Viewed from on high, the slope subtends the angle AO'B which is larger than AOB and much larger than that of the tree (CO'D).

Mistaken angular size:

Mistaken perspective may contribute to many slope and height illusions, but it does not explain the reported apparent raising of heights with ground-level viewing. If that indeed occurs, some perceptual scaling must operate over and above any effects that can be photographed. A possible contributory mechanism is the well-known phenomenon of size-distance scaling – the perceptual enlargement of the size of more distant objects (relative to their image size) that partially compensates for the diminution of the image with distance. The maximum size of this enlargement is typically voted by my student class to be a factor of 3.5: they were asked to estimate the apparent magnification of distant mountains with normal outdoor viewing compared to their relative size in photographs. An open field experiment by Gilinsky (1955) also showed that apparent angular size enlargement increases with viewing distance, reaching a factor of about 4 in the distance. Apparent angular enlargement must raise the apparent height of all objects, but particularly those viewed horizontally since they are typically farther away. Slight apparent steepening will also occur (Fig. 9).

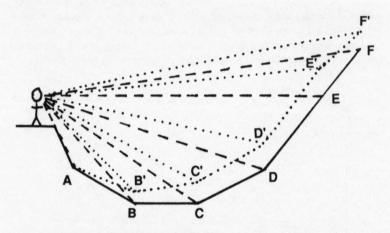

Fig. 9 Errors of enlarged angular size. All angular heights are apparently raised, but the apparent magnification is greatest with horizontal viewing.

Calculating the size of the errors:

Cornish (1935, p. 44) estimated the angular height error to be 6.5°, as measured from the mid point of the page containing his sketch of one mountain top viewed from another top. This method is questionable, but I found fairly similar errors from direct observation of several mountain sites. For example, from the summit of Beinn Bhuidhe, Inveraray (O.S. NN 204 187), when looking south-west towards the nearby top of Stac a' Chóirn, the latter appeared almost level with myself. The effect was so convincing that, as an honest Munroist (and lacking the confirmation of the promised Ordnance Survey pillar), I walked on to check out the next top. The true summit has a height of 948m, and the top about 830m, and the distance between them is about 1000m, giving an angular height error of 6.8°. Other sites gave errors between 3° and 7°.

It is interesting to consider how these errors of angular height compare with the angular size subtended by the mountain. The baseline is often ambiguous, but it can be assumed to be the nearest piece of level ground between the viewer and the opposite mountain. The situation is sketched for the Beinn Bhuidhe scene in Fig. 10, where the heights above plateau level are shown. Calculations give an apparent angular magnification ratio of 3.56. Other sites gave smaller magnification ratios of 1.5 to 2.0.

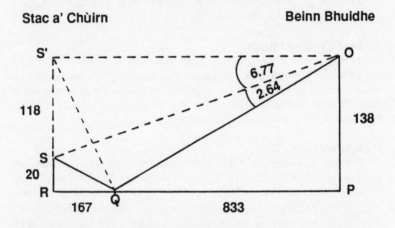

Fig. 10 Calculation of apparent angular enlargement. Beinn Bhuidhe has a height (OP) of 138m above the minor plateau (Q) at 810m. Stac a' Chùirn has a true height (SR) of 20m, but an apparent height (S'R) of 138m above the same level. The calculated angular height error SOS' is 6.77°. The true angle subtended by Stac a' Chùirn (QOS) is 2.64°, and its apparent angular size (QOS') is 9.41°, giving a magnification factor of 3.56.

Towards a conclusion:

These apparent angular magnifications are within the range usually reported for size-distance scaling and for other outdoor size illusions such as the moon illusion (the apparent enlargement of the moon on the horizon compared with its appearance high in the sky). The general explanation may therefore be similar for raised horizontals and enlarged moons: apparent angular magnification is greatest for objects viewed horizontally (normally farthest away) and is less for objects high or low in the visual scene (normally nearer).

To distinguish between this and other theories, further observations are needed. It is necessary to investigate angular errors at varied viewing distances and viewing angles. It is not known whether the angular height error is a constant additive (as predicted by the mistaken eye level theory); or whether it increases with viewing height and height in the visual scene (as predicted by the perspective theory); or whether it increases with viewing distance and horizontal gaze, and with the angular size of the object (as predicted by the angular magnification theory). We clearly have a long way to go before the perceptual scaling of mountains can be mapped with the precision of an optician's perimetry chart.

Request for observations:

The author would be pleased to receive detailed accounts of these and any other outdoor perceptual phenomena, particularly where estimates or measurements of the size of the effect are available. Please write to Dr Helen E. Ross, Department of Psychology, University of Stirling, Stirling FK9 4LA.

Further reading:

The early literature on mistaken eye level and mistaken slope is reviewed by Howard, I.P. & Templeton, W.B. (1966) *Human Spatial Orientation*. London, Wiley. A recent technical paper on the topic is: Matin, L. & Fox, C.R. (1989) 'Visually perceived eye level and perceived elevation of objects: linearly additive influences from visual field pitch and from gravity'. *Vision Research* 29:315-324.

Mistaken distance and some other theories are described by Minnaert, M. (1959) *Light and Colour in the Open Air*. (Trans. H.M. Kremer-Priest, revised by K.E. Brian Jay) London, Bell (Ch.9). Both mistaken distance and mistaken perspective are described by Ross, H.E. (1974) *Perception and Performance in Strange Environments*. London, Allen & Unwin (Ch.3).

Mistaken angular size is loosely described by Cornish, V. (1935) *Scenery and the Sense of Sight*. Cambridge: Cambridge University Press. It is more precisely described in relation to the moon illusion by McCready, D. (1986) 'Moon illusions redescribed'. *Perception and Psychophysics* 39: 64-72. It is supported by several authors in an edited book by Hershenson, M. (1989) *The Moon Illusion* Hillsdale, N.J.: Lawrence Erlbaum Associates. The field experiment on angular size matches was reported by Gilinsky, A.S. (1955) 'The effect of attitude upon the perception of size'. *American Journal of Psychology* 68: 173-192.

The early history of ideas on size and distance perception is outlined by Plug, C. & Ross, H.E. (1989) 'Historical review'. Ch.2 in Hershenson (cited above).

THE NO-HOLDS BARD

By Mike Jacob

MOVEMENT SLOWED to immobility and I was becalmed. I tried moving forwards a word or two but, no, it was all so misconstructed. How could I capture the reality of the moment, a fleeting feeling, and convey it across space and time? I retreated to the safety of a solid paragraph then scored through the offending phrases. They objected to being crossed out, like slighted friends. There's nothing wrong with you, I thought to them; just not suitable, like an inappropriate move. All manner of well-rounded holds available, yet I couldn't perform with elegance, precision or style. There was no doubt that I could get up the thing, sling down some well-worn clichés as aid, but I needed inspiration for a new metaphor or fresh simile so that they, you, would appreciate the artistry involved.

I fumbled through a lexicon of gear; no help there, everything seemed so stale and lifeless. Exasperated, I tried the sequence again, and again failed. Would I ever be able to just move from left to right and allow the words to flow fluently across the rock, an uninterrupted progression, as naturally as, say, the

> *sluice, chute, cascade, rush*
> *spout, fall, splash, gush*
> *of mountain Burns?*

I looked around, down the ramps of accomplished progression; a mistake, one that I recognised from past experience, a sure sign of broken concentration. Which way now?

The self-doubt: perhaps the problem was within, did it all matter much anyway? I could easily give up, nobody would know, I did not wish to add to

> *'all the cloud screen*
> *of human witness, dictionaried sport;*
> *and that these rainbows steal*
> *the selfless joy mountains can make us feel'* [1]

Was I not in danger of becoming like the tourists I had seen at Holyrood Palace, too preoccupied living through their camera lenses to see what they were looking at, that all they would have at the end would be negatives? But, deep down, I feel that this isn't a true analogy. I hoped that I was more like the photographer I met once at Camasunary who had been there two, three weeks; up and down Bla Bheinn and Bidein Druim nan Ramh with

---

[1] From *The Company of Hills* by G.W. Young.

extremely heavy equipment, bivvying out, waiting to capture that one coincidence of light and atmosphere that would transpose onto print with dramatic effect. He missed the one that we found and is now imprinted in the mind; the one at sunrise on the high gabbro ridge as a whole white sea boiled, billowed and flowed out of coire and over bealach as waves over rocks awash and, above, the calm blue sky and hot sun . . . Later, when we told him about it, he suffered agonies of frustration; not that he had not been there with his cameras but because he had not been there at all. So, yes, it was important to get it right, for although I could avoid the moves or even go down, I would have to come back sometime. My motive was genuine, I was doing this only for myself. I was trapped

> *for thoughts that breathe and words that burn,*
> *syntax, wordplay, parts of speech,*
> *this noun, that hold out of reach,*
> *expression, message, picture, surd,*
> *sentenced to search for THE WORD*

intangible, like the bond between climbing friends that ties them together more than the rope, like the resonant chord in mountain writing played by many composers.

And so, needing some kind of affirmation, I sought out my companions there, for although I was on my own I could choose whomsoever I liked. The clouds of doubt drew apart as voices rose from the pages with a direct impact. Donald Orr touched me with his 'nebulae of sodium streetlights in the blackness that always evoked a feeling of loneliness and melancholy' so that I cried out from deep down, having hovered over the same desolation, suddenly evoked. Then the creativity and originality of Iain Smart breathed wisdom and empathy in my ear. Jim Perrin, too, and he tells me, straight; to look, to think, to feel and see, you can be taught these things by words, this is how experience is shared . . . you feel it inside – synaesthesia. Then he, in turn, quotes from Dorothy Pilley, for him the one who comes nearest to the underlying why of mountain literature and there, in her words 'the sense of an uncapturable significance will arise, and its secret – for the mountaineer as for any other pilgrim of passion – is almost an open one. Therein, reflected, is the experience of being ardently alive'.

I realised that, after all, I wasn't off route. It does matter – the desire to communicate is really a voyage within, perhaps of perception, certainly of soul-baring. But, more than that, the difference between Holyrood Palace and Camasunary and the reason you would choose to be at one rather than the other, an uncapturable significance, an intangible word, will be a constant taunt.

Inspired, I tried the sequence again. Suddenly, it was all over. With relief, movement started to flow and I knew that, this time, I would achieve an end.

ANGEL FACE

By Andrew Nisbet

MY FAVOURITE cliff is Coire Mhic Fhearchair. Nowhere else so sharply highlights the special atmosphere of climbing in the mountains. As the drips run down your arm, says the cynic. Perhaps the answer is the spectacular backdrop, an expanse of wilderness out to the north spiked with such distinctive peaks, even as far as An Teallach. Surrounding you is the classical coire with lochan and steep walls neatly enclosed but not so close to be oppressive. Dream about the windless day when the whole atmosphere is captured inside the reflection on the lochan. And if it's your first visit to the coire and you've wisely chosen to approach from below to capture the sudden panorama as you breach the coire lip, then a windless day will provide a mountaineering highlight.

Curiously enough, this beautiful approach is a serious distraction from the real issue of climbing some rock. On only a handful of my visits, have I seen another party climbing in the coire, so my rating of it as equal to Cloggy or Scafell suggests that either I am biased or a lot of folk are missing out. Not that I should complain about the lack of competition for new routes, but it has intrigued me over the years (and now they're all done!). The walk is so memorably long and arguably tedious – once you've seen the view a few times – that from an armchair at home, it is easy to think of more appealing places to go. And even if you get as far as Torridon, there's always Diabaig. The new guide has hugely increased the popularity of Diabaig but as yet, made no difference to Coire Mhic Fhearchair. I only threw off the millstone of prolonged scenery when I awoke to the climber's functional approach over the top. My choice of line has varied over the years but the latest is the left side of a stream just left of the main screes which leads directly to the meadow down from Coinneach Mhor and the clifftop. This, of course, isn't described in the Guide.

And then the descent gully leads to Angel Face, close in profile, and impressive enough to convince me in the early days of its last great problem status. But a visiting rock star could never have found the same thrill as I did climbing near my technical limit on a line of outrageous appearance. Even pre-warned, you might have problems standing tentatively under it and trying to switch off the calculating mind which will divert you towards the more amenable Groovin' High.

Early days revolve around a weekend in 1980 when Brian Sprunt and Greg Strange climbed Pale Diedre and The Reaper while Neil Spinks and I climbed easier things. The Reaper was named after Brian's impression of their first attempt on the line. Brian was well known for his bold and powerful style of climbing and launched out on-sight up the wall heading for its most obvious feature, a big crack on the right side. About 50ft from his runners and running out of strength, he managed to rest with his chin hooked on a hold, hence avoiding meeting The Name. It's ironic that the much more improbable Angel Face is easier and safer, but the contrast is the origin of its name. So, when Greg commented on the impressiveness of our route, Olympus, and showed surprise at the grade of VS, he having just climbed what we assumed was the hardest route in Scotland (at least it should have been, based on Brian's colourful tales), it made me realise that the walls here were not always what they seemed. The ascent of Pale Rider, which we guessed at E4 and climbed at E1, confirmed the theory after a six-year gap and suddenly opened up the whole coire as climbable at a sensible grade (although Ling Dynasty later disproved that theory).

The quartzite is very smooth with little friction on the vertical faces but rough and often knobbly on the horizontal plane. I've heard from more than one geologist that the knobbles are metamorphosed worm casts but there must have been a lot of worms. The key to unmasking this improbable appearance is that there are square-cut holds composed of this rough surface but these are invisible except from close up. This lack of contrast also hides the line of Angel Face (a series of shallow ramps) from the ferocious surrounding walls. Edging-style boots are therefore most suitable for Coire Mhic Fhearchair and positive fingery climbing is the style. Again contrary to appearances, the quartzite has many thin cracks and these have often eroded into wedges, sometimes too small for fingers but excellent for small rocks and RP's. Logie Head is also quartzite and similarly well protected, although being newer and softer rock, the runners are bigger and finger jamming is more common.

There is a lot of chat here because my ascent – with Chris Forrest – of Angel Face went smoothly, with faith in the ridiculous reinforced by an abseil beforehand. Not a single loose hold was found nor any brushing done, so future cleanness is guaranteed. But, of course, there are problems. As a high north-facing mountain crag, it is a bit slow to dry and one has to wait until every last snow patch has melted to end the drainage. But the end pillars of the Far East Wall (Reaper wall and Groovin' High wall) are quicker than much of the rest, particularly as they get the sun from 3.30p.m.-10.30p.m. in June. So my impression is that a few dry days is plenty and the walls are quicker to dry than their reputation indicates.

The slow-drying section on Angel Face is the left-slanting groove just below the traverse ledge, which, unfortunately, happens to be the technical crux. After the big holds of the first pitch, suddenly the fingers have to work and as the groove leans away, the feet have to keep working out on small holds to stay in balance. There are continuous small runners but eventually those without steel fingers will be obliged to show some commitment. The traverse ledge itself initially seems a relief but slowly dawns the realisation that there are no runners so a bold wee wall above it before entering a tiny ramp increases the excitement. The ground above is ludicrously steep but every time you're forced against it, a step left gains a new crackline and keeps the angle conceivable. The improbability demands lots of runners, and backups to the lots of runners. So, however many you take, you'll run out of smallish wires. And just as you do, you'll have been forced out left under a roof into hostile territory. But as you reach 'the edge of nowhere', all is saved and even your diminished rack fits the crack, but some faith is definitely needed. Even when the tension is released, you're bound to remember the ridiculous exposure. The reassurance of those final moves provided a highlight which I will never forget.

SNOW ON THE HILLS

In the night, while we slept, the snow came
stealing over the hills with a soft step
and lying at the door
white in the dark
by morning deep and even.

And the country returned to the days of no roads
but ways through the hills
where man and beast passed on foot
and wind and buzzard and moonlight on wings.

Against the icy blast a tinker with his pack trudged on
longing for the shelter of the glen.
A messenger from the King, must cross the bealach before dawn.
A murderer from his crime, flees to high corries – fast.
And a few douce clergy and merchants, coin heavy,
abandon their carriages, held fast in the drifts,
to curse and trauchle on
to the yet too distant inn.

The armies of Montrose knew these white hills
spent bitter nights amidst the blizzard and the dark
in threadbare plaids,
before the dawn, cold water and oatmeal.
Yet still this frozen land was home.

But now the curtains open
children burble with delight
and quickly tourie bunnets, mitts and coats are struggled on
and Dad enjoys the snowball fight.
The sparkling snow lies pure and deep up on the hill
a shepherd and his collie cross the stile
and phantoms of the long ago are quiet awhile.

Lynne McGeachie.

YESTERDAY, TODAY AND TOMORROW

By I.H.M. Smart

Here are some serendipitously acquired memorabilia which shed a dim light on the frugal past, a wan light on the spoilt-brattish present and a gloomy light into the sadim market-oriented future.

YESTERDAY

REPRODUCED below is a letter from Robert Lawrie, one of the few pre-war suppliers of climbing equipment, written in May, 1946, in answer to a request to buy a 100ft length of hemp climbing rope. There appears to have been only one such length available in the whole country, possibly in the whole of Western Europe, and it was hanging on the market. (Nylon rope was still over the horizon). It indicates how quiet the climbing scene must have been after the war.

TELEPHONE NEWARK 766.
TELEGRAMS INLAND: ALPINIST, NEWARK.
CABLEGRAMS: ALPINIST, NEWARK.

ESTABLISHED IN 1867.

OFFICIAL SUPPLIERS OF CLIMBING BOOTS, ETC., TO
THE MOUNT EVEREST, POLAR EXPEDITIONS, ETC.
MILITARY BOOT AND SHOE MAKERS.

Robert Lawrie Limited,

ALPINE AND POLAR EQUIPMENT SPECIALISTS.

WARTIME ADDRESS

YOUR REF.   OUR REF. EL/CC.

53, Stodman Street,

Newark, Notts.

(LATE OF BURNLEY)

May 10th 1946.

I.H.M. Smart Esq.,
52, Arden Street,
Edinburgh. 9.

Dear Sir,

      We thank you for your letter of the 7th to hand and for your enquiry fir standard weight Rope.

      We have at the moment, a 100-ft. length in stock but offer this subject to being unsold at the time of ordering. We are enclosing a price list herewith, shewing other lengths available and would suggest that when ordering, you give an alternative length.

      Looking forward to the pleasure of serving you,

      We are,

        Yours faithfully,
        pp. Robert Lawrie Ltd.

        Director.

The leaflet that accompanied the letter is also reproduced; it, in its turn, indicates the minimal resources available at a time when happiness was having survived the war. At that time a schoolboy who could climb Severes hadn't done much compared to someone a few years older who had parachuted behind enemy lines at night or waded ashore at Anzio. We halflings kept very quiet; the day of the juvenile delinquent was yet to dawn.

Soft iron nails, like clinkers and hobs, by the way, were not all that bad for rock climbing and not as rock-destructive as tricounis. If they survived today they would have to be banned or the classic climbs would be abraded away; it is just as well that Vibrams were invented.

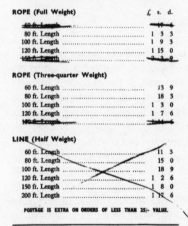

R. LAWRIE, LTD., 53 Stodman Street, NEWARK, Notts.

A limited supply of Best Quality

Manilla Climbing Rope

is again available and the following lengths can be offered subject to being unsold at the time of ordering

ROPE (Full Weight) £ s. d.

~~60 ft. Length~~	~~17 6~~
80 ft. Length	1 3 3
100 ft. Length	1 9 3
120 ft. Length	1 15 0
~~150 ft. Length~~	~~2 3 9~~

ROPE (Three-quarter Weight)

60 ft. Length	13 9
80 ft. Length	18 3
100 ft. Length	1 3 0
120 ft. Length	1 7 6
~~140 ft. Length~~	~~1 11 6~~

LINE (Half Weight)

60 ft. Length	11 3
80 ft. Length	15 0
100 ft. Length	18 9
120 ft. Length	1 2 6
150 ft. Length	1 8 0
200 ft. Length	1 17 6

POSTAGE IS EXTRA ON ORDERS OF LESS THAN 25/- VALUE.

R. LAWRIE, LTD., 53 Stodman Street, NEWARK, Notts.

IMPORTANT EMERGENCY WARTIME CONDITIONS.

1. Unfortunately, many of the goods shown in this catalogue are now discontinued with no hope of replacement until after the war. However, if you will let us know of any articles in which you are particularly interested, we will do our best to meet your requirements.

2. REGULATIONS.
Owing to present regulations, we regret that catalogues may not be sent out without a nominal remittance of 3d. having previously been paid.

3. SHORTAGE OF STAFF.
When sending in parcels, we should be grateful if customers would put their name and address on the outside as this greatly facilitates matters at this end. Also on account of this shortage, we are reluctantly compelled to adhere strictly to our terms of CASH WITH ORDER, and regret that we are no longer able to allow any credit.

4. NAILING.
Owing to the acute shortage of nails, we are compelled to reserve the more efficient types for the toe position and forepart of the boot only and are using hobs, or the nearest available, for the heels, waists and centres of soles.

5. SHORTAGE OF MATERIALS.
We regret that, owing to the very limited supply of leather and nails we now find it impossible to undertake repairs to footwear other than of our own make.

6. DELIVERY.
We regret that owing to special Service work which must of course have priority, it is impossible for us to give any definite delivery date, but you can rest assured that we shall do our utmost to complete any order you may place with us as quickly as possible. This particularly applies to handsewn boots stocks of which we are unable to accumulate owing to pressure of service work.

R. LAWRIE, LTD., 53 Stodman Street, NEWARK, Notts.
P.T.O.

TODAY

Here is a report of a rescue of a new-age hero from the Lairig Ghru as reported in the *Dundee Courier* on September 6,1993.

Emergency call-out—via Kent!

A PHONE call from the Lairig Ghru at lunch time yesterday set in motion one of the oddest mountain rescues the emergency services have tackled.

Two 17-year-olds, one from the Aberdeenshire village of Drumoak and the other, Neil Lawrence, from Kent, were walking from Braemar to Aviemore when the English teenager got into difficulties.

Equipped with a mobile phone in his backpack, he phoned his girl friend in Tunbridge Wells.

He left a message on her answering machine saying he was unable to continue.

When she returned home and heard the message, she contacted Neil's parents, who in turn contacted Grampian police.

A rescue operation was set in motion, controlled by RAF Pitreavie, who had a Belgian Sea King in the area on an exercise as part of an air force exchange.

The injured teenager was found a short time later and airlifted from Corrour Bothy by the Sea King to Raigmore Hospital in Inverness, where he was treated for a knee injury before being released.

TOMORROW

Things may have been difficult yesterday and indulgent today but what of tomorrow . . . Here is a conference program for 'Customer Care in the Environment'. It is a chilling document written in 'future speak'. In years to come we will no longer be citizens of our land or members of a community belonging to our own land but 'customers' having what was once our hope and glory marketed back to us by quangos and private interests who offer the topographical equivalent of commercial sex.

The market that these dull, humourless people serve has no loyalty, no culture, no morality. If market research suggested that it might be profitable they would turn Hallaig into a theme park with a diorama of men lying on the green at the end of every house that was and the girls returning from Suisnish, not as in the beginning, but every hour on the hour during the tourist season. These people are organised, have the ethos of a nasty regime behind them and mean business, in the several senses of the last term. If we don't actively oppose this sort of take-over and defend our land and community we will have our own mountains packaged and flogged to us as if we, the real owners, were mere 'customers'. England seems to have already fallen; the battle for Scotland can't be far off. Our national pastime of misdirecting our energies is now more than usually inappropriate. Surely, even we, in spite of our aptitude for easy subornation, can fend off these ponderous twits when they cross the Border. The alternative is to be 'managed' by bearers of the 'Sadim touch' which, you may remember, is the 'Midas touch' in reverse – all the gold it comes in contact with turns to lead. We have to find a better way for Caledonia – land of the mountain, flood, brown heath, shaggy wood and all. Sir Walter Scott when making up this list did go on to say that we were stern and wild – we should rummage in our collective unconscious and give these little-used attributes a try – for once.

COUNTRYSIDE
RECREATION
NETWORK

Customer Care
in the
Countryside

**A practical review of techniques to meet customer
needs and expectations in countryside recreation**

*29th September
to 1st October 1993*

University of Nottingham

COUNTRYSIDE
RECREATION
NETWORK

The Conference

We recognise the increasing importance of customer service and quality management. We need to develop new approaches and adopt consistent standards. This applies as much to those involved in managing countryside recreation as in any other part of the service sector. This Conference will bring together practitioners and academics to discuss the theory and practice of **customer care in the countryside.**

The Conference will:

- review the characteristics of visitors to the countryside and their expectations;

- review the need for customer care and quality management programmes in a countryside context;

- consider how such programmes can be undertaken; and

- investigate how performance can be measured and monitored.

Who Should Attend?

All those who are concerned or involved in countryside recreation and are keen to extend their knowledge and gain an insight into the latest thinking and practice in this area. This will include researchers, planners, managers and consultants and farmers concerned with providing quality countryside recreation. Participants are likely to work in local authorities, national parks, national agencies, voluntary organisations owning and managing land, higher education, consultancies and voluntary organisations representing users of the countryside

Conference Programme

Wednesday 29th September

18.30 Dinner

19.30 Welcome to the Conference by CRN Chairman Derek Casey (Director of National Services, The Sports Council)

19.45 **Experience Overseas**

Frans Schouten (Synthesis International): Best practice in caring for customers in countryside recreation and rural tourism in mainland Europe.

20.30 **The UK Experience**

Nick Allen (Human Resources Manager, Center Parcs Ltd): Caring for Customers at a major managed recreation site in the UK.

21.15 Discussion

Thursday 30th September

09.15 **Meeting Customer Expectations**

Dr Sue Walker (Centre for Leisure Research): A review of customers' expectations and barriers to participation at both managed and informal sites in the countryside.

09.55 **How to Care**

Speaker to be announced: The theory of quality management and customer care in the context of countryside recreation.

10.35 Coffee

11.05 **Review of Performance to Date**

A "question and answer" session to a panel of members of countryside user groups representing a range of activities and different interests.

11.45 **Training**

Gerry Carver (L & R Leisure plc): The role of staff training in caring for customers.

12.15 **Discussion on Morning Papers**

12.45 Lunch

14.00 **Workshops - Round 1**

15.30 Tea

16.00 **Workshops - Round 2**

17.30 - 17.45 Presentation of Results of CRRAG 1992 Conference Customer Survey

18.30 Dinner

20.00 Fringe Events

Friday 1st October

09.15 Feedback from the Workshops

10.15 Discussion on Feedback

10.30 Coffee

11.00 Making the Connection to Performance

Tony Bovaird (Aston Business School): What is the relationship between setting customer service standards and establishing performance indicators?

11.30 Customer Care in Practice

Professor Terry Stevens (Swansea Institute of Higher Education): The relevance and future of customer care and quality management in countryside recreation.

12.15 Discussion on the Morning Session

12.35 Chairman's Closing Remarks

12.45 Lunch and Depart

Workshops

Three Workshops will explore the practice of customer care programmes and quality management in various countryside contexts. Delegates will have the opportunity of attending two workshops on the Wednesday afternoon, and should indicate their preferences on the booking form.

The Workshops will each run twice and will consider the following topic areas:

Paid Access Sites (2 Workshops)
1. "The Big Sheep", Bideford (Michael Turner, Manager)

2. The National Trust (Hilary Lade, Manager, Fountains Abbey)

Training Schemes (1 Workshop)
3. Wales Tourist Board "Welcome Host" Scheme

Open-access Managed Recreational Sites (3 Workshops)
4. Inland Waterways (Ken Dodd, Marketing & Communications Manager, British Waterways)

5. Country Parks (Ian Fullerton, East Lothian District Council)

6. Forest Parks (Chris Probert, Forestry Commission, Kielder Forest)

Environmental Sites (1 Workshop)
7. Nature Reserves & SSSIs (Martyn Howat, Senior Site Manager, English Nature)

Footpaths & Rights of Way (1 Workshop)
8. Calderdale (Ian Kendall, Calderdale Countryside Service
   & the Pennine Way (Tony Philpin, Pennine Way Co-ordinating Project)

NIGHT ON BALD MOUNTAIN

By Colwyn Jones

MUSSORSGY, the composer of 'night on bald mountain' was Russian. If he had been Czech, our situation could not have been more appropriate. My sleepless mind drifted thus, as we sat in our rudimentary snow hole 7000ft up the North Face of Ganek on the Czech side of the High Tatras. At 3a.m. memories of a restless, hostile and warring Europe, from a restless, hostile and no less warring school history lesson, suggested a bleak possibility. Could Russia have been part of Czechoslovakia when Mussorsgy wrote this inspirational and predictive piece of music? I turned, intending to suggest this to my two shivering companions, when the Custodian suddenly asked: 'Have you any of that dental floss stuff with you.'

As I searched in the top pocket of the rucksack I was sitting on he added, by way of explanation: 'I'm hungry.'

'Ye cannae eat dental floss,' I chided. 'Anyway we shared the last food at midnight.'

'Naw, it's to see if I have anything stuck between my teeth.'

I didn't ask if he found anything to assuage his hunger, he may have offered to share it.

A week previously we had flown from Heathrow to the mausoleum of Prague's Ruzyne Airport, on a fresh spring morning. Customs had demanded two of us change the habit of a lifetime and shave our beards off. Could the harsh ethics of Czech winter climbing outlaw the beard as an artificial aid. Ethics which were enforced at national borders. A precedent, perhaps, to help in the preservation of the Scottish mountains? No, it was just a disenfranchised customs official longing for the power of the pre-perestroika days. We belatedly emerged, with whiskers intact, into the sunshine, to greet our hosts for the trip. The Czech State Bank Mountaineering Club.

A fleet of Skodas and a very comfortable BMW of recent acquisition, though dubious legality, conveyed us to various homes to enjoy the selfless hospitality of our hosts before travelling to the Tatras.

The overnight Prague to Poprad express was admirably priced. A bottle of whisky cost more than return sleeper tickets for eight of us. Though they were purchased at the local Czech price, not the western tourist one.

Next morning the delightful salmon pink peaks of the High Tatras turned searing white with the arriving dawn. We disembarked at the mainline Strba station and a rack railway, built to serve the local ski resort, took us up to Strbske Pleso with its ski jumps. We then walked the pleasant few kilometres through the pine woods of the Mengusovska-Dolina valley to the, grandly named, Horsky Hotel at Popradski Pleso. An adequate base for the first week.

The rough, clean granite of the High Tatras straddles the Czech-Polish Border and forms the northern end of the Carpathian range which stretches south into Romania. They are larger than the premier Scottish mountains, though not on an Alpine scale, so climbs can be completed in a reasonable day from the valley base.

Our first days were spent on ascents of Vysoka (2560m), Ganek (2459m), and Mala Basta (2285m) by fine 10 to 15-pitch mixed routes of Scottish winter grade 3/4. Ice falls on Kopky (2354m) gave excellent sport, though conditions were thin and by late afternoon the snow proved soft and tiring in descent. Our guidebook was written in Czech and gave only summer grades, while the advice of our two Czech hosts MD (Mad Dentist) and 'Bellybutton' only confused the issue when trying to gauge the difficulty of routes.

While climbing to the summit of Rysy (2499m) we found the enchanting Chata Pod Rysmi Hut (2250m) was open and from the col just above it we could gaze at the most intimidating cliff in the area, the Gallery.

The hut is normally closed in winter but Victor the warden was in residence. He had been to Scotland and after a few attempts we found the names of some mutual friends. Thereafter he insisted we stay and climb in the area and plied us with quite the most delicious tea. Next day nine of us arrived for an attempt at the Gallery on the North Face of Ganek.

MD, complete with home-made terrordactyls, joined Bill, the Raeburn Custodian and I in the obvious left-hand couloir. We think the summer grade was V. Diff., and it was imaginatively called Klasicka Cesta (the classic route).

A week had been spent finding the summer grades bore little relation to the difficulties encountered. A late start, three on a rope and thin conditions seemed a poor combination, but we started well, knocking off four pitches in the steepening gully. The virgin névé gave first time placements and the protection, which was excellent, appeared right on cue. The sun shone on the valley behind and we could see the three other parties on the distant Western Buttress, as we quickly rose above them towards the clear azure sky above.

The fifth pitch led to some tricky mixed climbing ably led by the Custodian, and he moved effortlessly up to another bomb-proof belay. After a week of climbing we were relaxed and enjoying the exposure afforded by the vertical wall.

No ice lined the gully, so MD led out left on to the face which overhung below us. Retreat was problematic from here, but we thought little of it, our sights were firmly fixed above.

From a crowded belay I led into an awkward but well-protected chimney and had run out half a rope-length before traversing to the foot of an icicle between two smooth buttresses of granite. A lovely drive-in to frozen turf helped me away and I was relishing the exposure when for once an axe placement didn't feel right. The pick was well embedded in the cold névé but felt alarmingly flexible. I hefted it out to try again and was concerned to see the pick remain in the ice. My mind wrestled with the problem, I had spare picks but the alloy head of the hammer had fractured, without prior warning, through the two retaining bolt holes. Then the penny dropped, the spare parts were of no value. My voice clicked into gear and I started to curse. My tirade harangued the hammer, the ice, the mountain, the world, but especially my conceited sense of patriotism which had prompted the purchase of the Scottish-made ice tools. I could hear righteous friends saying: 'I told you so.' Smiling Czechs reciting my acclaim of the quality of Scottish-made climbing gear back at me. Obscenities echoed around the Gallery.

The rope had gone reassuringly tight raising the stress on my sole remaining tool. The flow of invective stopped. The axe in my left hand was of the same manufacture as the broken hammer. It felt solid, but could it also fail without warning?

'A bit of slack please' I whispered.

The Custodian shouted: 'What's the problem?'

'Give me some slack please,' I hissed.

'What ?'

'Give me some slack you deaf b.......,' I yelled. And the profanity recommenced as I undiplomatically explained the problem to my bemused second.

Hanging on the vertical ice by one axe and my front points, I suddenly realised how slippery it was. I gingerly placed two Czech ice screws which seemed strangely thin. Is titanium really as strong as steel?

Diplomatic relations were re-established with the Custodian and he politely suggested step cutting. I was about to castigate him for being frivolous when, of course – step cutting. He had often reminisced about the technique during long bothy nights. 'An excellent form of retreat,' I could hear him say. Why hadn't I listened, and what a place to start using it.

I eventually trusted the ice-screws, clipped them, and pulled the axe out. Starting at knee height I cut huge steps and started to inch my way up the icicle. An hour later and about two metres higher, the step cut through to the underlying rock and I placed a No. 2 Friend in a purpose-made parallel crack. I belayed, and soon the Custodian climbed past, with a bearing best embodied in W.H. Murray's descriptions of J.K.W. Dunn, 'unflinching reliability'.

The rising timbre of a solid peg placement echoed down the main gully and I soon scrambled up on a taut rope, quickly followed by an ashen-faced MD. Safely on the belay, and after lengthy examination of the fractured hammer, he announced a preference for seconding the remainder of the route. We had carried a spare ice tool every day, but considered it an unnecessary burden on the long walk up to the hut. By some strange madness, which I still cannot explain, I volunteered to lead and continued with my sole remaining and suspect axe. In the narrowing couloir my crampons scraped the bare rock as I bridged breathlessly upwards. Almost a rope length out I reached a comfortable snow bay. The combination of a deep gully and, by now, late afternoon made it appreciably darker. My mention of the deteriorating light was initially met with a resigned silence, though the message was crystal clear: 'Get on with it.' However, a later couthy comment prompted me to take my sunglasses off. This admitted more light, but the loss of prescription lenses cancelled any improvement.

I belayed and was joined by my two panting companions. The light had suddenly gone. A surprise to those of us used to the extended twilight of more northern latitudes. The Custodian attached his head torch to his helmet and with 'studied ease' led the remaining 20m over the cornice – topping out in complete darkness.

Suitably relieved and illuminated, we readied ourselves for the descent. This followed a shallow gully before traversing onto a subsidiary ridge at the eastern end of the Gallery. We reasoned the three other parties would have used the same descent, however the poverty of footprints was disquieting. We yo-yo'd in the gully for over an hour but could find no trace of any route.

MD suggested we wait until morning. This stimulated further frenzied searching until, by a majority decision, we discontinued our nocturnal search and resigned ourselves to the ignominy of benightment. Perhaps we would enjoy company soon.

After digging a rudimentary snow hole, we sat on the gear. The Custodian and I had the luxury of bivvy bags. MD had a plastic raincoat. 'Czech Gore-Tex' he joked. We shared the remaining food and sat looking over the Border into Poland. The distant orange lights of Krakow glowed some 100km to the north, while the pure white, twinkling constellations above seemed closer at hand. Only seven hours until dawn.

We sang every song we could recall and many we couldn't. Autobiographies were told and dentistry was discussed at great length. After a few anecdotal stories, I was glad I had not admitted to losing a filling. We speculated at whose door the blame for our predicament could be laid. The others, by their absence we correctly surmised, had retreated by abseil. We also, rather prematurely I felt, boasted it was something we could tell our grandchildren. The night was magnificent, still and clear, as if the cold vacuum of outer space came down and claimed us. No one found respite in sleep.

At 5.30a.m. the sky brightened. Suddenly I felt strangely glad to be there. To survive a night of stress and uncertainty with such staunch companions was a privilege. An experience to be cherished, though hopefully, never repeated. We discovered the previous night's exploration had been too far down the gully. The descent soon warmed us and we arrived, albeit a little frost-bitten, back at the hut in time for breakfast and the good humoured, though relieved, jibes of the well-rested contingent of the party. And a cup of tea.

TILICHO SOUTH FACE

By Steven Helmore

When they were up they were up, when they were down they were down . . .

THIS WAS what happened on Tilicho South Face, Annapurna Himal, October 1990.

Our high point was a poignant moment: the red glow of sunset on Annapurna North Face, the inhospitable steep snow, and Pat and I trying hard to convince each other to continue into the freezing night. We are both beyond our previous experience, both tired after investing four weeks of effort on this face, both committed to a lightweight push beyond this never-ending headwall. Then Pat drops his gloves, and the sobering reality of 2000m exposure, a bone-chilling wind, the lack of ledges and the threat of frostbite tip the psychological scales. A groan of disappointment, an ice hammer smashed angrily into bare rock, and our numb minds were forced to concentrate on a dark, dangerous descent.

The British Army expedition to Tilicho 1990 was led by Matt, (Capt., Royal Engineers), Pat (Capt., Gunners), Ade (Paras), Dominic (cadet), Charles (doctor) and myself (taxpayer) made up the team. Sherpa Co-operative from Katmandu did a good job providing porterage and managing local admin. The climbing experience was pretty limited given the task at hand . . . nor had the team met or climbed together before. A brooding dissatisfaction with finances and horror at the sight of the route was polarising the party – Pat and I, Matt on his own and the other three, out of their depth.

Our base camp was the original Annapurna north side site, pioneered by Herzog in 1950. Indeed, inspiration for our line came from his superb black and white panorama in the back of 'Annapurna 8000m'. We shared this atmospheric place with a small Spanish expedition, and the ghosts of 20 or so unfortunate victims of the giant, whose names were inscribed in a simple memorial.

A closer inspection of our wall, the Grand Barrier, as it is known from the north, revealed only one likely line. The 7000m wall from Nilgiri in the west to Annapurna was for the most part guarded by seracs and avalanche swept walls. Above base camp, however, a ridge emerged from the bottom of a rocky headwall. Gaining this would solve the lower half of the barrier, and if climbable, would lead to Tilicho's summit plateau at about 7000m. From here a relatively short snow plod remained.

Our first task was to force a route up the very steep west side of this protruding ridge. Grass and exposed scree led to a campsite at 5000m, soon to be named Crow Ledge. Our military compo rations may have been chemical, biological and nuclear warfare proof, but they were no match for Tibetan crows. These combative creatures avoided poisons and traps but were finally defeated by a plastic barrel from Base Camp.

Our initial efforts to climb the ridge avoided Bertha, a prominent hanging serac, by taking a long gully to the right. This provided me with two days of loose entertainment at about HVS. And 300m of fixed line later, I was leading yet another crumbling pitch when a sudden storm produced conditions more reminiscent of Parallel B on Lochnagar. We were forced down to Crow Ledge to think again.

Matt and I then investigated Bertha from closer quarters. Though overhanging and the size of an office block, Matt coolly led right up into a cave under the front wall. Ominous creaks emanated as I jumared hastily towards him.

'Your lead,' he said, pointing at the traverse right – overhanging glacier ice dripping onto gritty, sloping ledges. Two bruising pendulums later, I gave up the arms-only ice axe traverse, and began half-heartedly sweeping snow from the steep slabs beneath. Hooking small holds beneath, I inched up and right. With grim satisfaction, I gained a gritty crampon hold and an ice axe driven into Bertha's base. After a much-needed snarg runner, the gritty overhung traverse continued to a small rock roof. Matt fell and pendulumed towards me. After some recovery of composure, he torqued his way up the overhanging rock corner, up to the steep but clear ice above.

I was quickly becoming very unhappy in the waterfall belay, and talked him out of further progress. Our day's work was done – the way to Camp 1 was clear. A heavy duty static line was hung here, avoiding the worst of Bertha's wrath, but every afternoon rock and ice slides made this a frightening place. The troops named it Bomb Alley.

Camp 1 was spectacularly positioned at 5350m on a snow platform cut into the ridge. Drops of 1000m on three sides gave tremendous views, while the way on led upwards towards the headwall. After a steep initial slope, the ridge thinned to a one-foot wide helter-skelter, half-a-mile long. This was superb climbing, but a lot of balance and nerve were required on this exquisite formation. We placed Camp 2 at 5650m, below the avalanche cone at the foot of the headwall now rearing above us.

The headwall was about 1200m high, and seemed most easily gained via a steep snow cone on the right. Bands of slabby limestone, ice fields and snow flutings hid an obvious line. After a very loose initial section, we were finally climbing less rotten rock and connecting steep snow.

At this stage there were only three fit climbers, with Ade and Dom incapacitated by altitude sickness. Our non-climbing doctor, Charles, learned to jumar by lying flat on the ground and dragging himself across base camp. He then proceeded to carry loads to Camp 2, filming us with a clockwork 16mm cine machine. His debut on the snow arete was carefully monitored by ropes from front and rear.

Steve Kennedy on the summit of Gerlachovsky Stit (2655m), the highest peak in Slovakia.

Morale could have been better among the troops. Matt's under-budgeting and 'hands off' leadership had lost their confidence and the increasing physical demands soon began to expose unexpected vicious conflicts. Our leader became increasingly isolated. By the time Pat and I had survived an interesting night descending the snow arete with one functioning head torch, exchanging tales of adventurous pasts, we had become good friends and a sympathetic climbing team.

Matt, Pat and I rotated climbing above Camp 2, and carrying loads. The thin 7mm line snaked upwards, and it was becoming clear this endless headwall would test our dwindling resources severely. The unremitting steep ground gave no respite in the form of ledges, and each pre-dawn commute to the top became longer. At the same time I could see the friction between the two captains getting worse. Rarely have a climbing pair been worse matched.

October 12 dawned clear as usual, and while Matt and Pat left before dawn to reach the rock before sunrise, I descended to the 5000m camp to fill a rucksack with food, fuel and rope. The journey up again was lonely, weighed by a large rucksack and balancing along the thin snow arete. But arrival was a relief, and I was soon relaxed in an open tent melting snow, contemplating the mist-shrouded walls above me. The sun dipped slowly behind Annapurna, bathing the peaks in a soft Alpen-glow – a beautiful spot.

High above me on the headwall, shouts from my invisible companions penetrated the still and cold air. I tried casually to make out what they were saying. Why was there only one persistent shout? With mounting alarm, I hauled myself out of the entrance to confirm my fears. It was a scream for help.

The unlikely climbing team had come to grief. After belaying Matt on two hard, mixed pitches, Pat had had enough and vetoed continuing in favour of a return before dark. In the inevitable ensuing argument, Matt untied the lead rope, and with a suitable expletive threw it away in favour of a 50m length of static line. While Pat started down the 500m of fixed line, Matt edged outwards towards a promising arete in search of a way on. When he fell, the long bruising journey to oblivion was halted by the 50m of static rope. Suspended tangled in gear, unconscious and with a broken arm, his situation at over 6200m was somewhat precarious.

It was Matt's pleas for help I could hear. Pat was out of earshot halfway down the fixed ropes. After a three-way shouting match, Pat set off upwards again. After packing water, clothes and a first aid kit I hurried upwards into the gathering darkness. I reached them just above a traverse at 6000m. To my astonishment they were still at it.

'Bloody incompetent belaying.'

'. . . . you, we'll leave you here and come back in the morning.'

'Pulled the bloody pegs out.'

Simon Jenkins and Martin Moran on the summit of the Aiguille du Jardin (4035m) during the Alps 4000 Traverse. Photo: Martin Welch.

My arrival restored some peace, and I placed myself squarely between the two combatant captains.

Matt was in obvious pain, with bloody face and bent arm, but was gritting his military teeth. Pat was sent ahead, while I fed Matt some Fortral and water. The abseil descent went slowly but surely, only the changeovers needed our help. Some overhanging sections added to Matt's bruises as he capsized and fell moaning on to the next belay.

At 3a.m. we were back at Camp 2, and decided to rest before continuing. The battered captain was examined, but not fed, and by midday we had negotiated the snow ridge and bumbled down to the top of Bertha. Matt free fell the overhanging abseil, landing on an unappreciative Pat. The mist and snow had arrived as we met the Doc, but at last we could relax in the presence of professional help and let others take over.

While Pat and I slept off our exertions, the hastily-assembled operating team of Ade, Dom, Sherpa Pemba and the cook helped the Doc set Matt's arm after heavy and alcoholic sedation. Ade and Pemba were then dispatched to summon help from Jomumsom. They reckoned on calling out an army helicopter, thus saving Matt a long and painful walk out.

Their run to Lete in 14 hours in new snow broke a few records, where they met our liaison officer, fortunately in residence at the local inn. After some tense diplomacy talking their way into the police station, and narrowly avoiding a British Embassy veto, a machine was summoned from Kathmandu. Two days' later, after a sluggish turn over the Annapurna Glacier, the clattering Allouette dropped onto our 'H' and Matt was on his was to the sanctuary of an army hospital in London.

After the noise had subsided, Pat and I adjusted ourselves to the task ahead. Our supplies at altitude were thin, and we were now just two. We reckoned on one visit to the top of the fixed ropes to tidy up after the accident, and then a lightweight push for the top. We lacked the resources and patience for a continued siege. The heavy new snow slowed us down, but after four days we were ready for the big push. We were glad at last to be 'going for it', but suitably nervous.

At 2a.m., October 20, we emerged into the windy Himalayan night and staggered towards the bottom of the fixed lines. Six hours of jumaring later, we started on new ground with very steep hollow snow which led after three pitches to a foot-wide, loose ledge under a huge block. The angle began to ease after another three pitches, and it looked as if the desperate mixed ground was giving way to moderate ice slopes at the top of the headwall. Still no bivi sites. Time and sunlight slipped away, and with wind and darkness the temperature plummeted.

We hung on a small poor belay and weighed up the odds. We had with us food, fuel and duvet jackets, but no tent or sleeping bags. There were no ledges up here even to sit on. We would have to continue upwards towards the summit plateau. Though the 18 hours of effort were beginning to take their toll, adrenalin seemed to be enough to force us on.

Then Pat dropped his mittens. Though we had emergency spares, the psychological scales were tipped, we had to retreat. Down climbing and three abseils found us on the small rock ledge.

At 6350m, we shivered until dawn. There was, however, one final ironic twist left. Our parched throats cried out for liquid, but the valves in two gas cylinders we had relied on were both damaged. Had we continued and committed ourselves to the summit plateau, this serious failure may well have been fatal. (It transpired that of the stack of 60 we had on the trip, two more were also unusable.)

Dawn came slowly, but fortunately there was no wind. Without water for 30 hours, the headaches had now set in, and the downward move was obligatory. Back at Camp 2, rehydration and sleep brought a new burst of enthusiasm, but physical and mental exhaustion were too much for my long-suffering partner. I was on my own. Better men than me would have tried to complete the climb alone, though better men than me have died doing similar things. There were fixed ropes up the headwall to within three pitches of our high point. The way to 7000m and the plateau was 'only' a steep snow slope away, and the summit a 2km glacier plod. The weather seemed stable. What frustration.

To my eternal regret, and probable continued survival, I accompanied Pat down to base camp and said goodbye to Tilicho's South Face.

ACHRIABHACH, GLEN NEVIS   JOHN MITCHELL 1984

CLIMBING IS ALL ABOUT HAVING FUN

By Rob Milne and Louise Travé-Massuyès

ROB: – 'What?' I shouted over the sound of the driving rain against my
Gore-Tex bivvy bag. I could hear a faint voice. 'I'm all wet!' was the reply
from my big wall partner. Her bivvy sack was just in front of mine on the
sloping bivvy ledge that is the top of pitch 6 on Half Dome's North-west Face
(VI 5.10 A2).

'Oh!' I replied unenthusiastically. 'Are you still warm?'

'I'm getting pretty cold,' Louise shouted back.

'Oh, that's okay, there is a dry jumper in the haul bag if you need it.'

I tucked deeper into my bag. I was still warm and dry, and after raining all
night, it couldn't rain all day also. After all, it hadn't rained for three weeks.
'It should stop soon, call if you get too cold.'

LOUISE: – For most of the night, buried quite cosily in my sleeping bag –
entirely made of feathers – I had so far been able to ignore the more and more
continuous plunk, plunk, of the water drops on my bivvy sack. But little by
little, I began to feel a wet sensation around the hip and the shoulder of the
side on which I was lying. Nothing alarming. My bivvy sack was Gore-Tex
and hence supposed to be waterproof. I decided that this was just my
imagination and fell asleep for another half-an-hour. However, the wet
sensation did not disappear, it got worse instead. My hands could now feel
the water on my clothes and the part of the sleeping bag between me and the
ground seemed to be a wet sponge. I had to accept that it really was raining
and that the bivvy sack I had borrowed from a friend was not as waterproof
as it was 10 years ago when it was new.

This is bad luck, I thought, three weeks without rain in Yosemite and now
. . . I was not happy, I had been looking forward to this big-wall climb for
years and now that I was here, already six pitches above the ground, it was
raining. Getting wet in a thunder storm in the Pyrenees is acceptable since
it's only two hours from Toulouse where I live, but getting such rain in sunny
Yosemite seemed senseless. Better not to think too far, my immediate
problem was that I was getting colder and colder. 'Quelle galere! Rob, I am
all wet!'

ROB: – In spite of the bad weather, I was feeling happy. It was the end of
May, I was part way up Half Dome, it hadn't rained in Yosemite for three
weeks and the climbing looked great. Not that we didn't have trouble getting
here.

I guess the first problem was when my bags got left behind at Heathrow.
Three days without my business clothes or climbing gear was okay. It was
only a technical conference and the weather in Seattle was great, so I was
happy.

I wasn't that bothered that the Camp 6 campground was full, I pretended to look for friends until we found a friendly campsite. It was all part of the adventure.

If I wasn't working on my sun tan, I wouldn't have enjoyed the approach. We tried to go direct from Mirror Lake to the base of Half Dome. Several people had said it was okay, but no one knew exactly how the path wandered between cliffs, slabs and dirt filled gullies. One of the problems with Americans is that they don't tell you that they don't know, they just say: 'I'm pretty sure it's obvious.' For most of the day we worked our way up a near-vertical torture chamber of dirt and trees. I was happy to be heading for the wall. Until we were misled by a cairn.

The next few hours were a nightmare. Fighting through the impenetrable willow with a pig of a heavy haul bag, in boiling hot sun. A series of cairns kept leading us deeper into a hopeless maze of dead-end willow paths. At least five times we backed off and tried another promising path, only to get ensnarled in the willows again. The face was close, but out of reach. Our plan to save a few hours turned into an all-day ordeal.

LOUISE: – I did not know what to think. In France, I would have decided long before that we were going the wrong way. But I had learned from an earlier experience in Yosemite, when trying to get the base of Snake Dike on the West Face of Half Dome, that a few simple sentences in the guide book like: 'Follow the trail up. After the second waterfall, bend to the left. Pass a dead lake and go up again to reach the base of the climb,' could actually mean more than six hours' walk, part of it in the bushes, without any trail or indications. Mother Nature wild style. That's American adventure, go for it and discover by yourself.

Now, our present adventure was becoming hell. After all, we were not in Brazil, where you need a machete to make your path in the heavy bushes to get the bottom of the climbs. C'est trop! I was getting tired, my bag was heavier and heavier and the face of Half Dome still far away.

ROB: – Finally, near dusk, we got back to the right trail, too exhausted to even reach the base of the wall. But the bivvy was great. As the sun turned the face the colour of gold, we found a large flat rock with a inspiring view right down the Yosemite Valley. I ceremoniously thumped that pig of a haul bag against the ground and said nothing until the tea was ready. It had been a real trial, but the wall looked great and the weather was good. It was paradise.

The next morning we felt recovered and ready for anything. In a couple of hours I was traversing the snow band to the start of the climbing. Three parties were above us already. That was fine, we didn't want to be hurried. It was so nice to be free of the haul bag that I didn't mind the giant rack of hardware.

Full of enthusiasm and energy, I started leading at high speed. Minutes later I reached the first hard section. I was here to have fun, so rather than work hard, I aided all the tricky bits. After all, we had only been in the Valley two days and done one warm-up climb. The climbing was very enjoyable, until I finished the aid ladder on pitch 4.

Snaking above me was a fist crack behind a flake. In my youth in Colorado I loved jam cracks. But after years of French limestone I was out of practice. It was rated 5.9, but felt desperate. I concentrated hard on each jam. The lower hand reaching up in the crack, the upper hand pointed down from above. I kept saying to myself: 'Relax, relax, work to get good jams and slam in Friends as fast as possible.' Working from one Friend placement to the next I struggled up the crack like a convulsive snake, but I did it. Five minutes after it was over, I decided it was one of the best jam cracks ever.

LOUISE: – This was my very first experience of big wall climbing and we had decided to go in pure style. The leader reaches the belay and pulls the haul bag, the second uses the jumars to go up and clean the pitch. Since I could not lead the hard sections, I knew that I would have to jumar most of the climb, although I hoped to either lead or second some pitches. Contrary to what one can think, the prospect of a lot of jumaring did not bother me, it seemed another attractive feature of the adventure. What was important to me was to live this trip, to be in the middle of the face, to see the bottom of the wall farther and farther away and spend three days – or more – out of the world.

Everything was going well so far, a sunny afternoon, little impressive crack pitches for beginning my jumaring experience. We were indeed slowly putting ourselves out of the world. We enjoyed the scenery and great rock. We took our time and stopped at the bivvy ledge in late afternoon. We were there to have fun, not work hard. The fact that the ropes got stuck just below the bivvy ledge probably influenced our decision to stop early. I proposed spontaneously to rappel down the pitch to release them. I was happy to be there and it was not a problem to go down the full pitch in order to pull the rope out of the crack where it was stuck, then jumar up again. That was part of the game. Next time, we would be more careful with the ropes.

Then it started raining during the night. The first rain for three weeks in Yosemite sounded like a monsoon on our bivvy sacks.

ROB: – Mid morning, it started to rain harder. I shouted over: 'This is a good sign, it will stop soon.' In her French accent she graciously replied: 'Bullsheeet, and I'm frozen.'

'Okay, Let me think.'

The first rule of big wall climbing, is that your most important task is to look after your big wall partner above all else. Take care of them before you take care of yourself. It was my duty to help, but I was warm and dry. It was clearly my obligation to get the dry clothes from the haul bag. Most people would consider our situation serious. I thought it was a great adventure.

Luckily the rain stopped before I made my moral choice. It slowly cleared and the sun eventually came out. We welcomed a rest day and a chance to dry everything. Louise's sleeping bag was the hard part. In spite of several recommendations, she had decided that it would not rain and that she would take her very comfortable feather sleeping bag. The result was that it was now flat and wet like a floor cloth. Another golden rule of Yosemite big wall climbs is – never use feather sleeping bags.

There was still a lot of cloud about. We considered climbing to the next bivvy ledge five pitches higher, but decided retreat was easier from here if the weather stayed bad. We fixed the next pitch and had a look at the easy traverse on to the main face. After that we felt a lot better, until after dinner.

We had just finished eating dinner, sitting on my sleeping bag, and had moved over to put the gear in the haul bag. Suddenly, we heard a sound like a rifle shot. Several large blocks were crashing down the face immediately above us. We dove under the haul bag and cowered. Rocks started to land on our bivvy ledge.

LOUISE: – I was absolutely terrified. I tried to get smaller and smaller against the wall with my arms and hands above my head. The terrible noise of rock fall I had heard several times during my Chamonix climbs. Every time, they produced the same electric discharge on me. Before, the rocks had always been falling elsewhere, but today they were falling directly at me. I could not believe it, Yosemite climbs were supposed to be extremely safe from this point of view. It was lucky that neither Rob nor I are superstitious, because the rain and now the rock fall would have been more than enough to convince us that the mountain gods wanted us to give up the climb.

ROB: – When the rock dust cleared, my bivvy sack was in tatters. The rocks had made a direct hit where we had been minutes before. My bag was hanging from its tie loop. My bivvy sack wouldn't keep me dry anymore. If it happened one minute before, we would have been seriously injured. I debated moving to a small ledge up the fixed rope, but it was getting dark and this was supposed to be a safe ledge. We rigged the haul bag as a roof against rock fall and went to sleep hoping it was the only incident, probably caused by the heavy rain. The clouds came back as we settled in.

At 5a.m. it seemed clear, but at 6a.m. it was foggy. It didn't matter, our enthusiasm was back, we were going up. A warmth generating jumar and two easy pitches led us to the bolt ladder across a blank slab. The sky had cleared to a beautiful day. The easy pitches looked like a catwalk onto a giant stage.

LOUISE: – I decided to lead these easy pitches. This was one of the few opportunities to lead a section of the climb. But I was not so sure when I put the gear rack around my neck. It was heavy like a millstone and the slings were adapted to Rob's size who is a foot taller than me. I felt like I was wearing a skirt made of carabiners, Friends and nuts. Qu'a cela ne tienne, I could not give up now.

I began an easy walk on a large ledge, then started a big staircase section and I put one Friend in a crack just in case. The pitch turned left and continued with a flake and crack section. As I went up, the rope was getting heavier and heavier. I had to pull a few metres of slack before making my moves because I could not climb with the rope pulling below me. This is the problem with easy pitches, they can become really hard because of rope-drag problems. I got to the belay out of breath and worse still, I now had to pull the haul bag. This was very hard work for me since it weighed almost as much as I did. Many times I was convinced that it was stuck.

ROB: – We were now on the face proper. Early attempts had failed here, until they decided to use bolts. On the first ascent, this bolt ladder was the key traverse to the chimney line up the face. The ladder ended with a 50ft pendulum. I had learned to enjoy these when I did the Nose on El Cap almost 15 years' earlier. The 900ft dead vertical drop added to my motivation. It was like being in a circus while I ran at full speed across the wall and lunged for the next crack. This was real wall climbing. I was so keen that I passed the next belay without noticing and linked two pitches together. Only the extreme rope drag slowed me down.

LOUISE: – When Rob began his lead he left me alone on my little ledge. He was concentrating so much that he did not even make a small joke as he normally does. The pitch above us looked impressive, it seemed quite impossible to go from where we were to the ledge that I knew to be the end of the pendulum way off to the right. I dreaded the time when I would have to use the sophisticated big wall techniques for traverse or pendulum pitches – and the next pitch had both.

It can be very tricky to go second cleaning the wall and a single mistake with the ropes or the slings can be disastrous. I tried to concentrate hard and to remember exactly the sequence of operations to be done when getting to a piece of gear. How to lower yourself down, then jumar up again to the next piece. I had never actually done this on a wall, all the experience I had was from France, practising six or seven feet above the ground or on the indoor climbing wall next to my home. This time, it was 900ft above the ground with a huge vertical mirror-like wall below me. This makes a big difference, believe me.

Suddenly, I realised that Rob was done with the pitch. My turn then. Once the haul bag began going up, I took a deep breath, avoiding looking down. I tried to convince myself the technique is theoretically sound, it should work. There should not be a problem if I did exactly as I had learned . . . Half-an-hour later, I was standing on the ledge, pretty satisfied with my performance. It had worked perfectly and I felt like I had climbed much higher on The Real Big Wall Climber scale.

ROB: – The next section was primarily 5.8 cracks and chimneys. I was warmed up and in my element. The soaking wet aid crack didn't make me upset. I thought of all those poor climbers in Scotland and the wet crags. But only momentarily, as I stepped up on a fixed nut and dry rock again.

The pitch ended in a sling ladder. I double-checked my last aid piece before using a 10ft knotted webbing ladder to reach a small pendulum bolt. I couldn't believe how rotten the slings looked, but I used them anyway to lean around the corner. Louise followed the short pendulum with the text-book technique of threading the rope. But it got stuck and 10 minutes of pulling hard didn't help. Another big wall rule is that you take turns unsticking the rope. I leaned around the corner to see an amazing spider web of tangled webbing. 'Oh! well,' I thought, this is what makes big wall climbing interesting.

Above us loomed one of the most dreaded sections of the climb. The chimney was mostly easy bridging, but it was blocked by an overhanging flake that created a 5.9 off-width crack. The guide warned that it is not as intimidating as it looks. And it looked bad. I put in our biggest Friend and sized it up. Fortunately, in my youth I was good at off-widths. I had fun on them when others just thrashed. This is largely because I learned to climb them with knee pads. Another rule of big wall climbing – climb in knee pads.

I adjusted all the gear and the haul-line to hang from one side, moved my chalk bag to the side and squeezed in. It was short but challenging. It felt good. Here I was more than halfway up one of the most scenic big walls, safely in a chimney system and enjoying squirming up another off-width. Minutes later, I let out a whoop as I pulled onto a good ledge.

LOUISE: – Chimneys are my favourite type of climbing. I kept thinking that this would have been a lot of fun to climb if I was not carrying a big pack with the day stuff and it was not already getting late. I began jumaring pretty fast, I had good technique now. But, the chimney was becoming deeper and I began to have problems with my backpack against the sides. To make things even worse, Rob had put all the protection in the back of the chimney so that I could not stay in the wide part. I had to squeeze as much as I could to gain every single foot. At each piece of gear, my weight on the rope prevented me from taking the rope out of the karabiner. I had to be very careful not to jumar too close. I stopped below each one and was forced to make a few free moves to take the gear out.

I was already in a sweat when I realised that the haul bag had been stopped above me for a while. It was totally stuck and did not want to move a single centimetre when I pushed strongly on the bottom. I could not get above it because my rope was going under the haul bag and against the rock. My jumars were already too high up. I re-tied my back tie knot and took the jumars off the rope. Without a belay, I climbed a few metres free and put my jumars on the rope above the haul bag. I could now seize it with my arms and, pushing hard on my legs, I could lean out of the chimney and give enough impulse to release the haul bag. It was going up again and I was exhausted.

ROB: – A few pitches later, we got to the pitch I wanted to do the most – the double cracks. When I was young, there was an article in the *National Geographic Magazine* by Galen Rowell showing a climber hand-jamming up a vertical crack, with the whole wall dropping below. It impressed me as one of the ultimate jam cracks. On an expedition once, I mentioned to

Galen how much that pitch impressed me. He then let me in on a secret. It is really a flake, with a good edge to grab inside. In other words, it was trivial.

To my joy, I discovered he wasn't sandbagging me. I hung from the flake for several minutes posing for photos, waving hello to everyone from my mom to the SMC members. Another rule – get photos when you can. Fifteen minutes later, I could collapse on Big Sandy Ledges, one of the ultimate bivvy locations. I was totally exhausted, but it had been a great day of climbing.

We ate dinner and watched the sun set on a bank of clouds moving in. We were only a few hard pitches from the top, but another night of rain could be very serious. The edge was taken off the fun by the serious proposition that if it rained we would have a real epic. I decided I was too tired to care and went to sleep.

Dawn was bright and clear. It had been a cold night and there was frost on my bivvy bag. Above us arched the zigzags – a strenuous section of free and aid. Everything I had read about them indicated hard work. I wanted to sleep longer and wait for it to warm up. Louise stuffed a mug of tea into my hands to warm them up and said to get going. I took some comfort from knowing that, after many winters of mixed routes, my fingers work well in the cold.

The laughing and joking had now stopped. I was about to do battle with the last barrier. I imagined I was climbing the arches of a gothic cathedral. Cold fingers were soon replaced by grunts and strains. I was a man with a mission, to get my climbing partner – and me – off the wall. As the warm blood forced me to take my wool hat off, I remembered that this was my favourite type of climbing. To climb all day, collapse at a bivvy and then start at dawn up the next section.

A hard step right and I clipped the belay. I shouted down about the great view and the neat crack above. The sun lit up the valley below and I could see lots of fixed aid points above. The fun was back.

The zigzags were hard work. I aided every move that I could and just kept going. I started to marvel at the lichen on the wall and the nice cracks. I could see the overhanging visor clearly now, a sign that we were getting close to the top. Soon, well actually, after a long time, I was belayed at the start of the most famous of all pitches, the Thank God Ledge.

Above us loomed the summit overhangs, 200ft of overhanging rock. The Thank God Ledge provides an easy horizontal traverse around the overhangs on to easier ground – hence its name. All my climbing career I had wanted to lead this pitch, and here I was. It starts 18" wide, narrows to 6" and then widens to 18" again. I had often thought about this ledge. I had seen many photos of people standing here. Would I be a show off and walk along it? Would I make a hand traverse? Would it be easy or hard? Now I had to decide what to do. I started to walk across it like Indiana Jones. But I had to kneel to put in a Friend. Then the rack got in the way, and I didn't want to risk a fall. In the end, I crawled on my knees. I had to slide one leg behind and one over the edge to pass the thin part, and I was across. I quickly led a hard step and a V chimney to the belay.

LOUISE: – Rob's style for crossing the ledge was not the most elegant. I was sure I could do better with the security of seconding. That was if I could get to the ledge. The hardest time I had on this pitch was trying to leave the belay about 7ft below the ledge. Because of my small size, I was missing some foot – or handhold, somewhere. The rope was running almost horizontal and the first piece of gear was 15ft away. Add to this the slack and the elasticity of the rope and I was facing a nice pendulum with a superb plunging view if I fell. I made the first moves and then back down to the belay three times. I was feeling desperate, the rope was even more slack now and my rucksack was too heavy . . . but I could not stay there.

I decided that on the next attempt I would just go for it. I must have done it right since I was suddenly standing on the ledge. I was not thinking of elegant style anymore. Once I had knelt down to take out the Friend, I stayed on my knees all the way across. Now, being smaller than Rob, I could traverse with both knees on the ledge even during the thin part. All things considered, it was not such poor style.

I was just thinking that I was done with all the problems when I reached the other end of the ledge. I had not been considering the pig of a haul bag. It had not moved for a while and I heard Rob throwing swear words. I got under the bag and tried to give it a shove far from the wall. This did not help much, the crack-chimney above me was oriented in the opposite direction of the haul-rope and getting narrower as it rose. This time, I had to crawl under the bag, lean my back against the wall and push the bag with my feet close together until it got out of the crack. I kept shouting: 'Pull now.' Finally, to end it all, it was impossible to jumar the crack, so I had to take off my rucksack and climb it free. This pitch took forever, a real mishap.

All that was left was an aid section – quite impressive though with 3000ft below our feet – and three easy pitches. We had cracked it. The mountain gods must have thought we now deserved a prize, for lying on the ledge was a brand new 50m x 5mm rope. Obviously, the parties above us had had problems in the rain. It would compensate nicely for the few new fixed nuts we had donated.

An easy traverse pitch, a VS slab and a steep step and we were on top.

In spite of the approach problems, the rain, the rockfall, stuck ropes and haul bag, hard work and cold weather, we were on top. Years of dreams and imagining what it would be like were over. We were really there. The landscape was cratered with wind carved sandy bowls. Clouds drifted in and partly covered the summit. This gave the strange atmosphere of being somewhere else . . . exactly where we wanted to be – out of the world.

We didn't have an epic, far from it. The climb had been fun, and we had had fun. And climbing is all about having fun.

NEW CLIMBS SECTION

OUTER ISLES

HARRIS: Like the authors, the New Routes Editor has no idea if the following routes are new.

Mangersta, Flannan Zawns:
Bubbles – 40m HVS 5a. C. King, R. Kenyon. 6th June, 1993.
An excellent route taking the groove up the centre of the slab taken by Flannan Slab. Start just left of Flannan Slab below a ledge at 3m. Gain the ledge, then move up leftwards to gain the base of the groove. Move up easily (possible belay), then follow the groove to just below the traverse on the second pitch of Flannan Slab. Now traverse leftwards to the arete and finish boldly up this.

Landlubber Zawn:
This is the zawn just north of Flannan Zawn, formed by a gentle-angled slab on its west side (end of Flannan Zawn) and a steep wall on its east side. The base of the zawn is easily gained by a walk down the gentle slab.

Dry Dock – 25m E1 5b. C. King, R. Kenyon. 6th June, 1993.
An impressive route taking the crack up the highest point of the steep wall. Start at the two large boulders at the end of the slabby tongue. Start easily up a corner crack. Move up leftwards and over an overlap. Continue up the crack to finish up a short corner.

The Painted Zawn:
The Prow – 25m VS. J. Ashdown, N. Dalzell. May, 1993.
Takes the front of the obvious black prow at the rear of the zawn. Scramble down (and up) from Painted Wall area and start to climb from a large ledge. Follow the easiest line up the prow to the top. Bold start on good rock.

Gloss – 20m E3 5b. N. Dalzell, J. Ashdown. May, 1993.
Scramble down to the neck of rock between two gullies on the north-east side of the zawn, left of Mick's Corner. Traverse awkwardly on to the pink undercut slab and then up to a series of breaks and footholds. Follow these rightwards to below an overhang (below top). Exit with care up a quartz vein that forms a short corner on the right of the overhang.

Legalibility – 25m E1 5a. D. Ashworth, C. Lofthouse. May, 1993.
Follows the right-hand side of the lower wall to the left and down from the previous route. Scramble down over the neck of rock between two gullies, left of Mick's Corner, to the above wall. Reach by abseil. Start up a rightward slanting crack through a bulge. Then climb leftwards through a quartz band to ledges. Follow the crack on the left and a wall to the top.
Black Foot – 30m E2 6a. D. Ashworth, C. Lofthouse. May, 1993.
This route takes the rightwards slanting line on the black triangular wall on the south side of the Painted Zawn, right of thewide middle gully. Start from a small black ledge reached by abseil. Follow a crack from the ledge through a bulge trending right and move up to a ledge with difficulty. Follow the obvious line left to the top.

Screaming Geo Zawn:

Whale Walk – 30m E2 5b. J. Ashdown, N. Dalzell. May, 1993.
Follow the initial right-facing corner of Claymore for 5m. Traverse left along good
handholds to reach a stance. Launch up a cracked slab through crux moves to reach
a sloping ledge. Climb the shallow corner above, trending left to finish on ledges.
A good line which avoids the loose rock of routes to the right.

I'll Try Up Here Again – 30m E1 5b. D. Ashworth, C. Lofthouse. May,1993.
Reached by abseil down an obvious VS-looking corner below ledges, approx. 15m
left of Claymore. The route takes an improbable line up some steep ground. Climb
an easy wall to a steep crack. Pull on to a small slab left of an overhang. Step down
to a crucial foothold at the bottom of the slab. Climb around the overhang (runners)
and follow the nose to the top.

SOUTH UIST, Beinn Mhor:

Western Gully – 120m I. B. Davison. 22nd February, 1994.
On the east side of Beinn Mhor are several broad gully lines. This takes the most
western (farthest right facing them). The back of the gully was lined with water ice
after two-three weeks of cold easterlies.

MINGULAY (1:50,000 sheet 31):

Mingulay is the second most southerly of the Outer Hebridean isles stretching from
Lewis in the north to Berneray in the south. Measuring 4 x 3k, its western seaboard
presents a continuous line of cliffs to the Atlantic, reaching a maximum height of
235m at the Biulacraig. Although many sections of cliff are vegetated or exten-
sively colonised by seabirds, there is also much clean rock offering great scope for
exploratory rock climbing. The island is uninhabited (although it once supported
a population of more than 100) and is normally accessed from Barra to the north.
Mingulay Bay, in the east provides the safest approach and good camping sites are
available adjacent to the ruined village.

Dun Mingulay (NL 543820):

Dun Mingulay is a cliff girt headland, in the south west of Mingulay, joined to its
parent island by a narrow neck of land (remains of a defensive rampart are visible).
Although much of Dun Mingulay's cliff line is broken or vegetated, a west-facing
section at Sron an Duin (overlooking two tidal skerries) forms a superb near 100m-
high wall of clean vertical to overhanging rock, providing climbing of an excep-
tional quality and situation. Access to the base is by abseil and is both an exciting
experience in its own right and very much dependent on relatively calm seas. A
100m rope is recommended (90m vertical drop). Very little loose rock is in
evidence on the cliff and the two routes climbed to date have been led on sight.

The Silkie – 105m E3. G.E. Little, K. Howett (alt). 31st May, 1993.
Two small cairns can be found on the west-facing cliff top near the western
extremity of Sron an Duin. Abseil from a point adjacent to the more southerly of
these to a rock plinth a couple of metres above tidal slabs. An impressive direct line
with sensational exposure on the third pitch.
1. 15m 4c. From the rock plinth climb a groove to distinctive red bands. Traverse
left along these to a small ledge and belay.
2. 30m 6a. Go straight up to below a black diagonal arching overlap and follow it
rightwards to below its widest point. Move up then pull through into a small scoop
on the left (crux). Step back right across the lip then climb flakes trending left up

a wall of compact rock to belay on the right below a square roof. A magnificent pitch.

3. 45m 5b. Turn the square roof on the left, then take a quartz corner breaking out right through a second roof. Step left on to its lip, then go directly up a juggy wall to another smal roof. Cross this to gain a cracked block ledge. Go up slightly right to a better ledge and belay.

4. 15m 4a. Climb steep but easier ground to the top.

Voyage of Faith – 125m E3. G.E. Little, K. Howett (alt). 31st May, 1993.
Abseil from a point adjacent to the more northerly of the two cairns to the base of a short square-cut corner immediately above tidal slabs. An outstanding intricate line with much atmosphere and stunning exposure.

1. 25m 5b. Climb the short square-cut corner to a small ledge at the base of an open groove (a more comforting belay if seas are running). Up the groove, then pull out left to belay on a small ledge.

2. 35m 5b. Move out left from the ledge, then follow a line of flakes trending left until a vertical flake crack leads to an obvious horizontal fault. Hand traverse left along the fault, then move up to a very exposed belay on a small nose of rock at the base of a slight corner (this whole area is undercut by a large sea cave).

3. 30m 5b. Climb the corner to a small ledge, then traverse 2m left into a parallel groove. Up this, then step left and slightly down to a very narrow ledge. Follow this until the overlap above can be bypassed giving access to a traverse line back right, above the overlap, to belay at blunt rock spikes adjacent to an obvious break in the main band of overhangs.

4. 35m 5c. Traverse out right through the overhangs (lower line) then climb directly up on steep rock via a groove to the base of a short, hanging corner. Climb this with difficulty to the top.

Guarsay Beag (NL 551845):

A clean west-facing wall lies at the north-west extremity of the Guarsay Beag promontory directly below an obvious cairn. The face is characterised by a shield-like section of rock, lichened in its upper part, defined by grooves on either flank. At the base of the shield, about 5m above the sea, is a curious hole in the rock, much favoured by seabirds.

With a View to a Shag (Left Hole Groove) – 35m Severe 4a. G.E. Little, K. Howett. 1st June, 1993.
Abseil to a ledge below the prominent hole. Ascend the groove bounding the left side of the shield.

Easy Day for a Shag (Right Hole Groove) – 35m Severe 4b. K. Howett, G.E. Little. 1st June, 1993.

After the same abseil, ascend the groove bounding the right-hand side of the shield. Well defined in its upper section.

From the Hole to Heaven – 35m VS 4c. G.E. Little, K. Howett. 1st June, 1993.
From below the prominent hole, climb the centre of the shield on excellent holds in an impressive situation.

West Face of Guarsay Mor:

A 100m of non-stretch rope recommended for abseil descents. There is a distinct inlet about halfway down the West Face of Guarsay Mor and the routes described go up the spurs on either side of the inlet.

Grey Rib – 70m H. Severe. C. Bonington, M. Fowler (alt). 30th May, 1993.
Starts from the highest point of the ledge just above the high-water mark at the foot of the buttress on the northern side of the inlet.
1. 35m. Climb 3m leftwards to gain a ramp leading up right into a short corner. Move up and left out of the corner on to the crest of the buttress and continue up for 12m to a stance.

No Puke Here – 65m VS. C. Bonington, M. Fowler. 30th May, 1993.
Follows the rib to the immediate right of a recess roofed by a huge overhang, to the left of Grey Rib.
1. 30m 4a. Climb the slabby rib on excellent rock moving left from a short crack to gain a good ledge.
2. 35m 4a. Continue straight up on good holds.

Stugeron –105m HVS. C. Bonington, M. Fowler. 31st May, 1993.
Up the groove line to the immediate left of the crest of the buttress to the immediate north of the inlet. Start from a cave immediately above the high-water mark at the foot of the groove line.
1. 30m 4c. Step left and climb a subsidiary groove until it is possible after about 10m to gain the main groove. Follow this to a ledge pulling out to the right.
2. 45m 4c. Up and right through the bulge above and on straight up to reach a ledge system below the headwall.
3. 30m 4c. Move left to a deep V-groove, pull over a small roof and continue to the top.

Pressure Band – 100m HVS. C. Bonington, M. Fowler (alt). 31st May, 1993.
Start as for Stugeron.
1. 45m 5a. Follow the groove line of Stugeron for 5m and then pull out left of the groove round a rib and follow the obvious steep crack line to a good ledge.
2. 25m 4b. Step up right, then back left to the ledge below the headwall. Traverse left for 5m to the foot of a steep groove.
3. 30m 4c. Climb the groove to the top.

North West Face of Slac Chiasigeo:
Liverbird – 125m E1. C. Bonington, M. Fowler. 1st June, 1993.
Start from the right-hand end of a wide platform with a small pond just above high water.
1. 50m 4b. Climb easily up to a ramp, then diagonally up the ramp into a steep corner and up this to a small ledge.
2. 35m 5b. Continue straight up a crack system and at 20m enter the obvious black, hanging groove. Climb this to a point about 6m below capping overhangs. Step and pull rightwards round an arete to reach a small stance in a corner.
3. 40m 5b. Climb through the overhang above, first using the left-hand crack and then pulling across round a rib to the right-hand crack, to reach a horizontal break. Move slightly left into a steep, deep-cut groove and follow this on excellent holds to the top.

COLONSAY:
Colonsay and its close neighbour Oronsay to the south (linked at low tide), lie to the north-west of Jura and Islay and offer a diversity of scenery unequalled on any other Scottish island of comparable size. Access is from Oban by a passenger/vehicle ferry. A bicycle is the ideal form of transport on the island. Although not

a major centre for rock climbing, the island does have a wealth of small attractive crags offering numerous one-pitch routes on a variety of rock types. Together with the many fringe benefits, rock climbing on Colonsay offers a delightful contrast to more traditional climbing venues.

Beinn Oronsay (NR 352981):
This south-facing edge lies to the north of the Priory and attains a height of 30m – not bad for an inland cliff on an island with a highest point of only 93m! The highest section of the edge lies immediately above the Priory and has a distinctive, open book, slabby, vegetated corner at its centre.

Hairy Habit Groove – 25m HVS 4b. G.E. Little, J. Finlay. 25th May, 1993.
The steep groove immediately right of the open-book corner with a pinnacle 3m up on its right side. Climb the groove throughout with the crux at half height gaining a small, grassy ledge. Copious drapes of hairy lichen add character to the route and mask many excellent holds.

Priory Slab – 30m Severe. J. Finlay, G.E. Little, W. Skidmore. 25th May, 1993.
The obvious clean slab left of the open-book corner with a distinctive slim rib at its start. Climb the rib and slab above to a grassy patch, then up an easy-angled slab groove trending right to finish.

Cailleach Uragaig (NR 382981):
This low headland can be accessed from the cottage of Duntealtaig by a vague path and exhibits an interesting jumble of coves, arches and crags.

Grooved Slab in the Dark with Bendy Boots – 20m H. Severe. G.E. Little. 22nd May, 1993.
Climb the centre of the clean, grooved slab on the south side of the headland – on the north side of Port nam Fliuchan.

Arch Crag:
This impressive little crag forms the south wall of an obvious shingle cove and the outer face of the leg of a natural arch. To the left of the arch the cliff has seen a major rockfall and is unstable, whereas the leg of the arch is composed of sound, vertical or overhanging clean rock with the odd loose flake high up.

The Jagged Edge – 30m HVS 4c. G.E. Little, J. Finlay, W. Skidmore. 22nd May, 1993.
Climbs the clean, hanging edge immediately right of the arch – the left edge of the outer face. Pull over overhanging flakes, then up the exposed edge to an arete and flake runners below the final steepening. Move left and up to a grass ledge and then to the top.

Waiting for God – 35m VS 4b. J. Finlay, G.E. Little. 23rd May, 1993.
Start as for The Jagged Edge and take an easy slab ramp leading up diagonally right. At its termination step down right at a big shaky flake. Then ascend a short steep groove to traverse back left above to gain easier ground. Take a slight groove running out right with an exposed finish.

Limpet Groove – 25m VS 5a. G.E. Little, J. Finlay. 23rd May, 1993.
Start at a crack leading into a groove on the right side of the crag (demarcating the right edge of the radically overhanging section of the wall). Climb the crack (crux) – not accessible at high tide – then up into an easier groove. Above a horizontal break, the final section is on strangely eroded, lichened rock.

Pat Hickey climbing Alpine style at 6300m on Tilicho South Face – Annapurna in the background. Photo: Steven Helmore.

Beachcomber Slab – 15m VS 5a. J. Finlay. 23rd May, 1993.
This route lies on the opposite side of the cove from Arch Crag on a black slabby face. Start at a polished wall below a shallow groove, left of a black hanging arete. Get off the ground (crux) then climb shallow groove/cracks to an overlap. Traverse left below the overlap to gain easy ground.

Meall an Suiridhe (NR 402993):
The grassy hillock of Meall an Suiridhe, to the west of the track leading from Kiloran Bay to Balnahard, is cut by a narrow cliff flanked rift. The most striking feature of this rift is a radically-overhanging wedge of rock (The Fang) well seen from the track.

Thrift is a Virtue – 20m V.Diff. G.E. Little. 22nd May, 1993.
West of The Fang, on the south side of The Rift, lies a crag at a more amenable angle, increasing in height towards the sea. This route tackles the high narrow slab with sea thrift at its top staying close to the right edge (this slab should not be confused with the wider slab to the right, more liberally covered in sea thrift).
At the North-west extremity of the headland, beyond The Fang, lies a north-west-facing, 20m vertical wall. Its base can be accessed at any state of the tide by descending rock steps to the south, then traversing back round on rock shelves to below the wall.

Walking on Sunshine – 20m E1 5b. G.E. Little, J. Finlay. 27th May, 1993.
Climbs a direct line, on excellent rock, near the left edge of the wall. Start at a plinth abutting the base of the wall. Climb just left of a diagonal crack for 4m to a fat flake. Step left to two small horns of rock then straight up, largely on side holds, to a tiny ledge below the slight groove in the headwall. Climb this strenuously to the top.

Port na Cuilce (NR 415002):
A 25m high, west-facing wall, of steep cracked slate, lies in the secluded bay of Port na Cuilce commanding an excellent view to Mull. The rock is superficially loose but once descaled, fundamentally sound – give or take the odd fragile edge.

The Mission – 20m E2 5b. G.E. Little, J. Finlay. 26th May, 1993.
This interesting route takes the line of the striking diagonal flake crack and the cracked wall above. Start at the 3m-high white cross. Climb the sharp-edged diagonal flake crack to near its end where a thin vein of quartz cuts it to create an X. Move up the wall to gain big flake holds, then directly up the rusty wall above to make crux moves gaining access to a small rock ledge and the top.

Meall a' Chaise (NR 363945):
Above the cottage south of Port Mhor an iron fence leads up the hill, terminating at the base of the crag. Left of the fence the crag forms a steep smooth slab. To the right the crag is steeper with a prominent thin crack running left to right.

Limpet Hammer Groove – 25m VS 4b. J. Finlay, W. Skidmore. 28th May, 1993.
At the right edge of the slab, above the fence, is a shallow groove. Climb the groove which gradually becomes less well defined.

Sliabh Riabhach (NR 367936):
Route 367936 – 30m V. Diff. W. Skidmore, J. Finlay, Jo Finlay. 26th May, 1993.
The narrow grey pillar at the back of the second grass bay to the south of Gleann Raonabuilg (cairn). Climb in three short pitches, a steep wall, blocks and final overhang by its right edge.

SKYE

Sron na Ciche:
Tennatte – E2 5b/c. G. Szuca. 22nd July, 1990.
On the steep wall left of Petronella and 10m up. Follow the steep layback crack to an obvious downward-sloping spike. Use this to pull up and right to better holds, then straight up to the *in situ* thread on Petronella.

Why – VS 4c. G. Szuca, A. Connolly. 23rd July, 1990.
Follows the slabby buttress left of Confession. Start by scrambling over a chokestone. Go up a steep corner until possible to move right on to a slab, just under a basalt bulge. Follow a line of big flakes rightwards, then back left to under the headwall (belay). A downward traverse left along a crack is followed by a finish up a corner.

The following two routes are on the slabby crags on the most southerly section of the West Face (MMS is scratched on the rock).
Protect and Survive – E2 5b. G. Szuca. 24th July, 1990.
Start 6m right of the large triangular block. Go up and right following a thin diagonal crack to an awkward move to gain a good ledge at a big flake. Keep moving up and right past a small spike to belay at a block in the groove.

Hindsight – E1 5c. G. Szuca, A. Connolly. 25th July, 1990.
There are two leftward-running cracks 8m apart. Climb the slab just right of the left hand crack.

BLAVEN, Lower East Face:
The Crucifix – 200m II. D. Litherland, M. Moran. 8th January, 1994.
Well down from the Great Prow is a deep gully which runs up leftwards to make a prominent cross with a transverse fault line. This ascent climbed the deep gully with one short iced chokestone, then took a right turn into the fault. The fault splits into three gullies on the upper face, and the route followed the right hand gully, gained by a very tight through-route behind a chokestone and followed to the top in two long easy pitches.

CLACH GLAS:
South East Gully – 250m II. D. Litherland, M. Moran. 8th January, 1994.
One pitch at the top of the right-hand finish.

EILEAN REAMHAR:
The following routes are on the south-east-facing sea cliffs around Eilean Reamhar, the island just more than 1k south of the Coruisg Hut. The first cliff encountered walking inland from the island is a 30m slab with overhangs at its top right and bottom left.

Sealsville – VS 4c. G. Szuca, A. Connolly. 25th July, 1990.
Start at a large spike at the bottom of the slabs. Go up to a V-notch, Pull through this rightwards, move left a few feet and follow the left hand of two thin cracks. At the top move leftwards to belay on a grass ledge just below the top.

Short Spurt – E2 5b. G. Szuca. 26th July, 1990.
The route goes through the overhang just right of an obvious protruding block 10m up and just right of the previous route. Flick the rope over the block as a runner. Bridge up a short corner on the right to gain a good hold on the lip of the roof. Pull over here, then easier to the top.

Nettie Diff. – A. Connolly, G. Szuca. 26th July, 1990.
The left edge of the slab left of the previous route.

The next cliff along has a crack running up its east face. This route follows its top half.

Half Crack – H. Severe. G. Szuca, A. Connolly. 26th July, 1990.
Start centrally and climb the wall on good holds to a big ledge. Go up and left, Then follow the superb crack to a block. Move left and follow the slab to the top.

The slab round the corner has two Severes. One goes up the right arete on a hanging ramp, then a bulge and roof, finishing up the headwall centrally. The other goes up the slab.

Slabsville – VS 4b. G. Szuca, A. Connolly. 27th July, 1990.
This route goes up the slab 6m to the left of the right arete (left of the mentioned routes above). Start at low tide in a small corner with a square block. Follow the slab on the left to a horizontal crozley crack. Move left a few feet, then straight up the white streak in the slab above, passing two pockets. Unprotected.

No Gain without Pain – E2 6a. G. Szuca. 27th July, 1990.
The route is on the barrel-shaped buttress left (looking inland) again. Start centrally and follow a line of very small sharp holds. Go up to a corner, move left and follow a basalt intrusion leftwards through a bulge. Unprotected.

NEIST POINT:
The following routes are best approached from the car park. Go down the hill using the concrete ramp to where the path goes through a stone wall. Turn right and in after five minutes, arrive at the first fence, which runs from the sea to below the crag. The following route starts about 100m right of the fence.

Abracadabra – E1 5a. G. Szuca, M. Limonci. 27th May, 1989.
Follow a black groove, then rightwards along a heathery terrace to a spike. Move left from the spike across a black slabby wall to a loose block in a layback crack. Go up a bit, then follow a line of pockets to better holds. Go up to a corner under a small bulge, turn this on the left and follow the crack in the steep headwall above.

Temgesic – E1 5b. G. Szuca, D. Heffernan, M. Limonci. 27th May, 1989.
This route is 50m left of the fence. Start at the left side of an obvious slab. Go up to a V-notch. Pull over, then move sharp right to a small footledge. Go back left using the flake in the middle of the wall to a horizontal slot. Go up the crack for a move, then move left using the break for hands. Move up the arete to finish on rounded holds.

Karen – VS 4b. G. Szuca, M. Limonci. 27th May, 1989.
50m right of the fence. Start at an obvious spike with three horizontal bands at its top. Climb the slab on the right to under the overhang. Move right, then up a few moves in the gully until possible to pul! on to the slab above the roof.

Farther on one comes to a crag and a stone wall. On the right-hand side is a big chimney. This route follows the hanging crack on its upper left.

Brass Monkeys – E1. G. Armstrong, G. Szuca. September, 1990.
1. 5b. Start up the chimney, then move on to the right wall and up to a ledge. Step
left across the void to a small ledge, then straight up on to a small slab. Follow the
rounded crack to a big ledge.
2. 5a. Move right and follow a corner with a big spike to under a roof. Move left
and finish rightwards.

Right of the previous route on the South Face, which rises uphill, are four prominent
cracks. This route takes the rightmost one.

Gritstone Reminiscence – HVS 5a. G. Armstrong, G. Szuca. September, 1990.
Follow the crack past a block for 15m. Move left and follow a continuation crack
to the top.

The next crag is approached by descending a gully just right of the stone wall at the
bottom of the concrete ramp. At the bottom of the gully (looking down), turn right
for about 50m. The next route is on the thinly-cracked slab next to a chimney on
its right (which is Diff.).

Sore Phalanges – E1 5b. G. Szuca, G. Armstrong. September, 1990.
Climb the slab centrally, moving left for protection to a niche at half height.

Smeg – VS 4c. G. Szuca, G. Armstrong. September, 1990.
An obvious corner crack 30m left of the descent gully.

Nothing Special – HVS 4c. G. Szuca, G. Armstrong. September, 1990.
Climb the slab centrally via a thin crack to below the bulge. Move left to finish.

The following route is 30m right of Temptation on a dark slabby wall.

Monkey Hanger – HVS 5a. G. Armstrong, G. Szuca. September, 1990.
Climb a crack to a recess, move right and straight up to a block belay. Abseil
descent.

Bay 3, South Face:
Trilobite Groove – 20m HVS 5a. C. Moody, B. Taylor. 24th April, 1993.
Climb the left-facing corner at the left end of the face, step left before it finishes and
climb a groove just right of the arete. Finish up a crack just left of The Ratagan
Strangler.

The Ratagan Strangler – 25m VS 4c. C. Moody, B. Taylor. 24th April, 1993.
Start between Trilobite Groove and Tinderbox. Go up easy cracks to the right side
of a ledge of loose stones. Climb the short corner crack.

Lushious – 30m VS 4c. M. McLeod, C. Moody. 20th June, 1992.
Climb the obvious left-facing corner crack, possibly overgraded.

TALISKER BAY:
Little Stack of Talisker – 20m HVS 4c. K. Milne, S. Richardson. 29th May, 1993.
Climb the seaward ridge, moving right at the top to surmount a short steep wall, to
finish along a rickety ridge. The state of the basalt is not quite as discouraging as
the guidebook suggests. Descend by abseiling the South Face having first fixed a
rope at the base of the North Face.

Note: The Great Stack of Talisker should be HVS 5a.
RUBHA HUNISH, South Stack:
Maol Groove – 30m VS 4c. S. Richardson, G. Muhlemann. 25th September, 1993.
Approach by swimming and climb the left-facing groove on the seaward face of the stack. The easiest descent is to down climb the South Ridge.

Split Stack:
Trodday Wall – 30m H. Severe 4b. G. Muhlemann, S. Richardson. 25th September, 1993.
About 30m south of the North Stack is a fourth stack which is split into two by a narrow gap. It lies close to the cliff top, and can be easily reached by scrambling down a gully to its south at low tide. Traverse round on to the seaward face, and follow a line of holds just left of centre to reach the south summit.

North Stack:
Shiant Corner – 30m HVS 5a. S. Richardson, G. Muhlemann. 26th September, 1993.
An involved and committing outing. Approach by swimming from the north-west corner of Split Stack, to gain a small platform on the south-east corner of the North Stack. Move right and climb the prominent left-facing corner on the North Fast Face, pulling through bulges to reach easier ground and the top.

NORTHERN HIGHLANDS

SOUTH AND WEST (VOLUME ONE)
KNOYDART, Stob a' Chearcaill:
North Spur – 260m II/III. S. Kennedy, D. Ritchie. 8th January, 1994.
Climbs the narrow spur immediately left of Para Handy Gully. Start up a short chimney just left of the toe of the spur. Move right and continue upwards keeping mainly to the crest.

GLEN SHEIL, Druim Shionnach, West Face:
Cave Gully – 110m III,4. S. Kekus, A. Nisbet. 16th February, 1994.
The crag is seen from the road but hidden on the approach up Coire an t-Slugain until a left turn is made a short way below the following crag. The summit of Druim Shionnach is 10 minutes from the crag top. The route is the prominent central gully, containing a cave (presumably the large gully mentioned in the guide and right of The Silver Slab). The cave is passed by a chimney on the right with a very steep entry. Fortunately, the chimney is wider on the inside than the out but still a wriggle. A long pitch but the rest is easy.

Capped Gully – 110m III. A. Nisbet, G. Vaughan, M. Webb. 20th February, 1994.
Left of Cave Gully is a slabby buttress and left of this is a shallow gully which tapers to a chimney slot near the top. Low in the grade.

Creag Coire an t-Slugain:
Pioneer Gully – 100m II. A. Nisbet, G. Wallace. 6th April, 1993.
This is the crag at the back of the coire, well seen when approaching up the coire. At the right end of the crag is an easy gully which extends down through a lower tier and was used as an approach to this route which takes a narrow gully starting 10m left of the upper section of the easy gully.

Ridge and Furrow – 120m III. P. Foulkes, A. Nisbet. 31st March, 1994.
The best ice-holding line on the cliff, just left of centre. A shallow trough with a bulging recess at half height and immediately left of a flakey ridge. The recess had an overhanging slush exit and the ridge was climbed for a pitch before regaining the ice immediately above.

AONACH AIR CHRITH, North West Face:
This is the large slabby face at the head of Coire nan Elrecheanach. The face has a steep compact buttress high on the left and a large slabbier section on the right. The two sections are separated by a right-slanting shallow twin gully, the following route.

My Mother Says No – 150m II. G. Craig, K. Lindsay, A. Nisbet, R. Patey, M. Valentine. 24th March, 1994.
The right half of the twin gully had two short pitches, which presumably could bank out in peak conditions and reduce to Grade I.

Mica Schist Special – 180m III. P. Coleman, M. Moran, S. Richmond. 20th March, 1994.
Takes grooves on the left-hand side of the slabby face, just right of My Mother Says No – sustained interest.
1,2. 60m. Climb a turfy groove just right of My Mother Says No, then trend right to a deeper and steeper groove.
3,4. 60m. Climb the steeper groove, then go easily rightwards across the crest of the buttress at an obvious block.
5,6. 60m. Take thin grooves in the slabs just right of the crest to gain easy ground 50m below the summit ridge.

SGURR AN LOCHAIN, North East Face:
A 200m Grade I gully, better described as a scooped ramp, in the centre of this face has been climbed often by M. Moran and parties (and descended very quickly by the New Routes Editor, who notes that it is steep for its grade). It has an alternative left finish starting just above half height on steeper snow (Grade II, but often with a big cornice). The shallow gully bounding the right side of the cliff is an easy Grade I and also has a steeper finish on the left.

Lochain Buttress – 200m II. N. Kekus, T. Masters, R. Reynolds. 1st February, 1994.
Climbs the buttress left of the main crag and separated from it by a wide easy gully. Start at the toe of the buttress and climb to a large block (50m), then cut up and left on to the buttress via a snow groove. Follow the buttress crest, generally on its left side, with one short rock wall at half height.

SGURR A' BHAC CHAOLAIS:
Snowdrop – 100m IV,4. D. Houfe, A. Nisbet, N. Sinclair, D. Wolfe. 1st March, 1994.
The deep gully left of Mayfly. The highlight was an 'ice pillar' falling from the lip of a big cave (and near subterranean belay). Probably III in better conditions, as there was deep sticky snow covering the ice. Few cracks; ice screws used.

THE SADDLE, Forcan Ridge:
Easter Buttress – 120m IV,5. R. Groth, M. Mauger, A. Nisbet, K. Rogers. 15th March, 1994.
A winter ascent probably of Easter Buttress. The buttress is the middle of three on the south-east flank of the Forcan Ridge. A distinctive tower seen from below becomes a Cioch (Skye)-shaped block seen from the side. The chosen line was initially a ramp just right of the crest (with an unreasonably hard start, the rest being Grade III) leading to a 2m block on the crest. The crest was followed until forced to traverse steeply left on flakes to a flake crack leading back to the crest, which was followed more easily to finish.

Coire Uaine:
Big Gully – 300m III. J. Ashby, J. Colverd, A. Nisbet. 7th February, 1994.
A fine route. Much steep snow and containing four ice pitches, the third being by far the longest (25m) and steep, though eased by being formed in a narrow chimney.

Little Gully – 300m I. B. Davison. 13th February, 1994.
To the left of Big Gully is a grass-covered face which runs into a narrow gully towards the top. The route starts up snow covered slopes and icy rocks to finish up the gully

BEINN FHADA, Sgurr a' Choire Ghairbh, North East Face:
Instructor's Gully – 140m I. R. Groth, M. Mauger, A. Nisbet, K. Rogers. 13th March, 1994.
The gully between Summit Buttress and Needle's Eye Buttress.

Needle's Eye Buttress – 150m II. J. Ashby, J. Colverd, D. Gunevan, A. Nisbet. 6th February, 1994.
Climbed by a central turfy trough.

The Wind Machine – 140m II. D. Houfe, A. Nisbet, N. Sinclair, D. Wolfe. 27th February, 1994.
The buttress left of that described in the guide with Guide's Rib and Porter's Climb has three rectangular ribs separated by gullies. The right gully is well defined in its top half and is this route.

Coire an Sgairne:
The Funnel – 180m I. D. Joynes, A. Nisbet, N.J. Worsey. 26th January, 1994.
The gully left of The Kintail Blanket. It slants in from the left and finishes up a square-cut slot.

LURG MHOR (GR revised to 060406):
Left Edge Route – 90m Severe. A. Nisbet. 26th May, 1993.
A scrappy route, not as good as it looks from below. Start just left of Munroist's Reward and climb the big inset slab with thin cracks to its top left corner. Pull across right to the top of a short arete. Climb a narrow rib close on the left of the big grassy corner to a more broken finish out right.

SGURR NA FEARTAIG, Coire Leiridh:
The Gully that Time Forgot – 150m II. I. Lee-Bapty, E. Todd, P. Westall. 16th March, 1994.
The narrow central gully on the crag at the head of the coire (NH 0245). The crux was wading the river on the approach. The bridge at NH 011482 no longer exists.

SGORR RUADH:

High Gully Direct – 155m V. P. Potter, A. Macdonald. 30th January, 1988.
1. 30m. Traverse in left from the Central Couloir to the foot of a left-facing groove to the right of the ordinary route.
2. 25m. Climb a corner to belay on the right.
3. 40m. Go back left and up a steep ice ramp to a niche below an overhang. Step up right (crux) to the upper slab and go up a grrove to the right of the main gully to join the main gully higher up.
4. 60m. Finish by the normal route.

Parallel Lines – 100m III. F. Bennet, J. Irving. 7th January, 1994.
Shortly after the start of Brown Gully is a right branch. This is easy until an awkward overhung wall about 3m in height. Easy snow grooves to finish.

Robertson's Buttress – 200m IV,4. B. Findlay, G. Strange. 16th January, 1994.
Takes a central line on the face right of Stepin. Start at toe of buttress and climb by snowfields, short rock steps, a shallow icy gully and a steep groove in the final rocks to reach easy ground.

FUAR THOLL, South-east Cliff:

Blue Finger – 120m V,6. A. Nisbet, G. Nisbet. 12th December, 1993.
The line was the same as followed by A.N. in summer. It fits the description but is just left of that marked on the new guide photo-diagram. The third tier was climbed by a steep spike-filled chimney and the last tier was climbed by working left, then finishing straight up.

Fuar Feast – 190m HVS. A. Nisbet, G. Nisbet. 24th June, 1993.
Climbs the crest of the buttress right of The Fuhrer. Start with the first few metres of Fuar Folly.
1,2. 55m 4c. Climb the lower buttress between The Fuhrer and Fuar Folly, zig-zagging to find the easiest line of clean rock and belay on the traverse of Fuar Folly.
3. 35m 5a. Leave the ledge just right of the crest, climb slightly leftwards and up the right of two short prominent V-grooves (obvious from the coire floor) to the ledge above.
4,5. 100m. Trend right up easier ground above to finish up Sandstorm.

11Duce – 200m VII,7. S. Richardson, D. Heselden (AL). 20th February, 1994.
Three parallel ice lines form down the central section of the South East Cliff. This varied ice and mixed climb takes the thin left streak to the left of Tholl Gate and The Ayatollah. Start midway between Tholl Gate and Sandstorm below a short steep wall topped by a narrow ice ramp.
1. 25m. Climb the wall and make a difficult exit on to the ramp which leads to a crescent-shaped snowfield. Belay below the wall above.
2. 15m. Cracks lead to a tongue of ice after 10m. Climb this to the terrace at the top of the first tier.
3. 50m. An intimidating pitch, but considerably easier than it looks. Move up and right to gain a narrow icy groove. Climb this for 10m, then traverse up and left past a precarious pointed block along a vague ramp to a ledge. Continue up and right on good ice to a stance on the left.
4. 50m. Climb the hanging icicle fringe on the right and continue directly to a stance.
5,6. 60m. Continue up the vague depression above, keeping left of Tholl Gate to the top.

Mixed Post – 100m V,6. D. Jarvis, A. Nisbet. 17th December, 1993.
Start immediately left of Pipped at the Post. Gain a shallow chimney from the right. Climb it and the continuation fault slanting leftwards to the top. It was climbed with no ice, but throughout February and March, 1994 became an icefall partly connected to Pipped at the Post but still offering a slightly easier separate line.

Lower Cliff:

The three parallel gullies mentioned in the guide have now been climbed. The left, Grade I, by M. Moran and party. The centre, Grade III,4 by A. Nisbet, G. Vaughan and M. Webb on 22nd February, 1994 (and repeated the following week). The upper icefall, which does not form readily, is the highlight but is avoidable (the gully has been climbed before but escaping below it, Grade II). The right gully was climbed by M. Welsh, M. Reid, M. Sizer and P. Sizer at Grade II on 20th February, 1994.

Mainreachan Buttress:

Nebula – 195m V,6. S. Richardson, R. Webb (AL). 15th February, 1994.
The summer route is an excellent ice trap, and is the natural winter line on the north-east face of the buttress. Start below the left hand of the twin grooves, 15m left of Nemesis (taken by Mainline Connection).
1. 35m. Steep mixed climbing (crux) leads into the groove. Climb ice to a ledge and belay on the left.
2. 40m. Continue up the icy groove to the terrace.
3. 25m. Move up the terrace to the foot of the ice groove cutting through the upper tier.
4. 45m. Climb the groove (as for Mainline Connection).
5. Continue up easy snow and mixed ground to the top.

AN RUADH STAC, North Face:

North Face Route – 300m III. A. Matthewson, A. Tibbs. 30th December, 1993.
An interesting mountaineering route. Climb the lower tier by a line based on Patey's North Face, then follow the terrace up right until it is feasible to break up and left to an amphitheatre below the summit.

Quartzice – 160m V,5. R. Everett, S. Richardson (AL). 20th March, 1994.
An interesting mixed climb approximating to the summer line of Foxtrot. Towards the right end of the lower tier, directly below the depression in the upper tier is a prominent icefall. Start in a snow bay just left of a big cave, about 20m right of the line of the icefall.
1. 45m. Climb a vegetated groove, trending slightly left, to a ledge.
2. 20m. Continue in the same line, and move left to the base of the icefall.
3. 45m. Climb the icefall and belay on the terrace above.
4. 50m. Follow the left edge of the depression via grooves to where the angle eases. 100m of scrambling leads to the top.

BEINN BHAN, Coire na Feola:

Man's Best Friend – 220m IV,5. G. Ettle, J. Lyall. 5th January, 1994.
This climbs the big corner line to the right of Y-Gully. Start as for Indigenous to belay at the foot of the corner. Climb the right-facing corner as directly as ice and turf allows, with a superb through route on the way. The final wall is easier than it looks from below.

Note: J. Lyall witnessed the first ascent of In XS and it is correctly shown and described in Northern Highlands Vol. 1. The line is obvious when seen from the foot of Y-Gully and will probably go at the same grade on turf (approx. V,5), although not of such good quality without ice.

Coire na Poite:

Teapot – 100m III. S.J.H. Reid, J. Rowlands. 14th February, 1994.
The buttress between the North Face of A' Chioch and the main crag is split by a prominent left-facing corner near its left side. Scramble up to a cave on the left just below the foot of the corner.
1. 50m. Climb snow and then a short but steep ice pitch followed by steep snow to a belay under a tiny roof.
2. 50m. Traverse right and follow a shallow snow trough to an obvious rock spike and the summit.

Coire nam Fhamhair:

C. Cartwright and D. Heselden note a free (and second?) ascent of Great Overhanging Gully. They graded it VI,7.

Coire Gorm Mor:

Flying Penguin Gully – 250m V. P. Potter, M. Welch. 18th March, 1988.
Takes the deep-cut gully in this, the sixth of the seven coires on the back of Beinn Bhan. Easy snow leads into the gully proper. Climb a steep ice pitch via three caves to a stance on the left below another steepening (45m, crux). Take the next step and continue up towards another short chimney. This was avoided on the right buttress before following the gully easily to the summit ridge.

SGURR A' CHAORACHAIN:

Note: The North Buttresses. Following the note in last year's SMCJ, No. 5 Gully was climbed by M. Moran and party. Under heavier snow conditions, the left branch had banked out and appeared Grade I while the right branch had a steep finish, perhaps II.

Chopper Chimney – 50m VS. M. Welch, M. Arkley. October, 1993.
Lies on a high crag right of the North Buttresses and approached from the Bealach na Ba (NG 787432).
1. 25m. Climb a steepening corner for 15m, then traverse out left on to the buttress.
2. 25m. Go left and up into a narrowing chimney.

South Face:

The following routes have been described as single pitches – ignoring the easier ground above and below. Gideon's Wrath was repeated the same day and in agreement with several others, was thought to be E1 5b 5b.

Sword Swallower – 35m E2 5c. J. Lyall, A. Nisbet. 15th June, 1993.
A fine direct line up the centre of the wall. The top half may have been climbed before as a direct version of Gideon's Wrath. Start 2m left of Sword of Gideon, direct start and climb easily to the right end of a ledge 3m up. Go up cracks (crux) until moves left lead to a small pod. Up this, then up and left to clip an old peg beside a small triangular roof (there is another triangular roof below and left). Traverse right and up a crack to an easier finish.

The Kings of Midian – 35m HVS 5a. J. Lyall, A. Nisbet. 15th June, 1993.
Climbs the right edge of The Sword of Gideon wall. Start just right of Sword of Gideon at the wall's right arete. Climb a parallel line to Sword of Gideon (which

has been used as an easier start to this route), then traverse right across a wall with twin cracks to gain a big ledge. An easier finish straight up the scooped wall above.

A' Chioch:

North Wall – VI,6. B. Davison, A. Nisbet. 27th December, 1993.
A winter ascent by the summer route. Well protected but sustained.

MEALL GORM:

Scampi Fries – III/IV. F. Bennet, J. Irving. 9th January, 1994.
Right of Stonner Falls is a fault. Climb this to a cave belay. Go up thin ice and two further steepenings (50m). Easy to the top.

Rattlesnake – 200m V,6. G. Ettle, J. Lyall. 13th December, 1993.
Followed close to the summer line. The first unavoidable tier was climbed by a groove line a short way right of the black patch. Climb the first and most impressive corner to half height, then move left to gain and climb the edge. Follow the corner system to the top with sustained and varied climbing.

Blue in the Face – 215m VI,7. G. Ettle, J. Lyall. 17th December, 1993.
A line up the wall between The Smooth Creep and Lobster Gully. Start at the foot of Lobster Gully and go up rightwards to a terrace. The first main tier is then climbed on the left by a zig-zag line which reaches a belay below the smooth vertical corner of The Smooth Creep (110m). The next corner to the left was followed up the line of a thin icefall to a ledge (25m). Step left and pull into a turfy groove which leads to a ledge and flake belay (25m). Traverse 10m left, past a blocky left-facing corner to climb an unlikely vegetated crackline up the wall. Belay in a right-facing roofed corner (30m). Step down to make an exciting axe traverse left on turf. Slant up left to a wide crack, climb this and finish straight up (25m).

BEINN ALLIGIN, Tom na Gruagaich, South East Coire:

Gardener's Choice – 100m II. B. Davison, C. Orrley. 8th April, 1994.
In the coire with the path from the car park to Tom na Gruagaich. There is an obvious easy gully on the left of the coire entrance. It is Grade I and was used as descent from the route. This route was the first gully rising out left from the bottom of the gully. Steep snow and vegetation.

LIATHACH, Coire Dubh Beag:

Head Hunter – 200m V,6. N. Kekus, S. Anderson. 7th February, 1994.
Immediately left of the start of Headless Gully is a prominent chimney groove raking up and left (from the Coire Dubh path, it appears straight up, whereas Headless slants right). There was evidence of previous attempts. The route starts up a steep icefall (crux, easier with more build-up) to gain the first terrace. A short awkward corner gains the bottom of the chimney. This is followed for 20m before leaving via ledges on the left to reach an excellent ledge and belay. Regain the continuation gully on the right and follow it to below a steep rock wall and icy slab on the left. Climb the slab to turn the rock wall on the left and reach a final steep ice pitch. Easy ground follows this to the top.

Coire Dubh Mor:

Under Thirties Icefall – 140m IV,4. R. Groth, M. Mauger, A. Nisbet. 17th March, 1994.
An icefall on the left wall of Way Up, starting just below Over Sixties Icefall. The large terraces are less spoiling than they look as the ice takes a direct line. The first

and crux pitch was steep ice (hidden from the approach behind two ice columns), the second mixed (the ice line being thin), the third a less steep wide icefall and the fourth an ice-filled chimney.

Over Sixties Icefall – 100m III. M. Johnston, A. Nisbet, D. Thompson. 7th March, 1994.
On the right wall of Way Up after about 100m is a lower-angled icefall (left of Hooded Claw and round the corner). It leads in two or three pitches of continuous ice to a big terrace from where a horizontal traverse leads left to the col (and descent). A shorter and quicker route than others in the coire – low in the grade.

Buttress Start – 160m III. B. Davison, C. Orrley. 7th April, 1994.
Provides some extra climbing, or useful if Way Up is avalanche prone. Start by a steep icefall on a ramp immediately right of Way Up. Continue leftwards in three pitches to join the normal route.

Foobarbundee – 200m VIII,7 (1PA). C. Cartwright, D. Heselden. 22nd February, 1994.
The route takes the obvious hanging icefall between Poacher's Fall and Test Department. Start directly beneath a long roof 30m to the left of Test Department.
1. 35m. Climb icy grooves trending right to belay in a right-facing corner directly below a large left-facing corner.
2. 30m. Climb up the corner and the roof into the left facing corner. Follow this for 6m, then tension left on to the hanging slab. Climb this on thin ice trending left above the long roof. The slab culminates at a small overhang; belay at its left side.
3. 30m. Climb the icy groove to the left of the belay and continue up the icefall.
4. 40m. Continue up the icefall trending right.
5. 45m. Move right to the obvious buttress, move around its prow to belay below an icy groove.
6. Climb the groove, then easy broken ground to the top.
The Stem – 50m VII,6. C. Cartwright, D. Heselden. 23rd February, 1994.
This route provides a direct start to Brain Strain. Climb the very steep corner immediately to the right of Brain Strain's initial chimney pitch.

Coire na Caime:
First Face – 200m III. A. Nisbet, G. Vaughan, M. Webb. 21st February, 1994.
Climbs an obvious wide icefall in the centre of the First Pinnacle Face. A start was made up a huge sheet of ice below and right of the upper icefall and leading into No. 2 Gully. A left traverse across the gully led to the upper icefall.

Echo Couloir – 250m V,6 (direct). S. Birch, C. Collin, M. Moran. 1st March, 1993.
III (left start). A. Nisbet, G. Nisbet. 19th March, 1994.
This route, claimed as an alternative start to Andes Couloir (SMCJ, 1993), is a completely separate route, the fourth of the five ice lines described in the Guide. The upper gully, containing 130m of ice, is a very obvious feature, more so than Andes Couloir to its left. The grade will vary with the chosen start. In good conditions a wide slabby icefall forms below the big final corner. This was usually complete throughout winter, 1994 and when Andes Couloir was climbed but not during the first ascent. It would presumably be climbed if present. The option is a right-facing turfy corner farther right. These options can either be gained by two consecutive icefalls (direct) or a diagonal line from the left on mixed ice and turf.

Toll a' Meitheach:
The Sneak – 90m V,5. D. Houfe, A. Nisbet, N. Sinclair, D. Wolfe. 3rd March, 1994.
The retiring icefall which forms up the left wall of Toll Gate East and which often
looks incomplete from below (if seen at all). In fact, it forms readily and is probably
usually climbable. It gave three steep ice pitches, particularly the third, with big
belay ledges and good rock belays between.

Sgorr a' Chadail:
The crag is at the very west end of Liathach, overlooking Loch Torridon and
contains the route Reflection Wall. Start just above the hairpins on the Beinn
Alligin road and flog up steep grass and heather to the crag base at 630m. At 60m
the crag is not as big as would appear from below and perhaps too much effort for
those who don't appreciate the sunny and spectacular outlook over Loch Torridon
(although as good as the sandstone crags nearer the road).
    Towards its left side, the crag has a wide square-cut slot with a sharp right arete.
12m right is a deep left-facing V-groove which leads into a crackline – Trench Foot.
12m right is a blunt cracked nose where the crag changes aspect from south-west
to south – Reflections of my Mind. Continuing right is a steep section with blocky
overhangs and discontinuous corners. After about 50m the crag changes aspect
again to a south-east facing cleaner wall with a light-coloured square wall low
down. This pale wall is the most distinctive feature from the road and its left edge
is a line of flakes which continues on to near the top – Reflection Wall. The routes
are described left to right.

Trench Foot – 40m E1 5b. A. Nisbet, G. Nisbet. 29th April, 1993.
The deep V-groove and its right arete, then the continuing crackline.

Reflections of my Mind – 50m E2. A. Nisbet, G. Nisbet. 29th April, 1993.
The blunt nose, starting just right of the crest. The best of the routes.
1. 25m 5c. Climb an overhanging groove (crux). Traverse awkwardly left into the
base of a left-facing corner on the left side of the crest. Climb the corner to a ledge.
A very sustained pitch with excellent protection.
2. 25m 5a. Continue up the corner line to easier ground.

The Pale Wall – 60m E1. A. Nisbet, G. Nisbet. 28th April, 1993.
Takes a crackline through the centre of the pale wall right of Reflection Wall.
1. 30m 5b. Climb the crack and its continuation to belay below a roof-crack.
2. 30m 5b. Climb the roof-crack and up into a recess. Up the crack at its back (the
right arete looks equally possible) and on to easy ground.

Mirror Image – 60m HVS. A. Nisbet, G. Nisbet. 28th April, 1993.
The crackline which forms the right edge of the pale wall.
1. 40m 5a. Climb the crack beyond the pale wall to an overhung groove. Pull out
right (or left at 5b) and on up cracks to a big ledge.
2. 20m. Finish up blocky walls.

BEINN EIGHE, Coire Mhic Fhearchair, Far East Wall:
Daughter of the Dawn – 100m E3. A. Nisbet, G. Nisbet. 28th May, 1993.
A sensational and recommended line up the vertical wall left of Kami-kaze.
1. 25m 4c. As for first pitch of Kami-kaze.
2. 20m 5c. Traverse 5m left and go up left to a smaller ledge. Step right into a crack
in a pale wall and climb it leading into a corner and a tiny ledge at its top.

3. 10m 5c. Pull out left into another corner and up this to a roof. Pull out left again and go up to a ledge on the left.
4. 45m 5b. From the right end of the ledge, climb up flakes, pull out right, place high runners and traverse right into a big left-facing corner, followed slightly left to a wide notch at the top.

Epilogue – 50m VS. J. Lyall. 14th June, 1993.
Start 5m right of Karaoke Wall at a parallel crackline. Climb this for 20m to a ledge. Traverse right along the ledge until above a large corner. Climb the wall above moving leftwards near the top.

Eastern Ramparts:
The Great Wall of China – 90m E3. J. Lyall, A. Nisbet. 14th June, 1993.
Climbs the wall between Heavy Flak and Turkish Delight. Start 5m right of the scrambly start of Heavy Flak below a flake-corner.
1. 30m 5a. Climb this to the low ledge. Step right, climb an open corner leading to the Upper Girdle and continue to a ledge below a roof.
2. 20m 6a. Climb the wall just right of the roof (crux), then traverse left delicately above its lip. Go up the right side of the huge flake (pinnacle?) and belay on top.
3. 40m 5c. Gain a ledge with perched block on the right, then follow a crackline to a small roof. Go left round the roof and up steps above.

The Unknown Soldier – 110m E1. J. Lyall, A. Nisbet. 4th June, 1993.
1. 45m 5a. Climb a parallel fault 10m right of Rampage, passing a ledge at 25m, to the Upper Girdle.
2. 20m 4c. Climb a right-facing yellow corner, move right and up to another big ledge.
3. 15m 5b. From the right end of the ledge, go up a steep wall. Step right and go up a second steep wall to a ledge out right (nut for aid). A short corner led to a block belay on the left.
4. 30m 5a. Go up the fault above, then move right to climb the very steep blocky rib between the final chimneys of Rampage and Forgotten Warrior.
Note: Pitch 3 was split due to the onset of heavy rain which forced the aid move. 5c/6a free and overhead protection?

DIABAIG, Beginners' Slabs (NG 825585)
An area of perfect pink slabs on rough rock just a short distance west of the first hairpin above Alligin Shuas where a large layby exists for parking.

Pink Slab – 35m Diff. R. Brown, J.R. Mackenzie. 18th September, 1993.
This is the largest slab which has a thinner slab to its right. Take a central line according to taste with an optional belay at two-thirds height. Rough rock and incut holds.

The Pillar:
Diabaig, the Hard Way – 35m E5 6b. N. Foster (unseconded). 1st June, 1993.
A very powerful problem through the obvious roof left of Diabaig Pillar (close to 6c). Start left of Dire Wall beneath a flat-topped pinnacle. Gain the top of the pinnacle via the brambly crack (or from the left). Step right and follow the open scoop to the roof. Tackle this using the obvious undercut flake, and continue up a crack just right of the arete. Where the angle changes, move right to the centre of the fine slab and wander pleasantly up this. The short headwall has an obvious

hanging V-notch – the 'Tail'. Arrange protection in a crack in the slab a few feet to the left, and boulder up into the notch – the 'Sting'.

The Dedo – 25m HVS 5a. M. Moran, A. Nisbet. 8th May, 1993.
Climbs the corner which bounds the upper right side of The Pillar and curves over leftwards into a roof. Climb the wall below the roof, place runners in the roof, then step down and traverse left until a finish is made past the left end of the roof.

The Freize – 25m HVS 5b. M. Moran, A. Nisbet. 8th May, 1993.
A ramp breaks right out of the corner of The Dedo into very impressive but surprisingly helpful ground.

Shunned – 20m HVS 5a. A. Cunningham, J. Pickering. 23rd May, 1993.
Right of Con-Con there is an awkward step in the grassy gully. Start just below this and climb into a crack. Where it peters out to the left, traverse right and up to finish via a right-facing corner.

Terrier Trauma – 22m E3 6a. K. Milne, J. Ashdown. 19th June, 1993.
On the steep wall to the right of the Condome Slab, facing west. Takes the crackline on the right side of the wall, starting at a recess. Climb on to a slab, then climb the overhanging wall very strenuously to a ledge and finish more easily up the corner crack. Detailed notes on protection and the suggestion of E4 5c were supplied.
Notes: Boab's Corner is undergraded. Certainly VS; the easiest line on Pitch 1 is slightly obscure and poorly protected (4b). Pitch 2, a short prominent groove above an old peg, is 5a unless tall, although it can be avoided round the corner on the right. The amenable start to Charlie's Tower is perhaps VS also (the writer's enthusiasm to have routes below VS!).
Dire Straights has a poorly protected 5b section, suggesting E2, and perhaps is harder than The Pillar.
The Con-Con has been suggested at E1 5b.
S. Crowe notes a direct finish to An Eyeful. The Gritty Finish continues slightly leftwards where An Eyeful moves into the crack. E3/4 6a.
Route One's top pitch, taken direct above the belay, has been suggested at 5b. The author considered 5b but decided top end 5a. Opinions?
Route Three: Pitch 1 is 4b (misprint), or even 4a.
Edgewood Whymper has been repeated and thought excellent but undergraded.

Midway round the peninsula between Diabaig and Inveralligin, and directly above the house, is a crag at NG 802578. M. Welch and M. Arkley climbed a 35m HVS in October, 1993. They climbed the initial slabs to a bulge, through the bulge into a steep groove and a direct finish. Nearby are two sets of slabs. The upper slabs are at NG 810577, have a 70° tilt and offer various 20m routes up cracklines at V. Diff to Severe. The lower slabs, at NG 810575, offer a 40m VS. Go up the steep slabs into a diagonal crack, then directly up, crux at the top.

CREAG NAN CUILEANN:
This is the south-east facing sandstone cliff which overlooks the hairpin bends on the road to Diabaig, shortly after leaving Loch Torridon. The black routes seep for weeks but several routes dry quickly. About 10 minutes from the road. Routes described left to right.

Becalmed – 30m E2 5c. I. Taylor, C. Moody. 10th May, 1993.
Left of a big left-hand corner is a tree-filled corner/chimney. Start here. Climb the

steep crack on the left to a ledge on the arete. Climb the arete to a horizontal break, move up left to the crack, then step back right and continue to the top.

Walsh's Groove – 30m Severe. M. Moran. 1990.
Climb up to the large corner, then follow the crack on the left wall. The rock improves after the corner is gained.

The Text Book – 30m HVS 5a. C. Moody, B. Taylor. 8th May, 1993.
The right-hand corner. Climb ledges to the bay, then take the corner crack till it closes. Traverse right to the arete and climb the jam crack directly above.

Bundle of Apathy – 30m E4 6a. I. Taylor. 10th May, 1993.
Right of The Text Book is a steep east face with a prominent crack. Climb the crack to the first overhang, move right and climb the finger crack.

Grey Matter – 30m E2 5b. C. Moody, R. Lupton. 8th August, 1992.
Gain the pine ledge. Climb the crack left of the pine till it finishes, step right and go up a short corner, then step left and finish up the wall.
Black and Blue – 30m E1 5b. C. Moody, B. Taylor. 8th May, 1993.
Gain the pine ledge. Go up the crack right of the pine and finish up the wide corner crack in the black streak.

Indian Winter – 30m E2/3 5c. I. Taylor, C. Moody. 9th May, 1993.
Gain the pine ledge. Step off the block and climb the wall just right of the holly bush to reach the left end of the ramp. The ramp leads right to the overhang, move left under it and climb the wall.

The Black Struggle – 30m VS 5a. C. Moody, B. Taylor. 4th July, 1992.
At the left side of the pillar is a corner crack in a black streak. Follow it, then move right and go past a holly to finish past a large corner.

Wind Break – 30m E2/3 5c. I. Taylor, C. Moody. 9th May, 1993.
Start at the middle of the pillar and move up left to a short corner on the arete. Climb the corner and continue up the arete to finish up a crack.

Nut the Rock – 30m HVS 5b. C. Moody, R. Lupton. 8th August, 1992.
Climb the wide crack on the right side of the pillar and step left. Climb the right arete of the pillar to finish up a crack containing a small rowan.

SEANA MHEALLAN:
Reject – 30m HVS 5a. C. Moody, I. Taylor. 12th May, 1993.
Climb the arete right of Rowan Tree Crack. Follow an obvious shelf right, then climb the corner crack.

No Brats – 30m E2 5b. I. Taylor, C. Moody. 11th May, 1993.
Start left of Mackintosh Slab. Climb the slab rib left of the undercut slanting roof, traverse right above the lip and follow thin cracks to finish up the final crack of Mackintosh Slab.

CREAG MHOR TOLLAIDH, Lower Tollie Crag:
Hostile Witness – 25m E2 5c. A. Fyffe, A. Cunningham. 26th May, 1993.

Climbs the wall left of Cloud Cuckoo Land, finishing up the fine flake crack at the top of the wall. Start at the top of the diagonal grass ledge and climb a set of grooves up the left edge of the wall to gain then follow the flake crack up and right. Move right and finish as for Cloud Cuckoo Land.

An Croabhadearain – 20m E3 5c. A. Cunningham, I. Rea, A. Fyffe. 25th May, 1993.
Climbs the obvious steep wide crack in the inset wall at the top of the grassy ramp left of Cloud Cuckoo Land (and left of Hostile Witness). Start up the black corner below the ramp leading into the crack.

SLIOCH:
Skyline Highway – 220m VI,7. R. Webb, N. Wilson. 23rd January, 1993.
An improved description. Start a few metres in from the right edge of the buttress below a shallow groove and below two obvious parallel finger cracks. Pitches 4 and 5 could be straightened.
1. 30m. Follow the groove past the parallel cracks, then via a finger crack to a stance.
2. 5m. Continue in the line of the groove to a better stance.
3. 20m. Above is an obvious roof. Pass this on the right and continue to the terrace.
4. 35m. Move diagonally up and left (easy) to gain a two stepped groove leading back right.
5. 30m. Climb the groove with increasing difficulty to gain a good ledge.
6. 10m, 30m. Move about 10m right to gain a crack system, climbed directly to easing ground.
7. 30m. Continue to reach the col at the top of the Main Buttress.
Either continue for 200m to the summit or descend diagonally rightwards to Easy Gully.

Bump Start Gully – 200m III. C. Hornsby, R. Webb. 21st December, 1992.
Start at the foot of Starter's Gully. Ascend Starter's Gully taking its right branch until an obvious broad gully with an icefall at its base opens on the right. Climb the gully to gain the col at the top of the Main Buttress.

The Slioch Slim Plan – 300m III. R. Webb, S. Richardson (AL). 1st January, 1994.
A left to right diagonal line up the imposing Main Buttress. Spectacular positions for the grade. Start 50m up Starter's Gully where a prominent parallel-sided gully cuts up right through the second tier.
1. 40m. Climb the gully, passing several steepenings, to a terrace.
2,3. 100m. Follow the obvious line of weakness up the ramp and wide gully to a broad terrace.
4. 30m. Continue up to a well-defined ledge cutting across the buttress.
5. 50m. Follow the ledge rightwards to near the right edge of the buttress where the angle of the upper section eases.
6,7. 80m. Climb mixed ground, common with Skyline Highway, to the flat top of the buttress where Bump Start Gully emerges from the left.

Stepped Ridge Direct – 180m VS. S. Richardson, R. Webb (AL). 15th August, 1993.
This attractive feature consists of seven distinct steps. The original line avoided the major difficulties by following the gully to the left, but if climbed direct it provides a fine sustained route on good clean rock. Start at the foot of Starter's Gully, and

scramble up a grassy gully to the right of the unpleasant first step to a grass terrace.
1. 45m 4c. Climb the second step, easily at first, up cracks, then make a difficult slabby exit on to a ledge. Move easily up to the base of the third step.
2. 40m 4b. Take awkward parallel cracks to the top of the step, then move to the base of the imposing fourth step which is characterised by a prominent right-facing corner.
3. 25m 4c. Climb the slabby corner to where it steepens and emerge on the top of an exposed tower. Climb the left edge of the knife edge arete above (crux) to a ledge. Continue easily to the base of a prominent tower.
4. 20m 4c. Climb the front face of the tower, and make an awkward exit just left of centre. Move easily along the ridge to the foot of the sixth step.
5. 20m 4c. Bridge the twin off-width cracks on the right side of the tower to the top, then move along the ridge to the seventh and final step.
6. 30m 4b. Climb the left of two wide cracks and continue up the prominent crack and corner system which splits the tower to reach the top of the ridge (junction with Starter's Gully). Drop down left and scramble to the top.

Sgurr an Tuill Bhan (Slioch east top), Coire an Tuill Bhan:
Far Away Buttress – 170m III. M. Irvine, R. Webb. December, 1993.
This is the prominent buttress on the north side of the coire. Start at the lowest point.
1. 40m. Climb a gully trending rightwards before breaking left at 25m to regain the crest. Belay below a fault line.
2. 40m. Climb directly up the fault line to belay in an open bay with no obvious escape.
3. 40m. Move hard right for 5m to gain a chokestone-choked chimney behind a giant flake. Continue to belay below the final wall.
4. 50m. Climb the wall to a spectacular narrow ridge which leads to the summit.

To the left of Far Away Buttress are a number of very turfy, more gently-angled buttresses and gullies which would give routes about Grade II. The buttress to the right of Far Away Buttress is as yet unclimbed.

AN TEALLACH, A'Ghlas Thuill:
Sixpence – 250m III,4. M. Johnston, A. Nisbet, D. Thompson. 9th March, 1994.
The wider buttress between the second and third prongs (2.5p?). Initially scrappy but improving to finish up a wide (3m) chimney in the centre.

Toll an Lochain:
Gobhlach Grooves – 350m IV,4. N. Kekus, M. Welsh. 29th January, 1994.
Climbs the Cadha Gobhlach Buttress. Start in the centre of the buttress where there is a choice of icefalls. Higher on the buttress it follows an obvious fault.
1. 45m. Climb an ice ramp and mixed ground.
2. 30m. Follow the ice line left into a corner.
3. 45m. Steep ice bulges, then easier grooves and mixed ground trending right.
4. 45m. Ice ramps, then a snowfield.
5. 45m. Go into an easy gully on the right with steep ice slabs on the left.
6. 40m. Go up the gully over bulges.
7. 50m. Including a short steepish ice pitch.
8. 50m. Up left into an easier gully.
9. Up final snow slopes.

Sail Liath, Central Buttress:
This is the largest of the three Sail Liath buttresses and lies left of the ramp which gives access to Bottomless Gully.

The Forger – 300m III. J. Lyall, S. Spalding. March, 1988.
The route starts at the right toe of the central buttress, much lower down than the access ramp for Bottomless Gully. Climb a gully leftwards on to a left-slanting snow ramp and climb it to its end. Continue diagonally left on intricate mixed ground to a snow terrace. Follow a snow ramp left to a second terrace and climb the obvious short chimney. Mixed ground leads up right, then a ridge is followed on to Sail Liath.

Sail Liath, Left-Hand Buttress:
This is the dome-shaped buttress which is separated from Central by a large easy snow gully.

Opposition Couloir – 180m II. J. Lyall. February, 1989.
This climbs the impressive deep gully cutting up behind a pinnacle on the right side of the crag. Finish up the buttress or enter the easy gully on the right to descend.

LOCH BROOM:
Bonar – 200m III. M. Buddle, B. Sparham. 26th February, 1994.
A heavily-iced burn in a shallow gully west across the head of Loch Broom and on the same grid line as Inverlael Farm. Cars can be parked at NH 169861 and a steep scramble gains the route. A steep line of crags (marked on the 1:50000 map) overlooks the route to the south-east.

NORTHERN HIGHLANDS

NORTH AND EAST (VOLUME TWO)

STRATHFARRAR, Coire Toll a' Mhuic, South East Face:
Middle Cut – 150m III. J.R. Mackenzie, P. Moffat. 12th March, 1994.
Midway between Best Back and Streaky is a narrow and well-defined gully which springs from a triangular snow patch. Reach it by following the snow ramp up right from Best Back to an icefall which guards the entrance. Either climb the icefall or an easier ramp which lies a little farther up the ramp (30m). The barrier immediately ahead is turned by ice on the right and the gully followed to belay below a prominent ice slot (35m). Climb the slot and the steepening gully above to a bottleneck exit which sometimes forms an ice bulge. Continue more easily to a short buttress (45m). Turn the buttress on the left and cross the snow ramp to a slabby groove which cuts across the rocks ahead. Climb the mixed ramp to easy ground above (40m). A pleasant route which readily comes into condition.

To the right of the icefalls on the South East Face, the nose of the buttress swings round to the north-east. The nose itself consists of a long easy-angled rib which then steepens into narrow ribs and gullies with a prominent slanting snow and ice ramp which exits just left of the true apparent edge. To the right of the nose, the much steeper North East Face rises above long Grade I slopes. The face is bottomed by a band of icefalls and rock with a girdling snow apron above. Above this apron the face is seamed by narrow gullies and grooves which gradually become less rocky farther right. The rock is extremely sound and is fairly massive though belays tend to be good where cracks occur. The routes are described left to right.

Porker – 120m II. G. Cullen, J.R. Mackenzie (in descent). 13th February, 1994.
A very exposed ramp of high-angled snow without pitches leads up from the easy-angled central rib below the nose up and left to exit up an airy headwall left of the nose proper.

Piglet – 110m II. J.R. Mackenzie, G. Cullen. 13th February, 1994.
Just to the right of the ramp of Porker the nose swings to the east. Piglet takes the first prominent shallow gully to the right. Climb the gully (40m), then continue up the steeper groove above (40m). Rather than escape up the snow to the left, the more interesting buttress ahead was taken on ice (30m).

North East Face:
Pearls Before Swine – 200m IV,4. G. Cullen, J.R. Mackenzie. 13th February, 1994.
This is a splendid route with varied climbing in an alpine position. It starts by climbing the steepening snow couloir to the right of the easy-angled rib and approximately centrally below the face. The couloir gives about 200m of Grade I climbing to rock belays below and right of a wide icefall.
1. 50m. Climb the icefall, which has two steep sections, to the snow apron.
2. 35m. Continue up the apron to the hidden entrance to a hidden gully on the right.
3. 35m. Climb up the gully to a seeming impasse ahead.
4. 50m. Move right into a chimney and follow this to another overhang. Turn this on the right and follow the rib up to the final overhang which blocks the exit. Difficult moves turn this on the right.
5. 30m. Continue up iced grooves more easily to the summit.

STRATHCONON, Glenmarksie Crag:
Helios – 60m E2. J.R. Mackenzie, R. Brown. 16th September, 1993.
This is the girdle traverse of the main crag. Despite having a contrived first pitch and the odd scrappy section, the climbing is good with an excellently sustained third pitch. Start as for Sea of Tranquility.
1. 20m 4c. Climb over the arched overlap and follow the lip of this boldly to the end. Descend the corner to belay on the birch.
2. 12m 5a. Cross the slab above the overhang of Dynamite and descend Proteus to the floor of the niche.
3. 15m 5b. Step down into the niche of Phobos and climb Phobos to the hidden flake hold. Step down and traverse to the foot ledge of Deimos and step down awkwardly to the small ledge on Callisto. A splendid pitch.
4. 12m 4c. Climb up Callisto's rib to cross to the bounding edge beyond Greased Lightning and belay on the small tree.

Glenmarksie Top Crag:
Bridging the Gap – 12m E3 6a. J.R. Mackenzie, R. Brown. 8th June, 1993.
Climbs the open groove left of Gritstone Corner giving a splendid and technical route which is well protected by RPs at the crux. A strenuous juggy start up the flake leads to altogether different climbing above, possibly easier for the very tall and certainly harder for the very short. Exit left under the overhang.

Man o' War – 15m E3 6b. J.R. Mackenzie, R. Brown. 28th June, 1993.
Takes the roof and wall in the middle of the crag left of Bridging the Gap. Start at a dead tree and follow the handrail up left to the roof. Surmount the roof strenuously (4 Friend) and continue up the overhanging wall to a mean exit. Excellent protection but a real test piece.

Scatwell River Slabs:
The Joust – 45m E3 6a. J. Finlay, J.R. Mackenzie. 3rd November, 1993.
Between The Tilting Yard and Grand Central is a cleaned area of concave slab with a prominent groove running up to a smooth headwall. A tremendous route with the crux right at the top. Abseil down Grand Central to the trees. Traverse left across the base of Grand Central to the start of the groove. Climb the increasingly difficult groove and flake to a small tree Above is a blank slab with a peg runner. Gain the peg tenuously and then the letterbox above (vital 0 Friend runner). The even-blanker crux follows.

The Tilting Yard – 30m E2 5b. J.R. Mackenzie, J. Finlay. 17th September, 1993.
This sustained and quite serious route takes the big corner which bounds the west end of the slabs (right looking down). Abseil to a ledge. Climb the thin diagonal line into the corner and follow this tenuously past two broken blocks to the prominent chokestone. Continue past the small tree to the top.

Boundary Ridge – 25m VS 4c. M. Hind, J. Lowe. 30th October, 1993.
This is the edge which bounds The Tilting Yard on the extreme right of the slabs (looking down). Abseil descent is possibly easier than a scramble well to the right. Climb the rib which has one awkward step.

Meig Crag:
Casting Out – 25m E3 5c. M. Hind. 30th October, 1993.
To the right of Limited Liability is a blank wall with a horizontal crack. Climb the vertical crack leading into Limited Liability and then traverse right (little protection) to the overhung nose at its end. Surmount the nose and gain an easier groove to finish. A sustained and bold pitch.

Hidden Crag:
Apocrypha – 12m HVS 4c. J. Lyall, G. Irvine. September, 1993.
Start right of Hoist at the base of the left-slanting crack. Climb up the brown streak, move right into a scoop and climb straight up.
Note: J. Lyall thinks that both Scoop Crag and Hidden Crag provide good little routes, but are overgraded and suggests the following.
Hidden Crag: Hoist by One's Own Bullshit – VS 5a. Chinese Eyes – HVS 5b. Shield Bug – HVS 5a. The Barker – E1 5b. Pledge – E1 5b. (Agreed).
Scoop Crag: The Spike – Severe. Fleetstreet Hack – HVS 5a. The Scoop – Severe. Confectionary Arete – V. Diff. (Agreed).

SGURR A' MHUILINN, Creag Ghlas, East Buttress:
Blue Moon – 265m III. G. Cullen, J.R. Mackenzie. 1st January, 1994.
Takes a central line up a snow strip to the right of Whoops. Climb the strip to poor belays on the left (50m). Continue in the same line to a belay on the left (50m). Climb over a steepening to a shelf (30m). Climb straight up heading for a bay to the right of the rounded buttress of Whoops, exiting to belays above (45m). Continue to the foot of the headwall. Turn this easily on the right and climb up to a steep pair of blocky grooves (50m). Climb the left-hand groove to a chockstone-blocked groove above and surmount this on the left (40m).

West Buttress:
Thumper – 90m IV,5. M. Hind, J.R. Mackenzie. 8th January, 1994.
The steep groove between Evening Arete and Glass Slipper. It produces a thin ice

streak and gives very good mixed climbing of a technical but well-protected nature. Start just right of Glass Slipper and climb the steep technical slab to the groove which is followed to the steeper groove above (35m). Climb this steepening groove to exit up a narrow chimney (35m). Climb the gully above and surmount a short chimney crack (20m).

Hall of Mirrors – 80m E1. R. Brown, G. Cullen, J.R. Mackenzie. 30th October, 1993.
This excellent route climbs the centrally placed striated side wall left of Sweet Charity, leading to a large overhung ledge. The long first pitch is well protected but requires a double rack of Friends – half to 3. Start centrally below an obvious crack system.
1. 50m 5b. Climb via cracks and flakes to a small overlap. Pull over and follow the main crack to a hanging belay beside a small spike about 6m below the overhung ledge. A very sustained pitch at the top end of its grade.
2. 30m 4a/b. Continue to the large sloping ledge and move left on to the arete. Climb this by delightful flake cracks to an awkward step right. Continue up and left to the right end of the heather terrace above. Either scramble down then up to reach the descent gully, or climb:
3. 15m. Climb the line of flakes into a shallow corner and exit left on to a big heather terrace.
4. 30m 4b. The wall of slanting cracks above has a projecting triangular block a few metres up. Climb up to and over the block and continue straight up to finish.

CREAG A' GHLASTAIL:
Waterfall Gully – 150m IV,4. J.R. Mackenzie, P. Moffat. 24th February, 1994.
This is the deep gully on the left of the crag. Vertical height not length is given. Though it can hold continuous ice, little is visible from below. The initial chimney pitch gives about 8m of vertical ice, followed by easier ground then another step. More easy ground leads to a step of about 20m which can be very hard in thaw conditions. More easy ground leads to an amphitheatre. Climb the pleasant 30m icefall to below the enormous wedged chockstone and cave. The cave is blocked except on the right where a short, but hard, groove leads to the roof of the chockstone. The gully is hemmed by walls on this side so walk along the roof of the chockstone to a cave below a fine icefall. Either escape tamely up a ramp to the right or climb the icefall (12m) to easier ice and the top.

BEINN WYVIS, Coire na Feola:
The Snick – 200m III. J.R. Mackenzie, P. Moffat. 3rd February, 1994.
About 250m left of the main crag is a prominent narrow buttress with an ice bulge at half height. It is flanked by a deep gully on the left and a less-pronounced one to the right. Start below the centre of the crag and climb shelves to just below the ice bulge (35m). Climb the very steep bulge (crux) which is quite short, to a ramp which leads to a small bay and spike belay (25m). Climb the iced ramp on the right, then trend back left and up to easier ground (40m). The route now finishes up the broad concave rib which has only a minor cornice (100m). A good route for doubtful conditions.

FANNICHS, An Coileachan, Coire nan Eun (NH 245685):
A cliff well seen from Beinn Dearg but only fleetingly from the road. Fatal Attraction is obvious from the road but the gullies are hidden.

Descent Gully – 110m I. A. Nisbet. 26th March, 1994.
Towards the left end of the crag is this left-slanting snow gully. There would be a pitch in leaner conditions.

Inner Sanctum – 100m III. A. Nisbet. 26th March, 1994.
About 20m right of the easy gully is a narrower and deeper left-slanting gully which remains hidden until the coire is entered. It had one very steep ice pitch which was chimneyed and was amazingly easy for the grade.

Fatal Attraction – 100m IV,4. A. Nisbet. 26th March, 1994.
The icefall just right of Inner Sanctum. A short right traverse near the top led to its continuation. Some thin sections on this occasion but turf was available and good rock cracks were noted.

Sgurr nan Clach Geala:
Skyscraper Buttress, Empire State Variation – 140m V,5. R. Everett, S. Richardson (AL). 13th February, 1994.
A highly-enjoyable expedition taking the left front face of the steep upper part of the buttress. Very exposed, but far easier than it looks. A complete ascent of the buttress with this finish merits VI,6. Start from the stance above the crux bulge at the end of Pitch 3 on the original route.
1. 50m. Follow the natural line up and right for 15m to a huge flake on the left. Move left around the edge above the flake to gain a small hanging snowfield, and climb a left-slanting shallow turfy groove which cuts into the headwall looming above. Belay in an overhung niche.
2. 45m. Climb straight up via cracks and grooves to reach a ledge and niche overlooking Gamma Gully on the left. An outstanding pitch.
3. 45m. Continue up the steep groove above to ledges, then take the turfy corner leading into the centre of the final overhanging wall. Step right into a second groove, then trend up and left in a spectacular position to the top. Finish easily along the horizontal ridge to the plateau (50m).

Sgurr Breac:
Turkey Time – 150m III/IV. G. Ettle, J. Finlay. December, 1993.
Climbs the buttress to the left of Ptarmigan Corner for 90m, then an easy gully on the left to the top.

BEINN DEARG, Glen Na Sguaib:
Orange Edge – 250m III. D. Broadhead, M. Dixon. 7th January, 1994.
Climbs the rib to the right of Orangeman's Gully. Start at the foot of Orangeman's Gully. Leave the snow bay on the right by a short steep corner to gain a series of grooves which lead eventually to the rib overlooking the upper reaches of the gully. A short steep groove (avoidable on the right) leads to easier ground.

Red Handed – 200m III. J. Lyall, A. Sutton, R. Wild. March, 1988.
Start at the foot of Orangeman's Gully and climb the icy ramp slanting left. Above this a V-groove is climbed, then trend up right to climb another groove. Continue straight up to gain a gradually steepening gully leading to the top.

No Surrender – 250m III. G. Borland, A. Fraser, M. Sillars. 5th March, 1994.
The buttress between Fenian Gully and Papist's Passage provides a pleasant mixed

route, well suited to bad conditions. Start at a grassy groove in the centre of the buttress. Climb this via a short bulge, then continue directly up the buttress.
Note: J. Lyall notes that Bonus is no more than Grade II, but a good climb for that grade.

Coire Ghranda, Lower Crag:
Stage Left – 150m II. B. Davison, A. Nisbet. 30th January, 1994.
On the left wall of the gully left of Yon Spoot is the short steep icefall mentioned in the guide. Lower down on the wall, near the start of the gully, a longer but less steep icefall runs up to the cornice, which was passed at the top of the buttress on the left.

Lillehammer – 250m IV,4. A. Nisbet, G. Nisbet. 25th February, 1994.
Climbs the crest right of Grotto Gully. The main feature of the route was an 80m right-facing, ice-filled corner (right of another less-defined fault). The base of the corner was gained by a right traverse from below Grotto Gully. Increasingly steep ice in the corner led to an easier finish.

Slush Puppy – 380m IV,3. B. Davison, A. Nisbet. 2nd February, 1994.
A wide slabby icefall with two overlaps in the centre of the main section of the lower cliff, about 150m right of Grotto Gully. Grade III should apply in better conditions, but still a serious route. Starting virtually at the loch, the icefall was climbed in four long pitches. Mostly 50°-60° with two bulges which should be climbed direct in future. A right-trending line with long easy sections led to the only break in a large cornice.

The Grander Icefall – 320m IV,4. S. Anderson, A. Nisbet. 10th February, 1994.
A thinner, but steeper, icefall about 50m right of Slush Puppy (the next icefall right). The same break in the cornice was used but was approached more directly by steep 10m icefalls in the preceding two tiers.

Right of The Grander Icefall are two more icefalls, each about 15m apart. After these ascents, a right traverse on steep snow led to the base of the Upper Cliff. This option is open for all the lower icefalls.

The Snake – 180m IV,4. A. Nisbet. 19th February, 1994.
The next icefall right. The ice flows over a small roof near the base. This was too thin and bypassed by stepping off a large block on its right. The icefall was gained soon above.
The Portcullis – 180m IV,5. B. Davison, A. Nisbet. 12th February, 1994.
Next right. Again incomplete near the base. A 4m vertical ice slot followed by a deviation on the left led to a thicker ice wall which was the main feature of the route.

Outer Crag:
As one curves round into Coire Ghranda from Loch nan Eilean, there is an overlooking frieze of crag with many icefalls. At NH 268799 its height doubles just before (south) of a spur which is met before the coire loch. This high section contained three icefalls but the ice was so extensive that thinner ice formed in places between them. The lengths are a guess but they will certainly provide two long pitches on continuous steep ice. A descent was made each time down a ramp which starts left of the icefalls (looking up) and slants down underneath them. This descent involves a short section of 50°-55° snow.

Left Icefall – 100m IV,4. A. Nisbet. 19th February, 1994.
Less well-defined at the start but steepens up with some very steep optional bulges.

Central Icefall – 100m IV,5. A. Nisbet. 19th February, 1994.
Slightly steeper, particularly near the top where an optional direct line was taken.

Right Icefall – 100m IV,4. A. Nisbet. 19th February, 1994.
The ice forms thickly in a long V-groove (with a larger left wall) leading near the top to a left rising snow ramp which was ignored for a direct finish.

Upper Crag:
Upper Class Corner – 120m III. A. Nisbet, B. Davison. 12th February, 1994.
About 60m left of the huge corner of Snort Trail (which looked excellent), is a much smaller right-facing corner containing an icefall.

The Toff – 120m IV,4. A. Nisbet. 19th February, 1994.
About 15m left of Upper Class Corner is a small right-facing, right-slanting corner. A thicker icefall flows straight down fron its upper section. The small corner itself could also be followed, probably Grade III.

ARDMAIR, Monster Buttress:
Over the Quota – 20m E1 5b. J. Hepburn, A. Fyffe. 1st October, 1993.
Left of Le Pontif is a vegetated fault, then a clean buttress. The route follows the obvious left-facing corner to a horizontal break, then the groove above to the top.

Mighty Atom – 10m HVS 4c. A. Fyffe, J. Hepburn. 1st October, 1993.
Climb the overhanging orange wall right of Little Red Rooster to a ledge. Finish up the crack as for that route or move left round the nose to finish as for Lagavulin.

Dancing Buttress:
We Can't Dance – 30m HVS 5a. A. Fyffe, J. Hepburn. 1st October, 1993.
Takes a line up the black-streaked rock in the gully left of Spider Jive. Start a short way up the gully just left of the vegetated corner.
1. 20m 4c. Climb the cleanest rock, then trend left on ledges. Move up and round a corner to the left, then return right to climb a black scoop to the heather ledge.
2. 10m 4b. Climb the corner on the left of the arete.

Edinburgh Rock:
Ten Seconds – 15m E4 6b. G. Szuca, D. Gregg, A. Wren. 14th April, 1993.
The crack left of Alliteration Alternative, moving right past an in situ nut.

Big Roof Buttress:
Unnamed – E2 5c. A. Cunningham, J. Pickering, K. Geddes. 4th September, 1993.
Right of Terrace Crack, crossing it leftwards near the top.

CUL BEAG, Red Slab (NH 129082):
This is a pair of slabs right by the roadside at the foot of Cul Beag. They are composed of first quality Torridonian sandstone.

Roadside Gem – 20m HVS 5a. G. Cullen, J.R. Mackenzie. 11th August, 1993.
The frontal face of the main slab has a shallow corner on the left. Climb this to step on to the front face where the corner fades and climb the left arete to the top.

Pink Panther – 24m E2 5b/c. J.R. Mackenzie, G. Cullen. 11th August, 1993.
An excellent bold climb taking the centre of the main slab. Start just right of a crack and climb the wall to a narrow ledge and sapling. Climb up to a flake right of the sapling to a hidden hold above, traverse left to stand on a flat foothold. Climb straight up the slab to the top. Half Friend essential protection on the traverse.

Red Slab – 24m V. Diff. G. Cullen, J.R. Mackenzie. 11th August, 1993.
To the right of the main slab is a narrow easier-angled one. Start on the road and take the best line. Probably climbed before.

Wicket Gate Crag (NC 090098):
Another crag probably climbed on before but considered good. On the north side of the road just west of Stac Pollaidh. It is set about 40m from the road and is approached via a small gate.

Garden Path – 25m VS 4b. F. Neilson, R. Webb. September, 1993.
In the centre of the crag is a dog-legged groove. Climb the lower groove to the roof. Traverse right through the overhang to gain the upper groove.

Black Crack – 15m H. Severe. F. Neilson, R. Webb. September, 1993.
The obvious black crack at the left end of the crag.

STAC POLLAIDH, No.3 Buttress:
The large buttress right of the scree gullies of Pinnacle Basin is Summer Isles Arete. The original route (V. Diff.) takes the easiest line, presumably big chimneys on the right of the buttress. The following route takes a more direct and obvious line.

Summer Isles Arete Direct – 115m VS 4c. A. Fraser, J. Dickson. 3rd September, 1993.
A pleasant civilised route with good positions. Just left of the toe of the buttress, next to the screes of Pinnacle Basin, is an obvious corner, the start.
1. 25m 4b. Climb the corner to ledges.
2. 15m 4a. Climb right on to the crest of the ridge beneath a pinnacle, then ramble left across a gully and walls to belay beneath a groove on the left of the buttress.
3. 25m 4c. Climb the groove, exiting right with difficulty to gain and follow an obvious crackline up the front of the buttress. Belay beneath the steep final tower.
4. 25m 4c. On the right side of the tower is a short vicious corner crack. Climb this, then follow ledges up and right to the final arete. Belay behind the final tower.
5. 15m 3b. Follow the arete directly to the summit ridge (this last pitch is optional, as is the Summer Isles Hotel Direct – five miles).

Outrageous Fortune – 50m E1 5b. A. Fraser, K. Douglas. 4th September, 1993.
To the right of Summer Isles Arete is a grass slope, at the top of which is a fine narrow tower, split by a steep bulging crack.
1. 35m 5b. Climb corners on the left of the tower to a ledge beneath the bulging crack. Climb this strenuously (rest used), then follow the ridge to large ledges.
2. 15m 4a. Climb up and over the pinnacle to the summit ridge.

REIFF, Bouldering Cliff:
Tidal Zone – 10m MVS 4b. A. Cunningham, J. Pickering. June, 1992.
The vague crackline in the wall 3m to the right of Sneaky Slab. Tidal.

Black Rocks Main Cliff:
Pot Black – 20m HVS 5a. A. Fyffe, J. Hepburn. 2nd October, 1993.
The wall left of Black Pig. Climb the lower easy section of Black Pig to a ledge, then move left on breaks and up to a pocket. Continue up, then move left to finish up a corner in the left edge of the wall.

The Sea Cliff Area:
NW Stars – 15m Diff. A. Cunningham and party. June, 1992.
The next open groove left of Carmine Corner.

Pole Position – 10m H. Severe. A. Cunningham and party. June, 1992.
The end of the promontary has a low-angled slab facing east.

Party Games – 10m Mod. A. Cunningham and party. September, 1993.
Climb a crack and corner near the left end of the slab.

Schnapps – 12m Diff. A. Cunningham and party. September, 1993.
Left of Party Games and at a lower level, climb a wide crack to a finish just left of Party Games.

Seal Song Area:
Falls of Leny – 12m HVS 5a. K. Geddes, A. Cunningham, M. Blyth. 24th April, 1993.
From a few metres up The Executioner, pull right into a sharp flake crack and finish up the groove left of Trout Mask Replica.

Bay of Pigs:
Impure Thoughts – 15m E6 6b. W. Moir. 13th June, 1993.
The route lies on the continuation walls south of Bay of Pigs, above the long flat platform 60m south of Eddy Current. At the right hand end is an obvious hanging corner line just left of an overhanging scooped corner. Practised, then led.
   Start on the right and work up and left to gain the obvious big pinch. Use this to gain an edge on the right and palm up to the base of the corner (serious and committing – rock 4 up in the corner). Continue up the corner and finish on the right.

Golden Walls:
The Road to Somewhere – 15m E5 6a/b. W. Moir, P. Allen. 12th June, 1993.
The arete right of The Road to Nowhere. Step off a big detached flake and climb the crackline, then the arete to the top. Sustained and superb.

Shakey Flakey – HVS 5a. G. Szuca, D. Gregg, A. Wren. 13th April, 1993.
Start 4m left of Dragons of Eden etc. Go up to an obvious spike at 3m. Follow the flakes up and rightwards to finish as for Dragons. Same as St. Vitus Gets On Down (Ed?)

Blood of Eden – 25m E1 5b. P. Allen, W. Moir. 12th June, 1993.
The right of two lines between Shades of Night and St. Vitus. Scramble up to ledges and belay. Start just right of the crackline. Gain and climb the crackline, then take the line of flakes running diagonally rightwards to finish by a short crack.

Forbidden Fruit – 25m E3 5c. W. Moir, P. Allen. 12th June, 1993.
The right-hand line. Climb corners with a tricky start to a ledge. Move left along this and gain a left-slanting crack in the black and gold streaked rock. Climb this and the crack above.

Jigsaw Wall Point (Guide p226):
Traditional Steps – 15m V.Diff. J. Pickering, A. Cunningham. 24th June, 1993.
The awkward stepped corner to the right of Traditional Chimney.

Desperado – 10m E2 6a. A. Cunningham. 24th June, 1993.
Right of Traditional Chimney on the seaward face. Climb a difficult left diagonal
crack near the right end of the face to a big break. Finish straight up.

Rubha Ploytach:
Bee in my Bosom – 12m E1 5c. A. Cunningham, A. Fyffe. 8th June, 1993.
The corner in the middle of The Black Back Wall with a steep awkward start.
Note: Excellence by Design (p184) is E2 5c* (misprint)

FOINAVEN, Ceann Garbh:
A Second Chance – 300m IV,5. D, Broadhead, G. Drinkwater. 20th February, 1994.
Climbs a large icefall high on the cliff, right of the Central Slabs, to the left of a
distinctive rock pillar. Start in the prominent easy gully (left of the North East
Buttress) to reach a moderate icefall crossing the right end of the Central Slabs,
leading to a snow bay below the main icefall. A full pitch of steep ice leads to a good
rock thread belay on the right. Continue more easily in the groove above as the angle
eases off again.
SHEIGRA:
The following is a rewrite by Andy Cunningham and includes many new routes.
Photodiagrams were also supplied. First ascentionists, other than those listed in the
Guide, given by initials:
AC – Andy Cunningham. IR – Ian Rea. AF – Allen Fyffe. SB – Steve Blagbrough.
JP – Jenny Pickering. AN – Andy Nisbet. GR - George Reid. JH – Jas Hepburn. CR
– Catriona Reid. AH – Alison Hepburn. KG – Keith Geddes. MB – Mark Blyth. JK
– Jim Kerr.

FIRST GEO:
This is the geo just to the north of the beach, the head of which is by the corner in
the fence. For the first routes, walk to the end of the promontory and turn back right
to below the climbs.

Shelob's Lair – 15m V. Diff. AN. November, 1989.
The chimney above the right end of the platform with a hollow block.

· *Slanting Crack* – 15m Severe. AN. November, 1989.
Left of Shelob's Lair is an overhanging wall and at the left end of this is a left
slanting crack leading into a shallower chimney.

The Ramp – 20m V. Diff. AN. November, 1989.
Between the above two routes and the overhanging central wall of the geo farther
left is a left-to-right broken ramp system starting above a short bulging wall. The
difficulty lies in the initial wall.

Remember the lines at the end of the promontory. Various at VS, mainly following
obvious cracklines. AC, JP. June, 1988.

The lines on the giant blocks. Access across a tidal channel east of the above
promontary. Mini routes from Severe to 5b. AC, KG. July, 1989.

South Wall (right to left):

Abseil in to the back of the geo, or walk round to the north side and descend by a wide obvious groove, or descend by the seaward end of the north wall at low tide. At very low tides, access is possible from The Ramp.

Monkey Man – 22m E3 5c. AC, AF, JK. 28th May, 1993.
The superb steep and strenuous vertical crackline to the right of Blind Faith.

Blind Faith – 25m E2 5b. AF, AC. November, 1989.
On the overhanging South Wall beside the largest high-tide boulder. Gain from the right a crackline curving rightwards. Follow its continuation up and left to the base of an obvious deep pink groove. Move right into a small alcove and finish right up a black crack.

BF Direct – 25m Grade and ascenders unknown. 5th-6th June, 1993.
From the start of the right curving crackline, climb straight up to the deep pink groove. Finish up the groove, which bounds the right side of the capping roofs.

Road to Reform – 25m E3 5c. AC, AF. November, 1989.
Follow a crackline leading up and left out of an overhanging niche 5m left of Blind Faith. Finish up the steep corner at the right end of the large ledge to the left of the big roof.

Unnamed – 5th-6th June, 1993.
Climb the thin crack in the steep wall to the left of Road to Reform. Finish the same. Chalk seen, no info.

Continuing left, the wall changes into blacker blockier rock with two large steps near the base. Above these steps is an apparent slab forming a left-facing corner.

Shiver me Timbers – 25m E1 5b. SB, AC. November, 1989.
From the top step, Climb the stepped wall on the right. Steep moves lead to a pull on to the slab. Traverse left and climb twin cracks in the slab above. Move left to finish up a short steep wall.

Same Old Story – 25m HVS 5a. SB, AN. November, 1989.
From the top step, climb the obvious left-slanting crackline in a corner leading to the same finishing wall as Shiver me Timbers.

The Only Way is Up – 20m HVS 5a. AF, AC. November, 1989.
Left of and at the same level as the top step is an overhanging wall. At its left end is an overhanging groove slanting right. Climb this to finish up the same short wall as Shiver me Timbers.

Gneiss Won – 20m H. Severe. AF, AC. November, 1989.
Towards the back of the geo is a distinctive black and pink cracked wall. Climb this through a slot to finish by a wide flake crack.

Rescue Alcove – 12m E2 5b. AF, AC. 28th May, 1993.
Left again the wall overhangs and becomes more compact. This route climbs a left-to-right gangway leading to a bulging finish. Awkward and fiddly protection.

North Wall:

At the back of the geo is a black bulging slab topped by steeper orange rock. The following two routes lie at the left end of this area taking two cleaned groove lines.

Casey Jones – 15m E1 5b. IR, AF. 28th May, 1993.
Trend left on to the slab by an obvious break. Enter the left-hand groove with difficulty and climb to the roof. Move left and follow the rib to the top.

Redneck – 15m E2 5c/6a. IR, AC. 28th May, 1993.
Take the bulge direct at its widest point leading on to the slab (crux, bold and artificial). Follow the thin crack into the right-hand groove. Climb direct to the top. Probably E1 5a avoiding the start.

Left of the above routes and just right of the descent groove is a small steep red buttress.
Second Option – 10m VS 5a. AC, GR. 12th June, 1993.
Takes twin left diagonal cracks above a low roof. Avoid the roof on the left. Not a classic.

The remaining routes are down from the descent groove.

Haddie – 15m Diff. CR,JP. 13th June, 1993.
Above the huge boulders, take a cracked black rampline rightwards and finish up a black slab.

Next is the main area with a series of black grooves starting by the huge boulders. The most obvious at the right end is capped by a large roof – the line of Original Route.

In the Pink – 15m V. Diff. AN, SB. November, 1989.
This route follows a crackline and groove in the slabby buttress right of Original Route, with an obvious pink vein.

Blackballed – 15m Severe. AN, SB. November, 1989.
In the left side of the In The Pink buttress, in the right wall of the V-groove of Original Route, is a wide crack. Climb the crack until it begins to peter out, then step right on to the buttress crest and climb a short groove to finish.

Original Route – 20m E1 5b. FA unknown.
Climb the black corner crack immediately left of Blackballed up to the smooth V-groove under the huge roof. Traverse right with difficulty to just above where Blackballed moves right. Trend steeply right and back left to finish.

R 'n' R – 20m H. Severe. AN, SB. November, 1989.
Just left of Original Route is another groove with twin cracks leading to a small roof. Climb to the roof, move right round this and continue up and left via a line of blocks.

Immediately left again are two grooves; the right one with a narrow black pillar leading to a short steep V-groove and the left one has a huge quartz-topped pedestal to half height.

Avoiding the Issue – 20m E1 5b. AC, AF. 28th May, 1993.
The right-hand groove. Climb the crack in the right side of the pillar and up to the base of the steep V-groove. Move left through the roof and climb up and back right to the top of the groove.

Two Step – 20m VS 4c. AF, AC. 28th May, 1993.
Climb a left-trending crack in the front of the pedestal to its top. Continue in the
same line up the wall above.

Aegir – 20m V. Diff. JP, CR. 12th June, 1993.
The groove to the left of the pedestal. Easier to follow the rib on the left in the top
half.

Blackjack – 15m Diff. AN. November, 1989.
The last black groove in this area is followed direct on satisfying sound rock.

At the seaward end of the North Wall and below high tide mark, is a diamond shaped
clean buttress with three left-slanting cracklines. This is the last buttress before this
side disappears.

Skate – 15m HVS 5a. AC, AF. November, 1989.
The right-hand crack going through a roof low down.

Cuddane – 15m E1 5b. GR, AC. 12th June, 1993.
The middle crack.

Flounder – 15m VS 4c. AN, SB. November, 1989.
The left crackline, passing a ledge at 5m.

Kippered – 10m HVS 5b. AC, GR. 12th June, 1993.
Takes the short wall to the left of Flounder via a thin crack.

SECOND GEO:
This consists of an impressive orange west face at its northern end running down
a huge slab to sea level and a large cave. At the top of the easy slab is a large 3m
sandstone erratic boulder and the routes are best seen from near this point. The
orange wall runs into a series of black corners at the south end of the cave with the
corner route of Dark Angel bounding the orange wall. The cliff turns south again
and runs out towards the First Geo.

Access:
1. For routes left of the cave (from Sideslip to May Tripper), start from the slab.
2. To climb the routes from Geriatrics, above the cave, to the rib of Lucifer's Link
left of the main black corner of Shark Crack, an abseil is made on to the Black
Pedestal, a good incut ledge at the base of Black Knight, 3m above the sea.
3. For Shark Crack and Fingers, abseil down Shark Crack to the slabby lower
section.
4. The route of Right-Hand Buttress is reached by abseil on to a sloping ledge at the
base, awash at high tide or in rough seas.

The routes are described from left to right from the top of the slab round to Right-
Hand Buttress.

Sideslip – 20m MVS 4b.
Near the top of the huge slab, start at the right end of a low ramp leading leftwards.
Climb the ramp and follow a subsequent curving vague crackline.

Sideline – 25m VS 4c.
From the base of the ramp, pull out right on to the wall and climb to a ledge left of a short left-facing corner. Finish up the wall above.

Juggernaut – 25m E1 5a.
Start a few metres down from Sideline and climb a short steep wall on to a small ledge. Continue in the same line past the left side of a large hole to finish up steep cracks right of the arete of the top steep corner.

Bloodlust – 25m E1 5b.
Start at the point where the slab meets the top of the cave and gain a small ledge. Go up a shallow corner and left up a gangway to the large hole. Make steep moves right to a small ramp and continue diagonally right to the top.

Bloodlust Direct – Finish E2 5b.
From the hole, go diagonally right and back left to finish direct up the right side of the steep red wall. Three stars.

May Tripper – 25m E1 5b.
As for Bloodlust to the first ledge. Climb diagonally right following a zig-zag quartz vein to gain and follow a small ramp to a large hidden pocket right of the black streak. Move up to cross Bloodlust and finish direct.

Geriatrics – 40m E2 5c.
From the Black Pedestal, traverse left into Dark Angel and continue left across the lip of the cave on a quartz band. From its end move up and continue left in a spectacular position to a ramp at the left end of the cave roof. Climb direct up the wall above.

Exorcist – 40m E2 5b.
Follow Geriatrics to the end of the quartz band and climb via black streaks above to a small ledge below the obvious shallow left curving arch forming a higher groove (the line of Presumption). Continue up the black streaks to gain a higher faint groove which is followed to the top.

Presumption – 40m E1 5b.
Climb Dark Angel to just past the first bulge. Traverse horizontally left crossing the black streaks of Exorcist and into the stepped left-curving arch. Finish direct just left of the top groove.

Muir Wall – 35m E2 5c. AC, JH, AF. 18th September, 1993.
Good, but eliminate, climbing between the corner of Dark Angel and the black streaks of Exorcist. Head for a hanging groove at the top.

Dark Angel – 30m E1 5b.
Step left from the Black Pedestal to climb the fine groove to the large upper shelf (possible belay). Make steep moves up the hanging corner above to finish (crux).

Black Knight – 30m HVS 5a.
Gain and climb the black groove directly above the Black Pedestal to the upper shelf. Finish easily on the right.

Lucifer's Link – 35m E1 5b.
Climb the rib on the right of the Black Pedestal in impressive surroundings.

Shark Crack – 30m H. Severe.
The crack in the main corner right of the Black Pedestal. Start from a ledge on the right of the lower slab reached by abseil. The route was originally ascended by difficult aid moves from a low tide ledge at the true base of the crack to gain the present start (HVS 5a, A2 with three pegs).

Fingers – 30m E1 5b.
The black wall right of Shark Crack is split by a thin crack. Climb the crack with a final steep section.

Right-Hand Buttress – 35m E1 5b.
This route is round the edge from Fingers on the west face above a deep tidal slot between the cliff and a small island. Abseil to a low tide ledge. Climb a steep wall to a large halfway ledge. Escape from the ledge with difficulty up the wall above to an exposed but easier finish.

Treasure Island Wall:
This area is basically a continuation of the Second Geo starting below the huge sandstone erratic block and running north opposite a low headland (Na Stacain) which is almost an island at high tide. There are two main approaches to the climbs.
    After about 50m north of the sandstone block is a burn draining down to the clifftop. A steep descent on big holds can be made to the right of the burn (facing out) at about Diff. Or abseil. From the base of the descent, move right to a platform.

The Nook, Tall Pall, Plum McNumb: As described in the Guide.
FA of The Nook: AN, November, 1989.
About 150m farther on from the shallow burn is a narrow gully lying between the main cliff and a rib dropping into the geo. Descend the gully underneath some immense blocks to sea level. Turn right under the rib and it is possible to traverse into the geo at mid to low tides. Otherwise abseil from near the top of the gully. The first routes are on the outside of the rib.

Will o' the Wisp – 20m M. Severe. JP, AH. 18th September, 1993.
This route actually climbs the rib itself. At the steepening, move left on to the front and finish by a steep crack.

Tickled Pink – 15m Severe. AC. November, 1989.
The first crack at the right end of the wall, curving leftwards.

Spare Rib – 15m VS 4c. AN, SB. November, 1989.
Climb the centre of the wall by a line of left trending discontinuous cracks.

After Dark – 25m E1 5a. AF, IR. 29th May, 1993.
Start left of Spare Rib at the left end of the platform. Gain an awkward ledge and trnd left up cracks until a move left can be made on to the black vein above a cave. Climb the weird flake crack to the top.
At mid to low tide, access is possible beyond the platform on to slimy boulders leading to further walls and to routes on the other side.

Necklaced – 25m HVS 5a. AC, AF, JH. 18th September, 1993.
Start to the left of a small cave. Climb blocky ground and a short groove to pull awkwardly into the flake at the left side of the black vein.

Flamingo – 25m Severe. AF, AC. November, 1989.
About 15m left of Spare Rib past the small cave, climb a left trending pink ramp with a good crack in the back.

Flakey Shakes – 20m E2 5c. AC, AF. November, 1989.
Immediately right and parallel to the ramp is a line of deceptively steep flakes – the route.

Squeeze to Please – 20m Diff. AN. November, 1989.
Farther left the geo narrows to a tidal pool, before which is an obvious left slanting black chimney. Climb this and the narrow rib on its left.

The Bluff – 20m HVS 5a. IR, AF, AC. 29th May, 1993.
Start just right of the Squeeze to Please chimney. Climb the corner and continuation flake to an easier finishing corner.

Sheep Sheigra – 20m E1 5b. AC, IR, AF. 29th May, 1993.
An eliminate up the pale wall above the start of Squeeze to Please. Start up the chimney and pull on to the wall. Climb direct to the top.

Rapture – 10m HVS 5a. IR, AC, AF. 29th May, 1993.
Short and sweet, this route climbs the overhanging wall at the far end of the pool reached by traversing above on the Stacain side. Climb by hidden jugs to a left-trending flake line and finish direct.

The remaining routes are on the Stacain side of the geo, starting opposite the gully descent on a fine gnarled wall. The base is awash at high tide.

King Rib – 15m VS 5a. JH, AF, AC. 18th September, 1993.
The left end of the wall forms a rib as it cuts back inland at a small geo. Climb the rib direct with a difficult start to a large ledge. Finish up the short wall above.

Blind Corner – 15m VS 4c. AF, JH, AC. 18th September, 1993.
A few metres right of King Rib is a chimney corner leading to a roof. Climb to the roof and move left under it and up to a large ledge. Finish up the short wall above.

Rough Trade – 15m HVS 5a. AF, AC. November, 1989.
Climb the gnarly wall about 2m right of Blind Corner with an awkward move left on to a small ramp. Finish up cracks leading right.

An Seachnadh – 15m E1 5a, b. AC, IR. 29th May, 1993.
Near the right side of the wall, climb via a line of pockets to a small roof. Pull left through the roof to a small black pocket and trend back right to a thin crack. Finish up a small corner.

Emotionally Disturbed – 15m E2 5b. AC, GR. 13th June, 1993.
The right arete of the wall.

The Green Channel – 15m VS 4c. SB, AN. November, 1989.
The well defined V-groove bounding the right side of the gnarly wall.

Open Season – 15m H. Severe. GR, AC. 13th June, 1993.
To the right of The Green Channel is a black slab with a right diagonal corner at the top. Climb a wide open scoop up the middle of the slab to the base of the corner and up this to finish.

Smolt – 15m Diff. CR, JP. 13th June, 1993.
Climb a black slabby ramp at the right end of the main slab and finish direct.

Dimples – 15m H. Severe. AF, IR, AC. 29th May, 1993.
Cracks in the next arete to the right.

Blacktail – 15m V. Diff. JP, CR. 13th June, 1993.
Right of Dimples is a V-groove leading into Y-cracks. Right of this is a wide crackline running through a recess and roof at 3m. Climb this on big holds.

Three short routes have been recorded on the west side of Na Stacain on the more obvious area of good rock at the south end. Left to right: Diff, Mod, VS. Climbed by AC and party, 22nd September, 1993.

THE NORTH GEO. (As in the Guide):

EILEAN NA H-AITEIG. (Northern Highlands Vol. 2, p287):
The following five routes are on a low-angled slab facing south-east at the end of the platform past Pebble Dash, by the gully with a huge jammed chokestone at its top. The routes are described from left to right and all starting from a small ledge 1m above high tide.

Wee Beastie – 12m Diff.
Climb the first obvious deep crack.

Winkie – 12m M.Severe.
Start 1m right at a small round pocket and follow the crack to a ledge and easier ground.

Bluie – 12m M. Severe.
Start 2m right again and climb a right-trending crack.

New Dawn – 15m Diff.
Start at the right-hand end of the ledge and climb a deep right -rending crack.

Dougal Doghead – 20m Diff.
From the end of the ledge, traverse right and down for 3m, then follow another right-trending crack.

From the grassy descent on the east side of the island, by hanging a left back towards the sand, the cliffs heighten again and the persistent will find the following three routes.

Quack's Corner – 15m MVS 4b.
Climb the first obvious corner moving right at three-quarters height and finishing up the continuation corner.

Guillemot – 15m VS 4c.
Start 8m right of Quack's Corner. Climb the wall trending left to a roof and move left to finish up a steep crack.

Big Konk – 12m V. Diff.
Climb a left-facing corner 3m right again.

The gneiss geo a few hundred metres farther west along the beach has two pleasant routes recorded on its slabbier west side.

Nice One – 20m MVS 4b.
Take the centre of the steepening slab to finish just right of middle.

Nice One Too – 20m Diff.
At the right end of the slab, climb up left of an obvious flake.

The above 10 routes by KG, MB, 23rd June, 1993.

SKIRZA, Salt Skerry (p301):
About 10-minutes' walk from Skirza Flagstone Quarries at the end of the road (ND 398693). The routes are 10m-20m long and climbed by A. Cunningham and J. Pickering.

Dead Friend – MVS 4b.
There is a black bay with a burn draining down the south-facing wall. This is the right corner crack at the back of the bay (facing) on to a platform below the top.

Fraser the Razor – HVS 4c/5a.
On the front face of the promontory to the south (left) of the black bay. To the right of the big central roofs, take short steep walls and ledges leading to a vague steep crackline to the top.

Brave New Seal – VS 4c.
To the left of the big central roofs of the promontory. An obvious smooth-looking groove at one third height gained by an easy traverse in from the right (or direct up the left arete at 5a). Finish by a huge flake crack. Good.

Scurvyless – V. Diff.
On the south face of the promontory south of the black bay. About 10m left of the arete, climb easily rightwards into a brown stepped shallow groove.

Skerry Monster – E1 5a.
A huge overhanging black groove to the right (north) of the black bay. An excellent route; steep and exposed but well protected. Climb the groove, step left of the overhang into a corner leading to the final roof. Climb by a flake through the roof.

Shrew Route – V. Diff.
Walk north 100m round the next arete to another bay with a black back wall and a staircase descent. Climb a deep chimney to the left of the descent.

Skirza Edge – E1 5b.
A cracked groove line to the left of the previous route and just to the right of the arete.

LATHERONWHEEL, Pinnacle Area:
Pippet at the Post – Severe. J. Pickering, A. Cunningham. June, 1992.
The 'vegetated crack' mentioned to the left of Freaker's Crack was cleaned to give this route.

Heavy Duty – MVS 4b. A. Cunningham, J. Pickering. June, 1992.
A vague crack in the pillar at the left end of the wall. Good.

Empty Bottle – Diff. K. Geddes. June, 1992.
An easy crack to the right of Eye in the Storm, gained from the Freaker's Crack platform.

The Big Flat Wall (p323):
Gle Mha – VS 4c. K. Geddes, A. Cunningham. June, 1992.
The crack at the right end of the wall. Very Good.

McCallan's Choice – HVS 5a. A. Cunningham, K. Geddes. June, 1992.
The crackline to the left rising out of a small cave. Avoid the cave by going out right and back left into a crack.
Note: The Serpent (p325) was considered E2 5b and excellent. The first ascentionist's opinion (S. Clark) is E3 5b. S. Clark also considers The Other Landscape to be HVS 5a and the route Flight from Sadness should be named Mysteries.

South Corner (p327):
On the steep back wall are two short cracklines. The left one (Night Shift?) was considered VS 4c. The steep crack direct in the middle of the wall was E1 5b (A. Cunningham, J. Pickering).

CAIRNGORMS

LOCHNAGAR, Shadow Buttress A:
Vortex – 130m IV,4. B. Findlay, G Strange. 20th March, 1994.
Start above and right of steepest section of lower buttress below the Spiral Terrace, about 40m down and left of Bell's Variation. Slant up left to gain icy grooves and follow these up and slightly right to emerge on the balcony at end of the Spiral Terrace. Cross this and continue directly on ice (just left of chimney crack on the 1944 Hendry/Walker Variation) to reach easy ground above crux rib on the Ordinary Route.

The Pinnacle:
Settler's Rib – 90m IV,4. R. Webb, S. Richardson (AL). 17th October, 1993.
The prominent rib to the left of Slab Gully.
1. 20m. Start just above the chokestone of Black Spout, Left Branch, and follow an easy turfy crack leading left up the crest of the rib. Belay on a flake about 15m below where the rib steepens.
2. 40m. Traverse horizontally right for 5m until overlooking Slab Gully, then climb straight up through a steep bulging crest just right of the buttress crest. Continue right up awkward rounded cracks, then trend left to a good ledge.
3. 30m. Continue up the crest of the rib (as for Twin Chimneys Route) to the summit of The Pinnacle.

West Buttress:
Isis – 210m V,6. B. Findlay, G. Strange. 19th February, 1994.
Climbs full height of West Buttress taking a line between Western Slant and West

End above the midway terrace. Start down and right of Black Spout Buttress. Climb obvious central corner on right flank Black Spout Buttress (60m). Trend right over snow to right end of short barrier wall, then go straight up across midway terrace to belay on left wall of narrow square-cut gully (70m). Ascend gully to its close. Climb out right, move right and go up corner to ledges below continuation corner (25m). Climb corner to cul-de-sac. Traverse out left on to face of buttress, then go up left and back right to gain snow slopes at top of Western Slant (35). Easy to plateau.

Southern Sector:
Quick Dash Buttress – 100m III,5. S. Richardson, R. Allen (AL). 6th March, 1994.
To the left of The Red Spout are some ribs, and then a well-defined buttress with a steep lower section, topped by a snow arete. Start at the left end of the front face of the buttress.
1. 30m. Follow a ramp trending right on mixed ground to a steep wall cut by a prominent crack (old peg). The crack is blind, so step left, climb a niche, and exit right at the top of the crack. Continue easily to a belay.
2. 50m. Pleasant mixed climbing leads to the snow arete. Follow this to its end, and belay beneath a short wall.
3. 20m. Climb easy snow to outflank the cornice on the left.

The Cathedral:
Transept Route – 100m V,6. S. Richardson, R. Everett (AL). 22nd January, 1994.
A good turfy mixed climb based on the summer line. It follows the prominent groove on the left side of the front face, just right of the mummy-shaped tower.
1. 40m. From a belay at the lowest rocks move up easily then step right into the groove. Climb this with increasing difficulty to a small triangular niche. Pull over the roof (crux) and continue more easily to a recess and large block belay.
2. 35m. Continue in the same line up a narrow groove to a small hanging snow field. From its top, exit by the right wall to reach the terrace which cuts across the upper part of the field.
3. 25m. Move left into the deep well defined-chimney and climb this to the top.

No Worries Groove – 90m IV,6. S. Richardson, G. Richardson. 30th December, 1993.
The buttress to the right of Cathedral Chimney is split by a prominent left-facing corner in its lower section. Start by following Forsaken Gully for 20m to below the groove.
1. 15m. Climb mixed ground on the left to the foot of the groove.
2. 30m. Climb the groove to its top and exit right.
3. 45m. Follow the easy snow arete on the right to the foot of a short impending wall. Surmount this (crux) and continue up the continuation groove to the cornice.
Note: Cnapan Nathraichean. G. Nisbet and F. Reynolds climbed a 70m icefall at the left end of Sleac Gorm on 20th February, 1994. Grade II/III.

CREAG AN DUBH LOCH, Broad Terrace Wall:
The Eye of Allah – 100m E3. W. Moir, C. Forrest. 7th September, 1991.
1. 30m. Start up Last Oasis and follow the fault easily to belay below a steepening (as for Alice Springs).
2. 30m 5b. Climb the corner above, then step left on to a rib and follow a thin crack left to a ramp. Follow the ramp easily to belay at its left end.
3. 25m 5c. Climb a finger crack to a shelf, use a good flange to traverse right and pull up into a little corner. Exit right to a belay ledge below a slanting corner.
4. 15m 5b. Climb exposed hanging slabs on the left and finish up blocks above.

White Elephant (original) – 330m VII,7. N.D. Keir, D. Wright. February, 1975.
A winter ascent of the lower part of Pink Elephant and the upper part of Dinosaur.
The line described gives a magnificent route climbing directly over the lower
overlap of Pink Elephant to enter the Dinosaur gully. Follow this to below the Sea
of Slabs. Climb the crack of Dinosaur and follow this to Labyrinth Edge. A direct
line was taken up a corner (3PA).
Note: The upper part of Pink Elephant had insufficient ice and presumably the
lower part had less than on the 1980 ascent. Whether or not the line will be followed
again, the ascent was a source of inspiration for modern Cairngorm climbing.

GLEN CLOVA, Winter Corrie of Dreish:
Diagonal Gully, (variation finish) – 70m III. A.B. Lawson, H. Davies. 12th February, 1994.
Start at the top right hand of the basin about 5m left of the chokestone pitch on the
original route. Climb a deceptively steep groove for 15m and then a right-slanting
ramp (15m). Continue up on steep snow to bypass the cornice on the left. Could be
harder under less favourable snow conditions.

CORRIE FEE, North Wall:
North Wall Direct – 280m IV,4. J. Ashbridge, G. Dudley. 23rd January, 1994.
A direct line vertically beneath the large icefall on the upper buttress, following a
snow and ice-filled depression. The route starts from a rightward trending ramp line
beneath the main wall at an obvious 15m icefall.
1. 50m. Climb the icefall, then continue up the depression to belay on the right
below a short buttress.
2. 40m. Climb an iced wall on the left to beneath the left overhang. Continue up to
the right of the overhang to belay beneath a buttress capped by a large roof.
3. 40m. Climb the icefall to beneath the roof with a slabby wall on its right. Make
a rising right traverse across the slab and a flake beneath the roof (crux). Continue
up icy slabs and steep ground to belay on the right of the depression.
4. 50m. Continue directly up through steep ground to belay beneath the large
buttress and steep icefall with a large overhang on the right.
5. 50m. The icefall would probably be V,5. Instead a right traverse was made until
possible to climb directly upwards.
6. 50m. Continue up through the buttress and up to the cornice following a rocky
rib on its right side.

Juanjorge:
Diagonal Crack – 70m V,8. S. Richardson, R. Everett (AL). 23rd January, 1994.
This short, but absorbing technical climb follows the summer route exactly. The
steep and sustained first pitch is the crux but the second is harder! Start 50m up West
Gully and scramble up vegetation on its right bank to below the prominent wide
right trending crack which cuts through the impending left wall of the buttress.
Belay on a platform at the base of the crack (old nut in place).
1. 30m. Climb the crack with interest to a good ledge. (Hex 11 and Friend 4 useful).
2. 25m. The crackline continues rightwards across the front face of the buttress, but
the route stays on the gully wall. Move easily up for 3m to a small tree, then pull
over a bulge on the left onto a slab (technical crux). Move left around an exposed
edge to a ledge, then climb up then back right to a stance directly above the previous
belay.
3. 15m. Step left and take the easiest line to the top.

BRAERIACH, Garbh Choire Mor:
Virago – 125m V,6. R.Everett, S. Richardson (AL). 21st November, 1993.
A good mixed climb taking the line of grooves left of Vulcan. Scramble up mixed ground about 20m left of Vulcan, directly below three prominent grooves situated midway up the crag, to belay on a left slanting shelf where the crag steepens.
1. 40m. Climb a short groove to a ledge, then take a steep slightly left-trending groove through the wall above. From the small alcove at its top, move right and go steeply up to a belay at the foot of a steep corner with a good crack rising above. This is at the foot of the prominent grooves visible from below.
2. 35m. Ignore the groove on the left and climb the crack straight above the belay past a small overlap. Step left into a steep flake groove and climb this with difficulty to a belay in an overhung recess.
3. 50m. Pull through the overhang and continue up the groove above to a small ledge overlooking Vulcan. Climb the smooth V-groove (crux) to easier ground which leads steeply back left and up to the plateau.

She Devil's Buttress (Original Line) – 120m V,6. R. Everett, S. Richardson (AL). 28th November, 1993.
This follows the summer line directly up the crest of the buttress, instead of taking the groove to the right. An excellent mixed climb with two contrasting pitches. Start at the foot of the rib to the right of Great Gully.
1. 50m. Follow slabby grooves up the crest of the rib to where the buttress steepens.
2. 25m. From the top of a spearhead of rock, step left onto a slab, then move up and right to crack which leads to fine eyrie with a table-top belay.
3. 45m. Climb the vertical wall above, move left into a shallow groove, then continue up grooves on the crest of the buttress to the top.

Hot Lips – VI,7. B. Davison, A. Nisbet, J. Preston. 22nd December, 1993.
A winter ascent of the summer route but with a more direct first pitch. From halfway up the initial ramp, a short traverse left led into cracks leading to the left side of the 'open groove'. Escape left on to Pinnacles Buttress is possible here. The open groove and the rest of the summer route was climbed. Icy conditions limited the protection but perhaps eased the difficulty. A fine sustained route.

COIRE SPUTAN DEARG:
Aurora – H. Severe 4b,4b. J. Lyall, R. Revill. 13th July, 1993.
Follow the winter line on Pitch 1, then follow cracks straight up to a grass depression at 15m. Continue straight up on blocky rock, then easier slabs to the top.

Cherub's Buttress:
Dark Horse – HVS. R.J. Archbold, R. Ross, G. Strange. 29th August, 1993.
Climbs the steep left edge of Cherub's Buttress. Start at some pale rock just left of short crack with chokestone. Climb the wall on knobbly holds until possible to make a difficult horizontal traverse above obvious square-cut overhang to gain more knobbly holds out on the right. Go straight up then slightly left and follow groove to find pull out right to ledges on crest. (25m. 5a). Finish up blocky edge.

Flake Buttress:
Flake Buttress Direct – 120m V,7. S. Richardson, G. Scott (AL). 14th November, 1993.
The triangular front face of Flake Buttress is cut by a right-facing corner crack.
1. 35m. Gain the crack from the left, and follow it past an awkward bulge to an

impasse formed by a roof. Pull through the overhang on the left and continue up a crack to a ledge.

2. 35m. Climb up to a prominent left-facing groove, and climb it making a difficult exit at the top. Move up easily to belay by the flake of the original route.

3,4. 50m. Follow the original route to the top.

Terminal Buttress:

April Wall Direct – 100m V,7. C. Cartwright, S. Richardson (AL). 4th December, 1993.

A rather disjointed route, with an excellent final pitch, based on the direct version of the summer route April Wall. Start 5m left of Terminal Buttress on the left side of sharp rightward-pointing flake.

1. 40m. Climb the groove for 10m, step right, then continue up a turfy groove to the left of the buttress crest.

2. 25m. Move easily up, then left to the foot of the steep depression of April Wall which cuts the right side of the upper wall.

3. 35m. Enter the depression via a mixture of ice and turf and follow the obvious line up a chimney through a bulge, and exit left on to a ledge. Make an exposed step left on to left wall and climb this (crux) to easier ground. Either continue up Terminal Buttress or descend the gully on the left after 40m of scrambling.

Note: Joker's Buttress (SMCJ, 1993) is HVS 5c, not 4c.

HELL'S LUM CRAG:

The Underworld – V,4. I. Dillon, J. Lyall. 28th March, 1994.

Following the summer line. The open corner was straight-forward, followed by a 50m pitch up the rib on good thin ice. The final corner was also sufficiently iced.

COIRE AN t-SNEACHDA, Mess of Pottage:

Trunk Line – 105m VS. J. Lyall, N. Forwood. 24th July, 1993.

A direct crack line up the middle of the crag which crosses No Blue Skies, Melting Pot and The Message.

1. 35m 5a. Start 6m left of No Blue Skies and climb a crackline up a 'green elephant's trunk'. Continue until the NBS traverse is reversed – go right. The wall above is climbed (crux) and the crack followed past the right end of a roof and a belay reached on the left.

2. 20m 4b. Follow the crack above until a diagonal line leads right across the top of a slab to belay on Melting Pot.

3. 50m 4b. Move on to the right wall and follow cracks up the pillar to a ledge below the final groove of the Message. Follow cracks up the wall right of the groove to reach the top.

The Three Decree – 45m V,5. S. Aisthorpe, M. Hind, J. Lyall. 24th January, 1994.

An alternative start to The Messenger, climbed when it was iced and The Messenger was not. Start down from and just right of the bay – 4m right of The Messenger. Climb a crack up the wall to gain and climb the thinly-iced left-facing corner to the right of The Messenger. Finish up the recessed icefall and snow as for The Messenger (55m).

The following route covers with much snow and ice in peak conditions but was described as a fine direct line in early season.

Yukon Jack – 90m IV,5. M. Sinclair, C. Schiller. 30th December, 1993.

Start down and right of The Messenger and The Three Decrees at a short wall with a wide crack directly below an obvious right-facing corner. Climb the crack, corner and its continuation (45m). Crossing the Haston line, follow this continuation until a steep snow shelf leads left. Follow this briefly, then gain and climb a chimney fault and capping bulge to easy ground close to the finish of the easy diagonal line (45m).

Note: J. Lyall notes an ascent of the thin and rarely-formed icefall which flows directly from the upper gully of Broken Gully down the left wall of its start (ie. separate from Broken Gully Left Hand). It gave 8m of near vertical, thin, but good quality ice.

COIRE AN LOCHAIN, No.3 Buttress:

The New Age Traveller – 100m VI,7. A. Nisbet, J. Preston. 31st December, 1993.

The Migrant is often started by a more direct (and easier?) line up a shallow groove leading directly to the short overhanging wall and the huge groove. If an initial cave is not banked up, then traverse left from the start of Nocando Crack/Vicar. This route starts up the steep initial groove of the original Migrant and continues in the same line immediately under the steep wall (40m). A short right traverse and a short wall leads to a ramp slanting left to a airy position under the headwall (15m). A right-slanting crack (very well protected) leads to the top of the wall (15m). Now easy to join and finish up Ewen Buttress (30m).

No. 4 Buttress:

Aqualung – 90m VI,7. G. Ettle, J. Preston. 17th October, 1993.

An excellent continuous line between Deep Throat and Gaffer's Groove. Start just right of Deep Throat underneath a rightward curving diedre.

1. 20m. Climb up into the curving diedre which is followed to a belay in the chimney of Gaffer's Groove.

2. 35m. Follow the chimney to a step left on to easy ground. Move back right into a steep groove and up to the large roof.

3. 35m. Turn the roof on the right by an awkward wide crack.

Occidental Discovery – 140m V,7. G. Ettle, B. Goodlad. 13th November, 1993.

A line up the frontal face of No. 4 Buttress which climbs through and to the left of Western Route. Start below the centre of the face.

1. 30m. Take the left trending easy line leading to a platform at the top of Western Route's first pitch.

2. 15m. Climb the steep corner for 3m, moving left to a flake, then an overhung niche. Exit the niche by a fine corner crack to blocky belays.

3. 50m. Step left and follow a rightward line of turf to large ledges. Move left into a wide chimney fault and continuing easier ground to below steep grooves in the final tower.

4. 30m. Climb the rightmost and longest groove to belay at the top of Savage Slit.

5. 15m. Easy gully to top.

Note: M. Bryan and K. Wilson note a 30m route on the far left of No.1 Buttress, starting in a gully and moving right (November, 1993). Probably banks out readily and probably climbed before.

NORTH EAST OUTCROPS

CUMMINGSTON:
J.R. Mackenzie notes that the original line of The Prophet started directly up the front of the buttress and worthy of E2 while the easier corner version was climbed later.

COVESEA:
Per Guano ad Astra – 10m HVS 5a. J. Preston, P. Amphlett. 28th September, 1993.
Start 2m right of The Sandman. Traverse right below a loose white block. Climb the crack on the right and the continuation corner above.

CLACHNABEN:
Shrew Rib – 30m III,5. S. Stronach, H. Taylor. 27th December, 1993.
The summer line was followed for 12m before taking a groove to the right of the crest to the base of a vertical wall. A possible hand traverse looked as though it might lead back left to the rib but this was ignored in favour of a traverse right round the wall and up a crack to a large ledge at the top of the slabs area. The 3m wall leading from this ledge to the top was the crux. The grassy descent gully mentioned in the guide was also climbed, finishing up right at Grade II, although a bit artificial.

LEY QUARRY:
Smego – 10m E1 5a. G. Szuca, A. Ramsey, C. Lampton. 25th April, 1993.
The wall left of the route with three bolts at the quarry entrance. Clip the first bolt, and climb the wall just left to finish in a chossy corner.

HIGHLAND OUTCROPS

BINNEAN SHUAS:
Comraich – 60m E2. A. Tibbs, A. Matthewson. 14th August, 1993.
Start 5m left of Blaeberry Groove.
1. 30m 5b. Climb up by a pale streak to a hollow at 10m. Step left and finish up cracks above to terrace.
2. 30m. Finish up easier rocks.

Tairnearn Tar As – 55m E2 5b. I. Taylor, R. Campbell. 6th June, 1993.
Between the right end of The Garden and Hidden Gully is a long roof. The route climbs the wall above the roof. Go up the left rib of Hidden Gully and either traverse past some saplings to gain the right end of the roof or continue up the rib and abseil 10m from a prominent tree to reach the same point.
1. 40m 5b. Above the roof make a spectacular, but easy, hand traverse left along a flake 2m short of a grass ledge. Climb the wall above using a short flake crack and continue up the wall, then slabs to belay on a ledge.
2. 15m . Scramble to the terrace.

ABERFELDY CRAG (NN 867512):
A schist crag, fairly steep, in the trees, and with good friction. Approx. 15 minutes approach.
Tartan – 30m VS 4c. D. Donoghue, C. Moody, L. Roberts. 29th August, 1987.
The left-hand corner. Move left just before the top, past a bush to a tree.

Shortbread – 30m VS 4c. W. Hood, C. Moody, I. Taylor. 6th September, 1987.
The wide crack left of Tae The Oaks. Move left near the top to a bush, then up to
a tree.

Tae The Oaks – 25m VS 4c. D. Donoghue, C. Moody, L. Roberts. 29th August,
1987.
Scramble to a tree. Climb the corner on the left which contains a tree. Move left at
the top to finish up an arete.

Domino – 30m Severe. W. Hood, C. Moody, I. Taylor. 6th September, 1987.
Scramble to the tree of Tae The Oaks. Go up the corner to the right and finish up
an arete.

CREAG DUBH:
Information of a winter ascent of Romp has been received. It was climbed by J.
Grosset, probably with C. Barley, in the mid-1980s. In good conditions it gives a
short ice climb of about 35m followed by an abseil from a tree.

BEN NEVIS, CREAG MEAGHAIDH

Note: Routes from 1993 have not been reported as they appear in the new guide.

East Face of Tower Ridge, Echo Wall:
The Edge of Beyond – 200m V,5. D.F. Lang, C. Stead. 26th March, 1994.
The route lies up the projecting edge of Echo Wall just before it bends in towards
the corner of Brass Monkey. It then continues up the east face of the Little Tower.
Start from Observatory Gully 15m up left from the edge.
1. 40m. Gain a ledge system with a Damoclean flake at 10m, traverse right, climb
the flake and traverse right until it is possible to go up to a ledge on the left.
2. 45m. Traverse 6m right, climb an ice corner and grooves to a ledge on the left.
Traverse right to an icefall which leads to easy ground.
3. 25m. Continue to the traverse ledge of East Wall Route below the east face of
the Little Tower.
4,5. 90m. Climb this to the top.

North Trident Buttress:
Left Hand Ridge – 150m IV,4. D.F. Lang, C. Stead. 12th February, 1994.
This buttress is described as being two ridges separated by a gully – Neptune Gully.
The Original Route ascends the right-hand ridge and the direct start climbs an ice
corner left of Neptune Gully and then appears to join the Original Route. This is a
winter ascent of the left-hand ridge. Climb the direct start icefall corner and
continue by the ridge crest, taking the rock tower by a central groove. Finish by a
horizontal arete level with the top of Original Route.

Nereid Gully – 90m III. D.F. Lang, C. Stead. 13th February, 1994.
This is the wide open gully between the Central Trident and left-hand ridge of the
North Trident Buttresses which finishes at the top of the latter. It is most easily

reached by a traverse below the buttress containing Metamorphosis. Climb the gully in three pitches, with an icefall on the second. The best sport is by keeping left. All difficulties could be avoided on the right, reducing it to Grade II.

Moonlight Gully Buttress:
Fifties Revival – 100m IV,5. D.F. Lang, C. Stead. 30th January, 1994.
The route follows a prominent groove line on the left flank of the lower tier of the buttress. Start 10m right of the lowest left hand rocks at an ice groove.
1. 25m. Climb the groove to the sloping ledges which Diagonal Route traverses right.
2. 40m. Climb the wall 2m right of a bulging crack, gain an ice smear and rejoin the groove line to belay below a chimney.
3. 10m. Climb the chimney to a pedestal.
4. 25m. Continue the line by a crack to easy ground and the buttress top.

Number Five Gully Buttress:
Slanting Slit – 140m VI,6. M. Duff, S. Greenhaugh. 26th February, 1994.
Roughly based on The Slant. The summer first pitch was banked out.
1. Gain the diagonal ramp (second pitch) and follow this to the cracked slab.
2. Climb the cracked slab (thinly iced apart from the top 2m) up corners above right to a roof with a wierd slit and bollard belay.
3. 4m. Descend to a ledge (backroped, peg and nut left).
4. 30m. Go along a snow ledge and around a corner to the foot of another corner with a large detached block.
5. 50m. Go up this and slightly left to an iceflow.

Castle Buttress:
The Keep – IV,5. M. Duff, I. Oates. 13th February, 1994.
Approximates to the summer line.

Castle Ridge, North Face:
Le Chat Noir – 225m IV,4. M. Duff, D. Horrox, J. Robson, H. Ousby. 17th February, 1994.
The buttress between Casino Royale and La Petite.
1,2. 80m. Easily up the buttress until it steepens.
3. 45m. In the centre of the upper buttress is a square turfy recess. Go up this and over a small overlap to reach the snow patch.
4. 50m. A very steep iceflow above, climbed by a runnel on the right side.
5. 50m. Easy ground to the top.

Cherry Pickers – 380m IV,4. M. Duff, D. Horrox, D. Potter. 21st February, 1994.
The icefall 40m left of American Pie, identified by a slanting right to left shelf at half height.
1,2. 75m. Climb the right side of the icefall to a corner belay. Gain the shelf and climb a steep icicle at its left end.
3,4. 90m. Go up the snowfield to belay under a small roof.
5. 45m. Go right then left to the foot of an icefall – which cannot be seen from the belay.
6. 40m. Climb the icefall.
7,8. 80m. Go diagonally left over mixed ground heading for a small tower on the slight ridge to the left.
9. 50m. The crack and shallow chimney behind the tower.

CREAG MEAGHAIDH, Pinnacle Buttress:
White Knuckle Ride – 60m VI,6. A. Perkins, N. Wood. 19th February, 1994.
Starts approximately halfway between Nordwander and Pinnacle Buttress Direct, with the main feature being a chimney choked by a 10m ice pillar at 30m, with a left-facing groove 5m to its left.
1. 50m. Climb diagonally and boldly rightwards, crossing several slabs and grooves until below the pillar. Climb up into a niche directly below the pillar, sneak up its left side, then swing on to the front, straight up before exiting right at its top.
2. 10m. Going diagonally left leads to the end of the traverse on Pitch 2 of Nordwander.

The Pedestal Variation – 75m IV,4. G.E. Little, C. Bonington. 26th February, 1994.
This exciting two-pitch variation is accessed via Staghorn Gully Direct Start (South Pipe Direct).
1. 40m. From the snow basin beneath the start of North Pipe, traverse right along an obvious snow ledge to below a short groove. Climb the groove on to a left-trending ramp. Follow this to a belay on a big spike overlooking North Pipe.
2. 35m. Traverse left in an exposed situation until an awkward move allows upward progress. Trend left, heading for what appears to be a rock keyhole. Enter this and squirm up to stand on a small rock pedestal. Climb straight up on steep terrain to the top of the gully wall. Walk left to belay at the base of a clean tower like rock wall. Two long pitches on snow, to the left of the tower, lead to the top.

CARN LIATH, Coire nan Gall:
An attractive slab of pocketed schist guards the entrance to the coire on the left (NN 487906). It faces south-east and receives the sun for much of the day. The best approach is from the sharp bend on the A86 at 513887 where the road crosses a stream. Follow the stream's west bank to a deer fence, cross this and strike directly up to the crag (3k). A deer fence runs up to the foot of the cliff.

Room to Roam – 100m E1. A. Matthewson, A. Tibbs. 16th August, 1993.
Takes a wandering line up the middle of the cleanest piece of rock. Start just right of the fence which runs up to the toe of the crag – bolt belay!
1. 20m 4c. Climb up and left to a corner and continue up its right arete to a ledge.
2. 35m 5a. Traverse hard left to a short corner which is climbed (crux) to a small heather patch. Continue diagonally left on a quartz band, then back up right and straight up (bold) to a small ledge on the edge. A committing pitch.
3. 45m 4a. Continue up the ridge to the top. Descend to the left.

Approximately 300m beyond the Room To Roam slab is a large gully/recess containing a waterfall high up on the left. The following route climbs the buttress left of the waterfall.
Waterfall Buttress – 120m II. A. Hume, A. Matthewson. 4th December, 1993.
A traverse left gains an obvious line of icy grooves leading to easy ground overlooking the gully on the right.

CREAG DUBH, LOCH ERICHT:
Swordfish – 100m V,5. G. Ettle, J. Lyall. 21st February, 1994.
This is the independent and much steeper icefall which is formed by the right hand section of the Neapolitan waterfall.

Re

1. 35m. Climb the vertical icefall about 15m right of Neapolitan to gain a rock amphitheatre on the right.
2. 35m. Continue up the icefall to gain a broad snow shelf.
3. 30m. The right hand icefall on the upper tier.

Fara Couloir – 100m I.
Left of The Hex Factor is this left to right slanting snow gully.

Far Away – 110m III/IV. J. Lyall, N. Nolan. 23rd February, 1994.
Starts in a bay left of Fara Couloir and climbs the iciest line out of this to gain and climb an easy snow gully. Move a short way right to climb the thin icefall just left of the imposing icicle hung wall.

Olympic Hare – 110m VI,6. G. Ettle, K. Grindrod, J. Lyall. 2nd March, 1994.
Left of Far Away is a short deep gully which is blocked by a large chokestone.
1. 40m. Go up this gully, passing the chokestone on the left side, then an easy gully to a bush belay.
2. 30m. Climb the icefall to a snow terrace.
3. 40m. A large ice pillar forms on the next tier, coming down from the right side of a rock rib above. This was climbed and steep snow to finish.

Knickerbocker Glory – 70m III. J. Lyall, N. Nolan. 23rd February, 1994.
Left of Wafer Me and Ice Cream is a gully leading into an amphitheatre. This lies directly above a small triangular peninsula on the shore of Loch Ericht. Go up the easy gully and climb an icefall on the right side of the amphitheatre.

GLEN COE

BUACHAILLE ETIVE MOR, South Gully, North Wall:
The following two routes were climbed on a small crag of very rough rhyolite about halfway up South Gully, on its north flank. To gain it, several fun crags lying between South Gully and The Chasm were climbed en route, providing several pitches of Diff. to V. Diff., probably climbed before. Above the highest of three crags is a small wall with a deep cave. Scramble left to the edge of South Gully and descend to the foot of the North Wall. The first route begins below the obvious crack/fault.

Starting Bright – 50m Severe. K.V. Crocket. B. Dullea. April, 1993.
Climb the obvious crack and fault line to a ledge and belay.

Hailstone Wall – 50m Severe. B. Dullea, K.V. Crocket. April, 1993.
Climb the wall on the left of the fault line, just right of the edge and passing a loose block to finish up a steepening wall.

Eagle Buttress:
Forever Red – 50m VS. A. Connolly, C. Higgins. 13th June, 1993.
The route ascends the prominent pink/red wall above and right of Eagle Buttress, maintaining a central line throughout. Start at a short fat crack just right of a narrow sloping gangway. Climb the crack and wall above trending slightly left to gain a line of discontinuous faint cracks which lead to a shallow mossy recess. Exit the recess direct to finish.

Central Buttress, North Face:
Central Chimney – 75m IV. A. Paul, D. Sanderson. February, 1992.
Technical climbing following the summer route throughout.

Rannoch Wall:
Fear of a Flat Planet – 90m VII,8. A. Clarke, M. Garthwaite. 27th December, 1993.
A three-star route, sustained and superbly steep.
1. 25m. Start 6m to the right of Red Slab at a very thin steep crack. Desperate hooking for 6m leads to a shake-out. Continue with sustained difficulty up the wider crack to a belay at the base of a shallow chimney.
2. 35m. Up the chimney to enter the right side of the bay of Route 1. Trend up and right following a shallow groove to a short steep wall. Up this to a stance and belay.
3. 30m. Make a desperate thin traverse to the left with not much gear to gain another groove which leads leftwards to the top.

North Buttress:
G. Szuca notes that he climbed the wall between Brevity Crack and Shackle Route (Shabity, MVS 4b).

Gibberish – 30m E2 5c. D. Greig, G. Latter. 16th August, 1993.
The hanging groove just right of The Gibbet, with the difficulties concentrated into the initial wall.

Shackle Route – VI,6. A. Clarke, M. Garthwaite. 20th December, 1993.
The summer route was followed in five pitches without the deviation from the crack on the first pitch.

Hangman's Crack – VI,7. A. Clarke, M. Garthwaite. 20th December, 1993.
An abseil approach from the previous route to an ascent by the summer line.

Bottleneck Chimney – VI,7. N. Main, S. Raw.

Cuneiform Buttress:
Central Chimney Direct – 30m VS 5a. J. Inglis, N. Suess. 10th May, 1993.
Central Chimney is a direct finish to Ordinary Route. This pitch is a direct middle tier which can be logically linked with Central Chimney – described as 'unjustly slighted'. Go to the left end of the first grassy ledge of Ordinary Route and climb the obvious steep corner crack past a ledge at 10m to a chockstone at 25m. This is passed on the right, whereupon the pitch relents, and rejoin the Ordinary Route at the second terrace.
Note: D. Sanderson notes ascents of Shackle Route in December, 1977 and January Jigsaw with T. Macaulay in February, 1985. Grade IV quoted for each but amount of snow not specified.

BIDEAN NAM BIAN, Stob Coire nan Lochan:
Leaning Jowler – 70m III,4. M. Duff, J. Knowles. 26th February, 1993.
The fins and towers on the left side of Pinnacle Buttress right of Pinnacle Groove form the left side of a corner system.
1. 35m. Climb to the foot of the corner, enter this by an odd mantle and up flakes to a snow terrace.
2. 20m. Climb the sharp corner above, traverse to the right and up to a snow terrace.
3. 15m. Move 5m right to an elegant steep V-groove.

Church Door Buttress:
Un Poco Loco – 120m VII,7. A. Cave, M. Duff. March, 1994.
1. 20m. First pitch of The Crypt.
2. 35m. Step left, then directly below The Arch by steep cracks to the left end of the span, swing into the groove on the left and up to the ledge. Belay in the centre of the span. Extremely steep.
3. 25m. Climb directly above the span to a groove with a flake crack, and trend gradually left.
4. 40m. More easily to the top.

Stob Coire nam Beith:
Scarab – 70m IV,5. J. Blyth, S. Lampard. 14th November, 1992.
Start just left and down of North West Gully to the right of Isis. Move up and left to the left side of a large flake. Go up to belay on a small ledge down and right of an inverted flake (35m). Climb direct up the rib above (crux), moving left at an overhang to finish (35m).

ALLT DOIRE-BEITH:
Fear is the Key – 16m E2 5b. G. Latter, T. Redfern, C. Grant. 1st July, 1993.
On the isolated dome-shaped buttress at the top of the gorge, on the opposite side from the other recorded routes. Starting a few metres left of the initial flake crack of Afraid to Walk, climb the centre of the wall to better holds and protection, moving slightly rightwards to finish at the same point as Afraid to Walk.
Note: Afraid to Walk, E1 5a (1989); recorded in SMCJ 1990, but omitted from the 1992 guide for an unknown reason.

AONACH DUBH, Lower Walls:
Thing of Beauty – 40m E4 5c. G. Latter, D. Greig. 17th August, 1993 (on sight).
A direct line up the left edge of the face, just right of the wet crack. Start up Lady Jane, and climb direct up the diagonal crack past a series of horizontal breaks to a bold run-out section. From the ledge, step left and up a blocky dyke to belay in short twin corners.

TRILLEACHAN SLABS:
Tufty Club – 55m E3. S. Kennedy, C. Grindley. 26th September, 1993.
A bold eliminate between the main corner of Hammer and the upper part of the original Pinch route. Follows in the main the cleaned crackline which runs up the slab a short distance right of the main corner. Start from the belay on Hammer just below the scoop.
1. 45m 5c. Follow Pinch up right to the obvious quartz pocket via the Pinch move. Climb the thin crack above the pocket for a short distance before traversing out left below a small undercut bulge. Step over the left side of the bulge and make thin moves up and left to reach a thin crack containing three small tufts. Climb the thin crack for a couple of moves, then move diagonally up leftwards to reach the obvious cleaned crackline (approx. 5m right of Hammer corner). Climb the crackline directly to reach the rightmost end of the delicate traverse on Hammer. Belay on Hammer just above the traverse.

GARBH BHEINN, North East Face:
South East Chimney – 325m IV,5. A. Matthewson, M. Shaw. 15th January, 1994.
Start as for Great Ridge up the lower buttress left of Great Gully to the lower rake (or traverse in along the rake) and continue up left via a shallow gully system to the foot of the chimney proper (200m). Climb the chimney (very narrow in one section) to belay below the arch (35m). Continue up and out to a surprising exit (10m). A further two pitches up Great Ridge lead to the summit (80m).

SOUTHERN HIGHLANDS:

BEINN A' CHREACHAN, Coire an Lochain:
A Bit on the Side – 85m II. G.E. Little. 15th January, 1994.
Start well up the wide gully between the central and right-hand buttresses where a steep rock spur juts from the flank of the latter – on the right side of the gully looking up, well above the rock island. Climb a runnel running on the right side of this rock spur with a steepening before access to a wide snow ramp is gained. Up the ramp and short snowfield above to gain the ridge.

BEINN DORAIN, Creag an Socach:
Days of Future Past – 120m IV,5. G.E. Little, J. Lowther. 13th February, 1994.
This route climbs the slabby area of rock where the vertical left-flanking wall of the crag gives way to the main face. It shares a common start with The Glass Bead Game and finishes at the same place as Kick Start, but otherwise stays well left of these routes for its entire length.
1. 35m. Climb a short slabby groove, then move left up an obvious fault line for about 10m to a little recess with an ancient peg (1950s vintage?). Traverse horizontally left to the base of a wide shallow scoop. Up this to a horizontal snow ledge. Traverse back right to belay about 4m left of an obvious groove.
2. 25m. A tricky move right gives access into the groove, then climb straight up to a narrow exit under a big hanging icicle. Move up right on a snow ledge to belay.
3. 45m. Traverse horizontally left, with one awkward step, to a snow bay. Move back right up a snow ramp to belay at a small rock recess.
4. 15m. Move right, then straight up to finish.
G.E. Little, after consultation, has compiled the following list of grades for Creag an Socach.

False Rumour Gully – IV,4. Days of Future Past – IV,5. The Glass Bead Game – V,5. Kick Start – IV,4. The Prophet – VI,7. The Sting – V,6. The Promised Land – VI,7 Antichrist – VI,7. Second Coming – III,4. Messiah – VII,7. School Daze – II,3

BEINN AN DOTHAIDH, Creag Coire an Dothaidh:
Beelzebub – 170m V,6. R. Everett, S. Richardson (AL). 16th January, 1994.
A direct line up the crest of the buttress in the centre of the crag between Lucifer Rising and BO Buttress. Start at the lowest rocks, 5m left of the first pitch of Lucifer Rising, and directly below a prominent smooth red wall 50m above.
1. 50m. Pull over a small roof and continue directly up the centre of the buttress following a series of turfy grooves. The left traverse and downward step of Lucifer Rising are crossed after 25m. Belay at the foot of the prominent red wall.
2. 50m. The easiest route through the steep slabs above the stance will depend on the amount of ice present. On this ascent, a broad snow ledge was followed left for 10m to below a 10m-high corner which lies 5m right of the short chimney of Lucifer Rising. From the foot of the corner (poor peg runners), a right-slanting ramp was taken to easier ground above the belay. Continue up, then left to a short right-facing corner. Climb this and belay on the snowfield above.
3. 40m. Move left and climb snow and ice to belay below a prominent roof.
4. 30m. Climb the ice step on the left, then follow icy grooves leading up and right to the top.

THE COBBLER, South Peak:
Sesame Street – 90m IV,6. J. Turner, A. Ogilvie. 3rd March, 1993.
Climbs the obvious line of weakness 30m down and left of Sesame Groove, starting

on a ledge at a large flake. Climb a wide crack until a short difficult traverse (crux) gives access to a left-trending line on frozen turf, joining Grassy Traverse for its final groove.

North Peak:
Wild at Heart – 60m E7. G. Latter (unseconded). 3rd and 27th September, 1993.
An outrageously exposed top pitch up the edge of all things. The main pitch attacks the stunning flying arete up the left edge of the scooped wall above the scooped wall on Punster's.
1. 25m 5c. Start up Direct Direct to the roof at 12m. Arrange protection, step down for 3m, then ascend diagonally rightwards across the wall to better holds. Up to the roof and follow this right to belay on the Punster's flake (originally aided as original start to The Nook?).
2. 35m 6b. Go up the wall directly above to a crack, then traverse left to quartz on the edge and up to a ledge. Make committing moves leftwards of the ledge, with a long reach to the first peg runner. Continue with difficult reachy moves slightly leftwards past a number of peg runners to good finishing holds near the arete. This pitch redpointed.

Punster's Crack – VI,8. A. Clarke, M. Garthwaite. 24th December, 1993.
The summer route was followed in three pitches, the crux being the top slab.

BEINN NARNAIN, Cruach nam Miseag (NN 278064):
The crag is on the north-east facing side of the south-east spur of Beinn Narnain.

Central Gully – 200m II. T. Archer, E. Ewing. March, 1993.
The obvious central gully up the broken cliffs of Cruach nam Miseag. Numerous short steps.

CREAG THARSUINN:
Anonymous Gully – 100m IV,6. I. Taylor, A. Robertson. 2nd January, 1994.
This is the 'unclimbed' gully on the left side of Sugach Buttress.
1. 30m. Easy snow leads to a blockage.
2. 30m. Gain a ledge on the left and make an awkward traverse to gain the gully edge. Go up a short groove on the gully edge until an exposed move rightwards gains the upper gully.
3. 40m. Easy snow.

BEINN AN LOCHAIN:
Megalith – 110m IV,4. A. Fraser, R. McAllister, D. McGimpsey, S. Mearns. 19th January, 1993.
An excellent companion route to Monolith Grooves, comparable in quality and scenery. Start at the first groove immediately right of the lower Monolith.
1. 45m. Climb a steep icefall on the right of the groove (or, in thinner conditions, the groove), continue directly to gain and follow a narrow left-trending chimney. Directly above this, climb a short desperate corner to a ledge and belay. Both the initial icefall and the desperate corner can be avoided on the right and left respectively, reducing the route to Grade III.
2. 15m. Traverse easily left to the left edge of the Table.
3. 50m. Beneath the upper Monolith is a right-trending flake system (conspicuous in *Cold Climbs*). Gain the left end of this by mixed climbing, then follow it easily rightwards to gain snow slopes which lead via an ice bulge to the top.

Note: Monolith Grooves. The guide over-estimates the length. At most it is 125m. The most obvious and direct start is the icy gully next to the left edge of the Monolith. This avoids the devious original start which takes shelves to the left. No trace of the rockfall was encountered in December, 1993, and the route was found to be a very scenic and worthwhile Grade IV,4.

Obelisk – 105m V,5. D. Macgimpsey, T. Prentice, A. Fraser. 10th February, 1994. An interesting route giving good climbing up the buttress between Monolith Grooves and Promenade Gully. Climb the first pitch of Monolith Grooves to ledges (20m). About 10m left of Monolith Grooves gully is a narrow steep chimney with an overhanging chokestone. Climb this with difficulty, then traverse right under steep rock for 6m. Follow grooves above to belay under Monolith Grooves upper chimney (50m). Follow MG chimney for 8m, then traverse left across shelves to gain an ice bulge and snow slopes (35m).

BEN LOMOND, North East Face:
Lomond Delight – 85m II. B. Swan, D. Ford, S. Donald. 23rd January, 1994.
Start 100m right of an obvious steep corner. Go up a shallow groove for 8m, then turn right up a ramp to a small cave and belay (45m). Exit on the left up over a bulge, then follow steep snow and exit on to the ridge (40m).
GLEN CROE:
Note: Pockets of Excellence has had its pegs stolen and has not been climbed without.

BEN CRUACHAN, Drochaid Glas:
The following routes lie on the East Face of the North Ridge between the two earlier routes, Into the Fire and Stonethrowers Buttress (SMCJ 1990, p514). All three routes start close to the foot of the obvious chimney groove in the centre of the East Face – Jamie's Lum.

Drumnadrochaid – 85m IV. D. Ritchie, D. Sinclair. 15th January, 1994.
Climbs the buttress just left of Jamie's Lum. Climb the righthand of the two parallel grooves trending left. Move back right and up the buttress crest, then trend leftwards to belay below an open corner (45m). Climb the corner, exiting left past a spike to easier ground and the top (40m).

Jamie's Lum – 85m IV,5. I. Blackwood, S. Kennedy, D. Ritchie. 13th February, 1994.
A fine route, following the central chimney groove referred to above. Climb a short ice pitch into a snow bay below the short chimney. Belay on the right of the chimney (25m). Continue up the chimney, well iced on the left wall, and continuation groove above (50m). Finish up easy ground above (10m).

Gaoth Mhor – 110m IV. N. Marshall, D. Ritchie. 23rd January, 1994.
Climbs the buttress between Jamie's Lum and Into the Fire. Start just right of Jamie's Lum and follow the vague crest by a steep turfy chimney to belay below a wall. Move 2m to the right and climb a short square-cut chimney and groove to a block belay (40m). Move straight up to below a steep wall, then traverse 15m right across ledges to belay close to Into the Fire (35m). Climb the fault line above leading up and left past a large block (clearly seen on the skyline from the belay) to finish on the ridge crest (35m).

ARRAN

BEINN TARSUINN, Full Meed Tower:
Along the Watchtower – 85m HVS. A. Fraser, R. McAllister. 29th May, 1993.
An interesting route of some character which climbs steep chimneys on the right or Coire a' Bhradhain side of the tower. Start 10m right of Voodoo Child at a deep chimney.
1. 25m 5a. Scramble unpleasantly to the back of the chimney, then back and knee up the chimney over a chokestone (crux). Continue up flakes to belay on a small grass ledge.
2. 15m 5a. Continue up the chimney, then easy grass to a spike belay.
3. 35m 5a. Traverse shelves leftwards to gain and climb the fine upper chimney.
4. 10m. Scramble to the top of the tower.
Note: R. McAllister and M. Reid freed Voodoo Child on 29th May, 1993. E1 5b and highly recommended.

GLEN SANNOX, Cioch na h'Oighe:
Klepht – C. Macadam and A. Fraser claim the FFA on 10th August, 1981.

Coire na h-Uamha, Lower Slabs:
G. Szuca and C. Lampton describe a route near Slapstick Wall, climbed in May, 1993. Start 10m left of Slapstick Wall and climb two pitches direct to the second belay of SW (35m, 35m; these pitches looked previously cleaned). Now take the variation but pull over the bulge above the belay, move right to the arete above the variation and follow it to the top. A very fine pitch; 30m, VS 4c.

LOWLAND OUTCROPS

Dalmahoy Hill:
The Lemming – 18m HVS 4c. J.D. Inglis, D. Buchanan, J.C. Eilbeck. 20th May, 1992.
The rib and shallow groove 2m to the left of Cleaned Sweep. Sustained, steepening to a bulge at the top where a long step right joins the exit of Cleaned Sweep. Little protection.
Note: Transcription (SMCJ 1992) is the same as an older route, Frustration.

Rosyth Quarry:
The Rust Bucket – 7m E2 6a. I. Taylor. June, 1992.
Right of Matinee Cracks is a tree. The route climbs the cleaned wall behind the tree without using the right-hand wall.

Auchinstarry Quarry:
The Seven Year Plan – 10m E2 5c. I. Taylor, S. Munro. 29th May, 1992.
Left of Block Pillar is a hanging ramp. Gain the ramp (old peg), then climb it finishing directly over an overhang.
Note: Dream Machine has lost a good hold at the crack base, making it harder, 6b.

Cowden Hill Quarry:
Earth Summit – 30m E4 6a. M. Garthwaite, A. Wren. 18th August, 1992.
The route follows the obvious flake up the black wall at the back of the quarry, passing two pegs. Move right below a small roof to the top of a small pinnacle. Finish direct up the wall above passing another peg.

GALLOWAY

A. Fraser and Kyle MC members have climbed about 80 routes. As the new Lowland Outcrops guide is scheduled for this year, they have not been duplicated here.

MISCELLANEOUS NOTES

BLACK THOUGHTS

Scott Johnstone recollects. The articles in the 1993 Journal about the Black Shoot of Beinn Eunich (Stob Maol) bring back some remote memories.

Hamish Brown is in error when on p.195 he suggests that Robin Campbell's ascent in about 1971 was 'probably the only ascent since early days'. I led a GUM Club party up it on August 30, 1942 – Bill Garden and Billy Fraser. While this probably constitutes 'early days', I don't think that is what Hamish meant.

This took me back to Robin's article of Vol. XXX, when on p.22 he mentions a 'malodorous hemp sling'. This was present, and already malodorous and rotten in 1942. As I doubt whether it was an original Lester or Raeburn relic from 40-odd years earlier, it indicates some other party before mine.

Still, 30 years between 1942 and 1971 shows that elderly slings may be much older than they appear. How would nylon fare?

SWINGING THE LEAD

The less aesthetically insensitive members will have noticed that the Journal has recently changed printers or, rather, that the Editor has done so. This is only the second change in our long history and, with his approval, I write a line or two about it.

When I took over as Editor in 1960 the Journal was still being printed by the Darien Press in Edinburgh. As recorded in the centenary number (SMCJ, xxxiv, 374, 1990) I changed to a clearer and less nostalgic typeface, and found the 'smoky and spirituous recesses of the Darien Press' surprisingly amenable to, and capable of, the transformation. There was still talent in Bristo Place and, as I suggested, they doubtless after 50-odd years liked to stretch a (little) bit. But they were soon absorbed within the miasmic cloud of Progress, taken over, engulfed by the larger and even less competent organisation, which in the process managed to lose our irreplaceable original copper plates.

So we had to switch for the 1967 issue. Editorial convenience and personal knowledge plumped for Culross of Coupar Angus, then under the imaginative guidance of R.J. Benzies, a weel-kent figure on these hills (even if insulated from them by club-foot boots and laminated plastic), sympathetic to our viewpoint; importantly, he was close at hand and could be visited and harangued almost daily on a commuter trip. So that, although we lost the beautiful typeface of the Darien Press we gained a reasonably clear print and most excellent co-operation (that at the Darien was agreeable but of a leisurely, glass-clinking, nature). Also, Culross could prepare photographic blocks and our previous – English – source of these appeared also to be succumbing to neoplastic Finance.

I would like to express more clearly now, what appeared as part of a niggardly footnote in 1990: my own – and the Club's – appreciation of the splendid personal help of Bob Benzies, whose keen eye and lively mind served this Journal so well when myself, Campbell and Brooker were editors, and of the ready assistance of his sons when he at length retired. Not only did he put up with continual editorial descents upon his office (despite keeping his car park defensively full), but he made a point – when commuting to the slopes – of returning these visits by popping, into the grimy editorial post-box out in the Bush, galley proofs, page proofs and first copies. Monumental displays of mutual patience (followed by exemplary remedial action) always sorted out the inevitable production crises. It was a great co-operation all those years with Culross, and I am happy to engrave it here upon the timeless annals of the Club.

G.J.F. Dutton.

MAKING OF A SERIES

If you were on Tower Ridge in mid-February and saw three figures in 1930s clothing and equipment making their way across Tower Gap it was not an hallucination brought on by the previous night's over indulgence in the bars of Fort William. As part of our series on history of Scottish climbing we are honouring the achievment of W.H. Murray. Such a celebration is not a moment too soon. A few days earlier we had recorded a moving interview with Bill where he spoke about writing *Mountaineering in Scotland* in POW camps; about the exploratory nature of Scottish climbing in the 1930s and about his friends from that period. Now we were recreating his ascent of Tower Ridge and our three climber/actors, Graham Moss, Alasdair Cain and Mark Diggins were discovering that the exposure of the Eastern Traverse is made more realistic by using the equipment of Murray's time.

In the same hectic three weeks of filming we had witnessed some impressive modern mixed climbing with Graeme Ettle and Rab Anderson on White Magic in the Northern Corries and Dave Cuthbertson showed us the merits of ice climbing by popping up Mega RouteX on Ben Nevis. Ken Crocket joined Andy Nisbet on Smith's Route, confirming that Robin Smith and Jimmy Marshall's achievment is not diminished by the absence of step cutting.

Farther north we sampled a winter classic gully with Paul Nunn and Clive Rowland on Beinn Dearg and were thankful for their patience in difficult conditions as modern technology tried to keep up with human endeavour.

Mick Fowler undertook a typical raid to put up a new route on Sgurr a' Ghaorachain, but by then we were all getting blase about filming in the best winter conditions of recent years and Duncan McCallum had proved that he can take more steady footage hanging on a rope than some cameramen can take on the ground.

Most importantly, many new friendships were formed and old ones rekindled. Cubby pronounced White Magic 'a West Coast Grade II or possibly III'; Rab proved it was possible at 5.30a.m. to eat copious Rice Krispies and simultaneously argue the merits of the new regrading system, and Mr Nisbet wondered how the Aberdonian contribution could be fitted into just three hours of television. But the storm clouds truly arrived when we produced a magazine that placed Duncan as only the 41st best climber in the country – or was it 43rd?

At the time of writing we are embarking on the first of our spring shoots and hoping to find good rock in the North West and on Skye. The programmes will be shown throughout Britain on BBC2 in early autumn and we hope to show the important contribution that Scotland has made to world mountaineering. Even with the luxury of six films hard decisions have had to be made and I am sure we have not been able to please everyone. What I can promise is some excellent climbing footage and a celebration of many outstanding names, but if your favourite climber *is* omitted do not write to the BBC to complain – demand a second series!

Richard Else.

THE SCOTTISH MOUNTAINEERING TRUST– A New Approach

Members will know that the Trust was formed in the early 1960s as the Club wished to become more seriously involved in guidebook production and required the tax-free status conferred by a charitable trust in order to sustain a viable publications programme. This situation continued reasonably happily until the mid-1980s with modest profits being shown for the Trust's efforts and consequently only small support being offered to the various requests for assistance.

The position, however, changed dramatically with the publication of *The Munros* which saw, for the first time, a situation where the Trust was faced with the disposal of a considerable income. The book is now on a seventh reprint and the money has continued to accrue. New powers conferred on the Inland Revenue to investigate the affairs of charitable trusts where the prime function is to do other than administer a capital fund (in our case run a publications company) meant establishing a subsidiary company, Scottish Mountaineering Trust (Publications) Ltd., which by covenanting its profits back to the Trust, enables the Trust to maintain its tax-free status and sustain its now considerable programme.

Trustees are, of course, all Club members and bring to the Trust a strong support for the interests of the Club, but members should realise that once appointed, Trustees act on behalf of the Trust which must act equitably towards all interests of Scottish mountaineering. Trustees are charged with a legal responsibility to administer the Trust's affairs in a business-like manner and this is particularly necessary in view of the scale of the Trust's operation and the amounts of money involved. I am pleased to say that Trustees have not flinched from this task and the work of the Trust has benefited enormously from the input of past, and present, Trustees. While recognising its responsibility to the wider mountaineering scene, the Trust has nevertheless managed to support Club projects in recent years – through the loan to finance the Raeburn Hut; the substantive funding towards the refurbishment of Lagangarbh; the relocation of the Library, and its annual support of the Journal.

Trustees, in the last few years, have become acutely conscious of the substantial funds at their disposal which have not always been matched by the number of applications received. Furthermore, footpath work which was a major beneficiary, has slowed down due, principally, to a seeming reluctance by Scottish Natural Heritage to renew commitments to projects at previous levels. At a specially-convened meeting last year it was therefore decided that the Trust should adopt a more pro-active policy towards the dispersal of its assets and much consideration has been given as to how this might be achieved.

Firstly, the Trust has now decided to advertise its existence more widely and it is hoped that this will attract more applications for financial support. Secondly, the Trust is considering an annual contribution to the winter skills course run at Glenmore Lodge which will provide benefit for many young mountaineers, and hopefully, improve their safety standards. Thirdly, and more radically, the Trust has created a separate land purchase fund which will be made available, possibly at very short notice, to bodies such as the John Muir Trust and the National Trust for Scotland to assist in the purchase of suitable mountain properties. These developments represent a radical change in Trust policy. The publications pro-gramme will continue as will grants for appropriate projects which benefit Scottish mountaineering, but through these new initiatives, the Trust can now be seen to be maximising the distribution of resources instead of the modest offerings of the past.

In the year since April 1, 1993, the following grants have so far been made. A full statement of these transactions will appear when the Trust accounts are made available at the AGM in 1994.

J.R.R. Fowler.

General Grant Fund

Grants paid	Scottish Rights of Way Society	£1000
	Dundee Film Festival	£350
	Kathmandu Environmental Project	£1500
	SMC Journal	£3380
Grants committed		£11,398

Footpath Fund

Grants paid	Stac Pollaidh	£2500
	Coire Lagan	£5000
	Blaven	£1320
	Ben Lomond	£1100
	Buachaille Etive Mor	£2165
	Glas Allt Shiel	£1500
	Wester Ross Survey	£1500
	Ben Nevis Footpath	£5000
Grants committed		£9250

Snart Bequest

Grants paid	British Mountain Guides	£1500
	MRCS Conference	£500
Grants committed		£1800

Sang Award

Grants paid	Cordillera Expedition	£750
	Charakusa Expedition	£500
Grants committed		£0

Lagangarbh Project

Expenditure this year	£1432
Phase 3 commitment	£18,000

MUNRO MATTERS

By C.M. Huntley (Clerk of the List)

This year's List takes up where the 1993 Journal finished, starting with number 1145. The traditional sequence of numbers, name, followed by year of compleation of Munros, Tops and Furths as appropriate. SMC and LSCC members are identified by * and ** respectively.

1145	*Jones W H	1993	1993	1192	Unsworth David	1993	1994
1146	Dobrzynski G	1993	1981	1193	Aiken Linda	1993	
1147	Robertson Robert M	1993		1194	Aiken William	1993	
1148	Wilson Colin	1993		1195	Hepburn Mary	1993	
1149	Thatcher David	1993		1196	Holmes Alan H	1993 1993 1993	
1150	Nixon David I	1993		1197	Morl George W	1993 1993 1993	
1151	Waterson David	1993		1198	Martin John	1993	
1152	Kerry R M	1993		1199	Williamson Roy D	1993	
1153	Keegan Alan	1993		1200	Brooker Margaret L	1993	
1154	Westmorland Mike J	1993		1201	Baker David	1993 1993 1993	
1155	Norrie Rita	1993		1202	Brown Kenneth	1993	
1156	MacLeod John T	1993		1203	Gayton Jean M	1993 1993	
1157	Douglas David	1993		1204	Tait Robert J	1993 1993	
1158	Knowles C	1993		1205	Baillie Carole	1993	
1159	Russell Margaret	1993		1206	Baillie Michael	1993	
1160	Collins Peter E	1993		1207	Jaap David	1993	
1161	Cook Eric	1993	1993	1208	Sinclair William	1993 1993	
1162	Stead Sandra	1993		1209	Morris Carl	1993	
1163	Heckford Mike	1993		1210	Berryman Jack	1993	
1164	Panton Brian D	1993		1211	Sutherland Charlie	1993	
1165	Mackay Charles M	1993		1212	Haworth David	1993	
1166	Bowden Iona	1993		1213	Whitehead Andy	1992	
1167	Bowden Roy	1993		1214	Wilson Dorothy	1993	1988
1168	Crabbe Stephen	1992		1215	Twentyman Maurice E	1993	
1169	Fenton Garth B	1993		1216	Donnelly Ian	1993	
1170	Fenton Elaine S	1993		1217	Cosby Joyce	1993	
1171	Kirkwood Harry	1993		1218	Cosby Brian	1993	
1172	Barr Jeanette	1993		1219	Moffat Valerie	1993 1993 1993	
1173	Lapp Bernhard	1993		1220	Moffat Andrew	1993 1993 1993	
1174	Collie Ian	1993		1221	Wilson John F	1993	
1175	Shipway W R	1993		1222	Strang Gilmour	1992 1992	
1176	Drummond Peter	1993		1223	Lee Chris	1993	
1177	McPhail Peter	1993 1993 1993		1224	MacDuffie Iain S	1993	
1178	Tulloch Christine E	1993		1225	Burgum Jeff J	1993 1993 1993	
1179	Hill David I	1993		1226	Maxwell W P	1993	
1180	*Peck Dave	1993		1227	Powell Martin C	1993	
1181	Cadoux Theodore	1993		1228	Ogorman Heather	1993	
1182	Upson Chris J	1993		1229	Holder John	1993	
1183	Fry Mike	1993		1230	King Iain	1993	
1184	Matthews John B	1993		1231	Convery James A D	1993	
1185	Johnson John	1993		1232	Bryn Levan	1992	
1186	Lincoln Peter	1993		1233	Ager Arthur W	1993	
1187	Bowers Bill J	1993	1993	1234	Stanford Dave	1993	
1188	Froebel Karin	1993		1235	Graham Winifred	1992	
1189	Burrows J S	1993		1236	Plumb Robert L	1993	
1190	Rich Donald	1993		1237	Coakes Heather	1993	
1191	Slater David	1993		1238	Anderson R J	1993	

1239	Henshaw Roger C	1993	
1240	Atkins Michael	1993	
1241	Carrie John G	1993	
1242	Baxter James L W	1993	
1243	Griffiths Richard T	1993	
1244	Foster Duncan	1993	
1245	Carrington Norman	1993	
1246	Brogan Janey	1993	
1247	Brogan David	1993	
1248	Singleton S G	1993	
1249	Wylie Morag	1993	
1250	Hopper Gordon	1993	
1251	Sutherland Innes	1993	
1252	Martin Frank	1993	
1253	May Christine M	1993	
1254	May Timothy J	1993	
1255	Woods Una S	1993	
1256	Yates Keith	1993	

1257	Cryle David A	1993	1993
1258	Hanlin Michael	1993	
1259	Gray Ian	1993	
1260	Cowie Brian	1993	
1261	Hunter L	1993	
1262	*Boyd Tom W	1993	
1963	Donaldson Michael J	1993	
1264	McIntosh Iain B	1992	
1265	McLean Dorothy	1993	
1266	Wilson Joan	1993	
1267	Kennedy Dave B	1993	
1268	Welsh Brian	1993	
1269	Sutton Aida	1992	
1270	Sutton Alan	1992	
1271	Deall Tony M	1994	
1272	Johncocks Bill R.	1994	
1273	Ritchie G. Fraser	1993	
1274	Swindells Peter	1994	

AMENDMENTS to the List. Multiple rounds only showing the last year.

112	Roberts Peter	x3 1993	1975	624	Vaughan John	x2 1993		
315	Paton Robert	x2 1993	1983	859	Smith Ivan	1991 1991 1993		
				881	Carter Geoffrey D.	1991 1993		
334	McCreath Garry	x2 1992	1986	1045	Fallon Steven	1992 1993		
				1108	Deas George	1992	1994	
336	Ramsden Stephen	x2 1993	1989					

In addition, there are the following corrections to the List in the SMCJ 1993. Tim Pickles (1087) was incorrectly listed as Tom, and Dave Park (1041) was not credited with compleating the Tops. Sorry!

It would appear that the alarming exponential rise in compleations of 1990 to 1992 is now over, and that Munro-bagging has perhaps reached its peak. Not withstanding this, there are 127 new entries to the List, which is over 100 more than compleated a decade ago. It certainly appears that the publication of *The Munros* guidebook may have prompted many who were well into their round to see out those last few summits.

Of course, Munros is almost a word of everyday usage and the whole activity has spurred a whole range of support paraphernalia. You can climb the hills, read the books, watch the videos of the Munro Show, watch the Golden Cagoule, and now the latest is the Munro Mania board game (not bored game) which 'will bring back memories of your walks', and with the help of a 'fitness dice you'll allow even the slowest to achieve Poetry in Motion'. In addition, for the really comprehensive record of your day on the hill you can get the PC Mountain Diary to ensure you have an accurate pictorial summary of your tally so far.

Behind every name and number there is a fund of tales on and off the hills and I have tried to condense a few of the details I receive in the letters of compleations.

M. matrimonialis is as strong as ever with 10 more couples this year. The Bowdens (1166/67) talk of starting down the slippery slope/primrose path together and seem to have found searching out the hills very therapeutic from the pressures of Total Quality Management, although there is a mention of telling the fridge of their exploits, and even promising to take it on their second round. The Hill/Tullochs (1178/79) seem to have rattled round the hills in only five years which is pretty good going for an exiled Scot in Lancashire. At the other end of the scale the Aikens (1193/94), spread their ascents over 40 years, although 13 years ago they were almost compleat with only the Skye Ridge and Sgurr Fiona on An Teallach to do. The Tait/Gaytons (1203/04) recorded their compleation in a nine-verse poem to me which is really worth an item in the Journal. It takes the reader through the early days of finding the hills, giving up smoking to the inevitable 'Galloping Munroist' phase from where there is no return. The Moffats (1219/20) have gone for the full round of Munros, Tops and Furths and thought they'd better include Beinn an Lochain as an 'honorary' Munro. They've also supplied some observations on potential new tops based on altimeter readings – more work for the Master of the Tables to sort out! The Mays (1253/54) also went for *M. brevis* compleating on Ben More after 31 to 32 years and mention that the next round should be accompanied by Munro-lets. The Crosbys (1217/18) finished nearer the other end of the *M. longus* timetable, spreading their saga over 40 years, giving them a pleasant start to retirement and '277 prizes'. Finally, on family matters, Iain King (1230) follows his father, Graham (70), and mother, Heather (928).

Many of those compleating are not resident in Scotland and two are particularly distant. Bernhard Lapp (1173) resides in Bremen, Germany and began his round on Slioch in 1979. He compleated this year after 13 separate holidays and 106 days (not including eight aborted days) and expects to be closely followed by his brother who is only 70 hills behind. The second, Gordon Hopper (1250), had a head start by compleating 195 before emigrating to Canada. Also, while on issues from abroad, I should mention that there are opportunities of further 'furths' in Kenya. Sir John Johnson (1185) reports that while on colonial service in 1955 he was intrigued to find the country was full of mountains which had not been tabulated. He drew up an indicative list and presented it to the Mountain Club of Kenya around 1961, and this has been the basis of a guide to the mountains of Kenya republished in 1989.

The Celebration on the Last One figures highly in the reports I receive. Charles Mackay (1165) being a Highlander by birth and having shinty 'connections' was presented by his brother with a fine 'Munro' camman, and before the collected throng made to hit a ceremonial shinty ball from the summit. He reports: 'It is a number of years since I hit a shinty ball in earnest, and that, coupled with the champagne, ensured I didn't surprise anyone on the Rannoch Wall.' Moving 'upmarket', Jack Berryman (1210) and Chris Suth-erland (1211) compleated together on Ben More Assynt to find, much to their surprise, that their companions had laid on champagne on a tray served by two friends dressed in white shirts and black bow ties. Bagpipes figure high in the priority of all Last One celebrations and Arthur Agar's (1233) was no exception. However, he also had a formal printed invitation to the party, numerous kilted companions, a Saltire, guitar and a parapent which the owner used to glide from the summit (while also kilted). Brian Welsh (1268), although accompanied by a piper and pipe, had to content himself with strong winds and driving rain which caused a severe dose of frozen digits and damp reeds emanating not a note. Margaret Brooker (1200) had far better weather for her celebration which seemed to attract many more than the original party once they reached the top. From this year's reports it certainly seems that if you are ascending any of the popular final Munro choices on a Saturday in May and June there's a good chance of finding a celebration.

Some of the most enjoyable letters I've received have come after *M. longus* campaigns. No fewer than 11 in the list have spread their round over 40 years, with the longest being Tom Boyd (1262) who ascended his first hill, Ben Ime, in 1940 having just recovered from measles, and he recalls the highlight of the day was a 'solitary spitfire flying overhead, no doubt about to take part in the Battle of Britain which was approaching its climax'. Frank Martin (1252) and Innes Sutherland (1251) compleated together on Gulvain after 40 and 50 years respectively. This was particularly appropriate for Innes who nearly ascended the hill in 1943 while on Commando training. However, the exercise didn't include the summit and that had to wait until this year. Later, on training in the Cairngorms with an instructor called F.S. Smythe they regularly ticked the summits and camped in Coire Etchachan. The pair's ascent of the Inn Pinn in 1992 was in true 1940s style with 9mm hawser, two slings and two crabs. I note that the Inn Pinn is often kept until late in the round, and Winifred Graham (1235) is no exception. Having started in the 1950s it was not until recently in her 65th year that the necessary combination of weather and 'someone with a rope' combined. Another *M. longus* is Roy Williamson (1199) who started in 1950 but only really accelerated since his 50th birthday in 1986. This acceleration was halted after one day-trip from Perth to Beinn Sgritheall when he realised while lying in the bath back home that he had only visited the first top. Three days later the 'problem' was corrected. Donald Rich (1190) decided that his 45-year round should be compleated on Sgorr Dhonuill (Donald's Peak) and feels that he is now free to revisit those where he missed the views.

Our elder statesman of the year is Theodore Cadoux (1181), *M. venerabilis,* who compleated at the age of 76. Nudging Theodore fairly close is Bill Jones (1145) compleat at the age of 68, who was introduced to the hills by one of the finest approaches – Crowberry Ridge in 1950. It obviously made the right impression!

Almost NOT compleat tales abound in the letters. Peter Roberts (112) nearly ruined any future hill walking by rupturing his Achilles tendon when a snowbridge collapsed near the summit of Mullach Clach a' Bhlair while on his third round. His descent back (after ticking the summit of course) sounded grim, but surgery and plaster seems to have sorted the leg out and he is duly onto his fourth round. Margaret Russell (1159) could have been defeated, not by weather, age or injury, but her ophidiaphobia. This seems to have induced Margaret to only venture into the eastern hills in winter, but the reptiles had the last laugh when a snake surprised her on Suilven. W.R. Shipway (1175) feels he may have only just made it due to age, but imparts his advice to others searching out the hills to 'first gather about you a number of staunch and steadfast friends'. Andy Whitehead (1213) could have failed at a very early age due to his inability to keep his breakfast down while travelling to the hills in his school teacher's car. This obviously made him a much less welcome companion in the car and he does mention often finding himself making his own transport arrangements. Michael Hanlin (1258) nearly didn't make it after a brush with wet snow on Slioch which prompted him to leave the hill for a 'better day'.

The medical state of *Chronic Munrosis* first published in the October 1984 edition of *Scottish Medicine* has now thoroughly ridden its author Iain B. McIntosh (1264) who is now compleat, although there was a delay of a year before he was prepared to acknowledge the fact and write to me. A further condition referred to is from John Martin (1198) who describes *M. lactiferculensis* (Munros by milk van). This seems to have involve his landlady's milk van being used unofficially to transport him to Ben Lawers for his first hills.

Finally, a report I have just received of a Round of the Extremities; Alec Keith and Derek Bearhop (259) report that they have completed a circuit of the four extreme Munros in a frenzy of motoring endurance. The round started and finished at Perth and took 23 hours and 25 minutes, ably driven by Pete Smith and Allan Amour who it is said observed all speed limits. Hopes of completion within 24 hours were nearly dashed when they had to stop to help a drunk try to remove his car from a bog near Achnasheen. The bog appears to have won leaving the team free to press on. However, in closing, Alec does comment that 'the expense and stamina required by this excursion renders its performance unjustifiable'. Well said!

For entry to the List: Notification of compleation should be sent to Dr. C.M. Huntley, Old Medwyn, Spittal, Carnwath, Lanarkshire, ML11 8LY, enclosing a SAE to ensure a reply. I leave the style of notification to the writer, but generally I like to know the names and dates of your first and last hills plus whatever anecdotal evidence you feel would be of interest. I note that the older writers often include their ages but remember I may use the information in the journal article. Also I know that the 'Unknown Munroist' position at 277 is getting very crowded and any who wish to 'come out' would be welcome to record the fact. Once registered in the List, Munroists can claim a tie and/or brooch. (Tie for £8.50, brooch/lapel badge for £8.50, all prices including p.&p. from the Keeper of the Regalia, Gordon M. McAndrew, Bishop's House, 4 Lansdowne Crescent, Edinburgh EH12 5EQ.)

Footnote: (All eight of them . . .) Readers may recall the request in the 1992 Journal by Isobel Baldwin of the Royal Museum of Scotland, to collect spiders while hillwalking and send in specimens for research purposes. She writes that since the start of the project, some 869 adult spiders have been collected, 601 of them true montane specimens contained in 21 species. She thanks those who helped, and adds that more specimens are welcome. The Editor, in a continuing fit of scientific zeal, will publish an article on these montane arachnids next year, by Isobel Baldwin, complete, we hope, with maps, drawings, and even, perhaps, a close-up colour photograph of one of our most accomplished climbers, the spider. Send in any captured beasties to: Isobel Baldwin, Royal Museum of Scotland, Chambers Street, Edinburgh EH1 1JF.

SCOTTISH MOUNTAIN ACCIDENTS

REGIONAL DISTRIBUTION

(Geographical Divisions are those used in SMC District Guidebooks)

| REGION | CASUALTIES (of which fatalities are bracketed) | | | | INCIDENTS | | | | | | | Non-Mountaineering | |
| | | | | | Actual Rescues | | Other Callouts | | | | | | |
	Injuries	Exhaustion/Exposure Hypothermia, Hyperthermia	Illness	TOTAL CASUALTIES	Incidents with Casualties	Cragfast	Separated	Lost	Overdue or Benighted	False Alarms	TOTAL INCIDENTS	Animal Rescues	Incidents
All Regions 1992	164 (31)	26 (1)	16 (11)	206 (43)	194	20	11	13	46	14	298	4	7
Northern Highlands	17 (3)	2 –	5 (3)	24 (6)	22	2	2	2	10	1	39	–	1
Western Highlands	9 (1)	2 –	3 (3)	14 (4)	13	–	–	–	4	–	17	–	–
Ben Nevis	23 (4)	5 –	2 (1)	30 (5)	27	3	2	1	3	–	36	–	–
Glen Coe (inc. Buachaille)	30 (10)	1 –	– –	31 (10)	26	7	1	–	6	–	40	–	–
Other Central Highlands	12 (3)	– –	– –	12 (3)	12	–	1	1	–	1	15	–	–
Cairngorms	31 (6)	3 (3)	7 (2)	41 (11)	38	1	3	5	4	3	54	3	5
Southern Highlands	36 (9)	– –	5 –	41 (9)	38	2	5	2	8	1	56	1	4
Skye	14 (4)	– –	1 –	15 (4)	14	5	–	–	1	1	21	1	–
Islands (other than Skye)	7 (1)	1 –	– –	8 (1)	7	–	1	2	4	–	14	–	–
Southern Uplands	15 (8)	2 –	2 (1)	19 (9)	18	–	1	–	6	–	25	–	5
All Regions 1993	194 (49)	16 (3)	25 (10)	235 (62)	215	20	16	13	46	7	317	5	15

TOTAL MOUNTAIN RESCUE CALL-OUTS, EXCLUDING AIRCRAFT, MARITIME AND ROAD INCIDENTS, AND ANIMAL RESCUES.

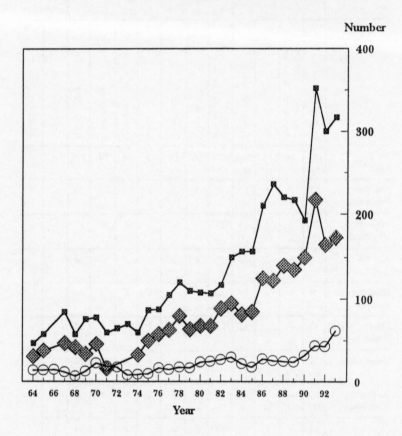

Number

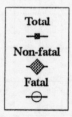

MOUNTAIN RESCUE COMMITTEEE OF SCOTLAND

CONTRIBUTORY CAUSES OF SOME INJURIES
(fatalities bracketed)

The mountain injury lists exclude casualties from the following causes, although they are included in the rescue narratives:

Not known	7 (6)
Sea cliffs (other than rock climbing)	7 (2)
Suicide	4 (4)
Piste skiing	4 (1)
Drowned	2 (2)
Suicide attempts	2
Total	26 (15)

SUMMER

Hillwalking summer slip/trip/stumble	41 (9)
Hillwalking slip etc.descending	33 (2)
Illness	18 (5)
Rock climbing roped	11 (1)
Rock climbing sea cliffs	3 (1)
Rock climbing unroped	3
Mountain biking	3 (1)
Foothold came away (Skye ridges)	1 (1)
Exhaustion	8
Rockfall	3
Loose handhold (scrambling)	2
Old injury causing trouble	2
Hypothermia	2
Loose rock dislodged by leader	1
Fell running slip on scree	1
River crossing instruction	1
Jolting on disabled hill climb	1
Rockfall during animal rescue	1
All terrain vehicle accident	1
Total	136 (20)

WINTER
(Snow, ice, frozen turf underfoot

Hillwalking slip/trip/stumble	14 (3)
Hillwalking descending	23 (8)
Mixed climbing/snow climbing unroped	6 (5)
Hypothermia	5 (3)
Blown over	5 (1)
Ice climbing roped	4 (1)
Illness	3 (2)
Ice or rockfall during mixed climbing roped	3 (2)
Avalanche	2 (2)
Ice-axe braking practice	2
Mixed climbing roped. Piton failure	1
Mixed climbing roped	1
Ice climbing unroped	1
Exhaustion	1
Polybagging	1
Cornice collapse during rescue	1
Total	73 (27)
Total mountain injuries	209 (47)
Full rescue total	235 (62)

Rescuers are generally named in, or just after, the narratives, with the number of rescue person/hours at the end of each incident. Police are not usually mentioned since it is well known they are always deeply involved – being ultimately responsible for all Scottish rescues. More than one-third of winter injuries have been fatal, whereas less than one-sixth of summer injuries have proved so.

I know that the list is far from complete, staggering as it is, because reports have not been received from all services. I hope to make more demands for information in 1994.

Scottish Mountain Safety Seminar – Dunblane Hydro, 6th May, 1994.
The Editor was invited to attend this seminar at the last moment, and duly turned up, as distressed as the rest of us at the high numbers of recent fatal accidents. The meeting had been arranged before the 1993-94 winter, a timely coincidence, with 170 delegates from both sides of the Border. Many weel kent faces were there, from a broad spectrum of the interested. In part, it was a group soul search, a discussion on whether mountaineers should continue to accept the dangers that attend mountaineering. The best prepared speech was perhaps that by Bob Reid, outgoing President of the MC of S. He made the acute observation that while it is possible to go hillwalking in summer, in winter there is only mountaineering. Many accidents, it would seem, have as a contributary cause either incompetent navigation, or even a lack of navigation aids. Indeed, I was shocked at the prevalence of such ignorance. Ben Humble's 'simple slip' will always be with us, and will take its annual cull of the tired, unwary, or downright unlucky. The Government, unsure as how to catalogue hill-users, promised more funding for research into accident statistics (they seemed to be oblivious of the annual reporting in this journal for one). The analysis presented shed little light, excepting the navigational shortcomings. An in-depth interview of each and every survivor might help, though even this would be full of traps and pitfalls. At the end of the day we left the hotel breathing gratefully the balmy spring air. And perhaps some of us drove home more carefully than usual.

SCOTTISH MOUNTAIN ACCIDENTS 1993

Compiled by John Hinde

NORTHERN HIGHLANDS

JANUARY 1st – With inadequate lighting (one working head torch between all three) three males attempted Ben More Assynt. Two climbed a gully to meet the third on top, but they were slow and he alerted Assynt MRT. The two from the gully searched for the third before descending. 2.

JANUARY 3rd – Old Man of Stoer Original Route (MVS). Hillwalkers saw two climbers, P. Morgan (31) and M. Austin (21) abseiling. Their ropes got stuck. Assynt MRT and Lochinver Coastguard were alerted. The two climbed back to the top and eventually got themselves off in wind, rain and darkness. 10.

JANUARY 20th – An Staonach, NE of Beinn Bhan, Applecross. Peter Robb (30s) weight 23st or 146kg, driving a 4-wheel ATV to a remote fish farm on a high hill loch, struck a rock, fracturing a tibia and fibula. He was stretcher carried by Torridon MRT (Is this a weight record?) to an airlift by RAF Sea King. 36.

JANUARY 29th – Jon Beard (21) traversing Liathach, was seen by the rest of his party falling into the northern coire, when cramponing down névé west of Coire Dubh Beag. Trying to brake he lost his ice-axe. He struck a boulder and was thrown off the ridge into Coire Dubh Beag. Two went for help and one tried to find Jon, but could not do so. His body was found by SARDA dog. He had fallen 240m. Torridon and Kinloss MRTS, RAF Sea King. 160.

FEBRUARY 11th-18th – Mist came down after Christopher Nicholls (30) had reached the summit of Slioch. Running about to keep warm he fell and sprained his ankle. He found a stone shelter and bivouacked to await better weather. He had carried a bivvy bag and sleeping bag but he had not left a route plan. His food ran out on the third day and he sucked ice to prevent dehydration. On the seventh day the weather improved, so he decided to move from his bivvy, descended 900m (taking two days in his weak state) and was found by a local farmer on the eighth day stumbling around a field. Evacuated by Torridon MRT ambulance and slowly rewarmed for hypothermia. He suffered frostbite of both feet but did well to survive such a long bivouac. 12.

FEBRUARY 20th-21st – Two men, Geoffrey Main (29) and Ciaran Grogan (28) attempted the south route of An Teallach traverse, which avoids the ridge proper. The route was in harsh condition with snow, ice and verglas. Gales with snow forced them to retreat. They lost one torch and smashed another. They bivouacked at 058827 when their descent gully appeared to end in a drop. Found by HMCG helicopter at Shenavall on second check. The bothy had already been checked when the pair were bivouacking. Dundonnell MRT. 213.

FEBRUARY 21st – Meall a' Chrasgaidh, Fannichs. One of a party of two, Bernard Hynes (55) had a cardiac arrest near Loch a' Bhraoin and had to be left alone. He was dead when winched by HMCG helicopter. Dundonnell MRT. 14.

MARCH 7th – Body of John Oag (19) found at the foot of 35m cliffs below ruins of Old Wick Castle, Wick. No suspicious circumstances.

MARCH 13th-14th – Starting late to climb Cioch Nose (VD), Applecross, John Maclachlan (35), Gail Burton (27) and Gary Wroe (27) were benighted. Torridon MRT met them on the ridge above the climb and walked down with them. 30.

APRIL 5th-6th – Routed from Glencalvie Lodge to Eileanach Lodge, Glen Glass, 11 pupils from Elgin High School, aged 15-18, grouped into two parties of five and six on an award hike were overdue reaching their rendezvous in Kildermorie Forest, a wild area north of Ben Wyvis 'riddled with peat hags up to six-feet deep, filled with water and snow'. There had been no midway check and some of the clothing was inadequate. One party was found at 425764 (Loch nan Amhaichean) by parties from Dundonnell and Kinloss MRTs, the other party at 449781 (Feur-lochan) by RAF Sea King. One teenager had hypothermia and another was in the early stages. RAF Nimrod aircraft involved, and Police SARDA dogs. 334.

APRIL 10th-11th – In a party of four, Mary Stoddart (32) sprained ankle on Beinn Liath Mhor, Fannaichs. She and a companion spent the night in a tent lent by a couple they met. She was stretchered out by Dundonnell MRT. 146.

APRIL 12th – On a coastal walk to Greenstone Point (headland west of Gruinard Bay) in a group, James Chapman (65) had a fatal heart attack. Bristow helicopter recovered him with his wife and took him to Alltbea Police. He was declared dead by doctor on board R119. 6.

APRIL 13th – Two men, Newton and Chapman, attempted to climb West Buttress, Stac Pollaidh, but leader, Newton, got arm cramps and they abseiled off. A late start, queueing for the route, and retreat delay caused benightment. They got lost and descended away from their car. Dundonnell MRT alerted.

MAY 25th – Mountain trail of Beinn Eighe Nature Reserve. Harsheta Patel (9) separated from a group of 24. She was seen to slip on scree and fall into a 50m gorge by other walkers. She was unable to say how she reached the bottom without serious injury. She suffered bruising and cold trauma. Winched by RAF Sea King. Torridon MRT. 25.

JUNE1st-2nd – Separating from three others on Meall nan Ceapraichean (Beinn Dearg group) David Andrews (39) went east instead of west and got to Glenbeg Bothy. In mist he tried to find the path over to Inverlael, but his compass seemed to have become demagnetised so he returned to Glenbeg Bothy. He was found there by Dundonnell MRT. Kinloss MRT and RAF Sea King called out. 208.

JUNE 8th – Ewan Mackay (21) soloing a south-facing gully on Liathach to the ridge (west of Stuc a' Choire Dhuibh Bhig), slipped on wet rock and fell 12m suffering extensive injuries. After first aid from Torridon MRT and RAF Sea King winchman, the helicopter managed to winch him on a 70m wire. 30.

JUNE 19th – Descending the path in Coire Dubh after a day on Beinn Eighe, Hugh MacKay (38) suffered severe chest pains. Torridon MRT provided first aid for a suspected heart attack. Airlift by RAF Sea King. 27.

JUNE 28th – J. MacInnes (18), suffering from an old knee injury, was evacuated from Shenavall Bothy, An Teallach by Bristow helicopter. Dundonnell MRT. 5.

JUNE 29th – Mapping Morefield Quarry, 1.8km north of Ullapool, geology student Helen Jarret (20) tripped on a rabbit burrow and hurt her ankle. Lifted by Inverness Air Ambulance.

JUNE 29th – Duncan Campbell (41) usually walked down from his work site at Farrmheall (BT project) to base at Cualin Lodge, Rhiconich in 30 minutes. On this occasion, mist came down after five minutes and he had not been following Argocat tracks. He turned up safe after four hours. Assynt MRT alerted. RAF Sea King. 12.

JULY 5th – Hillwalkers lifted by helicopter when Derek Scott (51) broke an ankle on Ben Loyal.

JULY 16th – Coast walking Achiltibuie to Blughasary, Ivor Marriot (53) slipped into a gully banging his head. He returned to Achiltibuie unaided. Dundonnell MRT standby. 6.

JULY 20th-21st – Between A'Mhaighdean and Ruadh Stac Mor five walkers ran out of daylight attempting the Fisherfield Six. They bivouacked and two went for help at 0630. Jill Adams (60), Jennifer Thompson (50) and Fran Revell (40) were found walking out and lifted by RAF Sea King, as were the three Dundonnell MRT who were out looking for them. 48.

July 31th-August 1st – Angus MacLean (40) became separated from his friend on a fishing/hillwalking trip near Dundonnell. Overdue, he turned up safe at 01.30. Dundonnell MRT alerted.

August 4th – Ian Cox (29) got stuck on a ledge above Camusnagaul when descending the north side of An Teallach in mist. His whistle was heard by a fishing boat on Little Loch Broom. Winched off by Bristow helicopter. Dundonnell MRT. 5.

August 14th – Man (21) fell on to rocks on Gairloch foreshore. Recovered semiconscious by HM Coastguard and Ambulance Service.

August 19th – Two tourists trapped by tide at Durness, got cragfast on cliffs at Sango Bay. Talked down by HM Coastguard.

August 19th-20th – Without a torch, a 46-year-old man set out at 13.40 to walk from Corrie Hallie near Dundonnell to Poolewe via Carnmore, a distance of more than 20 miles, without bivouac gear. After dark he sheltered about six miles short of Poolewe. Dundonnell MRT passed him at 05.30 but he did not know if it was a vehicle or torches. 24.

August 29th – Gordon Nuttall (48) slipped on a stone, rupturing Achilles tendon, descending Beinn Liath Mhor, Fannaichs, with two companions. By the time Bristow helicopter arrived he had hobbled to road with one friend. Dundonnell MRT. 13.

August 29th-30th – Separating from three friends on summit of Cona Mheall, Beinn Dearg group, to go down Gleann na Sguaib, Duncan Kirkhope (29) went down Choire Ghranda before realisation and retracement of steps. Found by Bristow helicopter but walked out. Dundonnell MRT. 70.

Late August – Walker. Cliff path Thurso. Fatality.

September 5th – Sgurr a' Chaorachain, Applecross (probably on Summit Buttress). Bristow helicopter with a doctor aboard evacuated two casualties from a rock-climbing slip. A runner pulled. Brian Cross (38), leading, had head injuries and a dislocated shoulder. Richard Vernon (42) also suffered shoulder dislocation. Torridon MRT and Fairbridge Drake. 20.

September 20th-21st – People camping in a corrie of An Teallach reported red flares. Three members of Dundonnell MRT climbed an unnamed top of the main ridge, immediately north of the summit, finding nothing. HM Coastguard were out on the Moray Coast for flares reported about the same time near Inverness. 32.

October 2nd – Dundonnell MRT helped Mary Langridge (48) down to the road after she slipped descending path from An Teallach injuring an ankle. 27.

October 3rd – Dundonnell MRT member checked Shenavall Bothy as part of search for a German couple missing in Skye from September 7th and later found dead in Trotternish. 5.

October 10th – Five hours overdue on a low-level four-hour walk from Glasnock to Balgyby Loch Damh; Torridon MRT found Jane Farargue (55) and Hilary Gosling (55) and three dogs. They had under-estimated time and terrain and taken a wrong turning. 30.

October 23rd – Separated from a group of five, Adrian Moore (48) got benighted descending from west end of Liathach (Sgorr a' Chadail) direct to Torridon village. He flashed a light and was guided down, uninjured but grateful, by Torridon MRT. 30.

October 30th – Companion of Archibald Hannah (78) returned and said they split up at Eas Chual-aluinn (waterfall), Kylesku. Assynt MRT searched the track, then RAF helicopter and Police dog were summoned. Hannah had got lost and was found walking along the main road towards Inchnadamph about midnight. 40.

November 24th – Searches for John Hendry (60) crofter, of Smerlie, Lybster. Found dead two miles from his home.

WESTERN HIGHLANDS

FEBRUARY 6th-7th – Two walkers overdue from Sgurr na Ciche took a wrong turn and spent night at Sourlies, Loch Nevis when they should have reached A'Chuil, Glen Dessarry. Sarah MacCumber (20) and Dylen Huws (18). 120.

FEBRUARY 27th – Doreen Thomson-Watson (50) suffered a heart attack descending Sgurr nan Ceannaichean, Glen Carron, with a friend. Torridon MRT commenced CPR within an hour of callout, but she was dead on arrival at Raigmore Hospital by RAF Sea King. Leuchars MRT. Helicopter made its own white-out, so that the use of night vision goggles was very difficult. 109.

MARCH 29th – Police searches for woman (64) later found dead in hills behind Corpach.

APRIL 15th-17th – Helped by a stalker with ferries across Loch Quoich, Kinloss MRT eventually found three girls aged about 18 who had changed the route of their award hike due to poor weather and rivers in spate. Other searchers involved were Leuchars and Lochaber MRTs, SARDA and RAF Sea King. The ambitious intended route had been: Kinloch Hourn, Barrisdale, Bealach Unndalain, Loch Quoich south shore to Kingie Forest. They camped at Lochan nam Breac on their first night, then took a shortcut round the head of Loch Quoich to their second camp by the road 9km east of Kinloch Hourn where they were found on 17th. 631.

MAY 16th – Coire Dubh (NW of Ardgour House). In a party of seven walkers, Barbara Vaughan (61) was descending a wet, grassy slope beside MacLean's Towel (waterfalls) when she slipped breaking an ankle. Evacuated to Raigmore by Air Ambulance. 10.

MAY 23rd – William Kay (31) suffered head injuries and multiple fractures and cuts from a 30m fall on Great Ridge, Garbh Bheinn of Ardgour. Lowered by his companion Bernard Shaw (see incident below). Lochaber MRT, Lomond MRT, RAF helicopter. 54.

MAY 23rd – Helping in above incident, Bernard Swan (41) Lomond MRT sustained a broken arm from a boulder dislodged by climbers above.

MAY 25th – James Andrew Harkin (44) was walking the Loch Quoich Munros with two friends. Near the Gleouraich/Spidean Mialach bealach he collapsed with a heart attack. RAF helicopter from Plockton, with GP aboard, found him dead. 15.

JUNE 3rd – Dennis Barker (63) slipped descending An Caorann Beag off Ciste Dhubh injuring an ankle. Stretchered down by Kintail MRT. 27.

JUNE 5th – Solo hillwalker, Ian McNicol (48) slipped descending steep gully on SE Face of Druim na Maodalaich, Kingairloch, Ardgour. Body found by staff of Ardgour Outdoor Centre.

MID JUNE – West Pier, Lochaline. Schoolgirl (14) got minor injuries from 10m cliff fall. Stretchered by HM Coastguard.

JULY 7th – Helen Torbett (62) missing. It was she who, using her maiden name, compiled the list of 'Grahams' (Scottish hills between 2000ft and 3000ft). Car left at Inverinate, Loch Duich on July 7th. Searches of Beinn Fhionnlaidh and Carn Eighe, Loch Mullardoch, on December 4th, 1993 (snowline 650m) by Kinloss and Kintail MRTs. 360. Searches (with gear found) up to April 1994 at Inverinate.

JULY 22nd-23rd – Kinloss and Kintail MRTs called out to search for a walker who had not returned to his tent at Glen Affric YH. He had been seen at Mullach na Dheiragain (978m.) heading NE on 22nd. RAF Sea King checked the hostel. He had just returned having spent the night on the hill. 36.

AUGUST 7th – Totaig Broch, Glenelg. Wearing smooth shoes descending a wet path, Denise Stewart (44) slipped and broke her ankle. Stretchered down by Kintail MRT. 14.

AUGUST 8th-9th – Kinloss and Lochaber MRTs in an RAF Sea King searched for Monica Rottinger (45) and Christian Rottinger (45) overdue walking from Glenfinnan to Morar. They were spotted at Swordland having stayed at Oban Bothy, Loch Morar. 28.

Note: The delay was supposed to be caused by rivers in spate, but I do not think it rained heavily until after dark. However, the distance is considerable and the terrain rough, so they may have under-estimated their timing – J.H.

SEPTEMBER 16th – A couple got lost heading for Falls of Glomach without map and compass. Marlene Davis (56) slipped on a muddy path and broke her ankle near Bealach an Sgairne. Stretcher carry by Kintail MRT. 30.

OCTOBER 23rd – Walking near Kyle Rhea, Elizabeth MacFarlane (31) slipped on a path, falling 25m. Transferred to Broadford Hospital by HMCG helicopter where she regained consciousness and was treated for a fractured elbow. Glenelg MRT, RNLI. 16.

OCTOBER 28th – Walking NE of Beinn Sgritheall, David Waddington (63) and Lindsey Waddington (58) got fatigued and cold, walking in a circle with no idea of direction despite having a map. No compass, torch or food. A younger woman stayed with them and son went for help when it got dark. RAF Sea King and Glenelg MRT. 88.

BEN NEVIS

JANUARY 3rd – After climbing South Castle Gully, James Stalker (30) was cramponing solo down No. 4 Gully when he was blown over by wind and fell 65m breaking an ankle and a thumb. Helped to CIC Hut by a Lochaber MRT member and another climber. Later double strop-lifted by RAF Wessex. 11.

FEBRUARY 1st – David Glover (33) fell running on screes of Carn Dearg NW tore leg muscles. Airlift from Halfway Lochan by RAF Sea King on another mission. 6.

FEBRUARY 2nd – Descending foot of Tower Ridge after doing Italian Climb, Jeremy Birtles (35) sprained ankle. Kinloss MRT saw torch signals, lowered him to CIC, and stretchered by Lochaber MRT. RAF Sea King unable to assist because of weather. 139.

FEBRUARY 13th – Richard Cuthbert (22) and Jess Woodridge on Raeburn's Easy Route, went off route in mist and spent night on a ridge at 1200m. Climbed to plateau at dawn. Found by Lochaber MRT going down the path. RAF Wessex. 50.

FEBRUARY 21st – Michel Dennis Bou (40) soloed up towards the start of Point Five behind a companion – who was waiting at the start of the climb, heard a rattling noise and turned to see Michel trying to ice-axe brake. He slid 50m then went over a buttress to land head first among rocks. He wore a helmet, crampons and was using two axes. Stretchered to CIC by other climbers, then lifted by RAF Wessex. Died in hospital from severe head injuries. Lochaber MRT. 26.

FEBRUARY 22nd or 23rd – Climber dislocated shoulder in Gardyloo Gully. Hoisted to plateau by Glenmore Lodge team

FEBRUARY 23rd – Search by Lochaber MRT and RAF Sea King had started when a pair overdue from climbing Tower Ridge turned up at Golf Club. Peter Loftus (47) and James Kenyon (41).

FEBRUARY 28th – Daniel Gibson (19) fell 38m when pitons failed, as he led a route between Point Five and Hadrian's Wall. He banged his face and shoulder, becoming unconscious for a time. Second had a good belay and lowered him off. Kinloss MRT monitored and lowered him to easier ground, then back-roped him, walking, to CIC for double-strop airlift by RAF Wessex. 28.

MARCH 3rd-4th – John O'Brien, London (40) was not reported missing, but was believed to have been on Ben Nevis since 3rd-4th March 1993. He was found in Surgeon's Gully by Herbert and David Brooks on May 31st 1993, when they got lost coming down the path. Remains were left till June 3rd then winched by RAF Sea King and Lochaber MRT. No footwear was found and no technical equipment. He had sustained multiple injuries. 30.

MARCH 4th – Caldwell Jones (35) and David Meigh (31) airlifted at night. Cragfast on Slalom, Little Brenva Face at 1200m. Shouts to other climbers raised the alarm. Lochaber MRT, RAF Sea King. 30.

MARCH 9th-10th – From a tent at CIC, Paul Birchell (26) and Lucas Heathcote (23) climbed Hadrian's Wall. Paul was struck in the eye by falling ice, which affected vision and slowed them down, so they got benighted. On 10th, cragfast, they were helped to plateau by other climbers. Thought to be suffering exposure they were airlifted from top of No. 4 Gully to Belford Hospital by RAF Sea King, but did not require treatment. 11.

APRIL 11th – Richard Collie (45) airlifted by RAF Sea King from Red Burn with head cut and fractured rib. He had left the path to descend a snowfield, slipped and slid 100m colliding with a boulder. Other walkers mobile-phoned police and nearby RAF. Stafford MRT members helped. 11.

APRIL 18th – Nabaz Malaly (40), soloing Green Gully was seen to fall 65m from which he got severe head injuries. No helmet. Airlifted by RAF Sea King. Died on transfer between hospitals. Lochaber MRT. 20.

APRIL 30th – Solo, descending soft snow near Coire Leis abseil posts, David Price (57) slipped and failed to ice-axe brake. He came to among rocks 30m below. Three people heard his cries. Winched by RAF Sea King with fractured arms, head and back injuries. Lochaber MRT. 26.

MAY 1st – Climbing, roped, the last 6m to CMD Arete, Kyle Pearce (22) dislodged a boulder which struck his second, Ian Warren (18), breaking his right forearm. Ian was helped to the ridge, where they attracted the attention of a passing helicopter and were taken to Fort William. RAF Sea King. Lochaber MRT. 4.

MAY 29th – Leader fall on Secretaries' Buttress, Poll Dubh, Glen Nevis. Colin Whitehead (26) slipped and fell 18m, hitting his second, Simon Cooke (25), then falling a farther 9m below Simon. Colin had spine, chest and abdominal injuries. Simon got bruising to his lower leg. Kinloss MRT exercising nearby summoned help. Lochaber MRT and RAF Sea King. 54.

MAY 31st – Herbert Brooks (40) and son David (12) rescued from Surgeon's Gully, Glen Nevis, by RAF Sea King and Lochaber MRT. Reaching top of Nevis by CMD Arete they had lost contact with their companion in mist, and strayed into the gully from the Ben path. They got cragfast trying to descend. Cries for help were heard by walkers in Glen Nevis. 116. Remains of John O'Brien were found. See incident March 3rd-4th.

JUNE 4th – Between Coire Leis and Nevis summit, Glen Mason (33) stumbled on wet scree and hurt an ankle, but he was able to continue over the top and down the Ben path with two companions till they met someone who went for help. Stretcher carry by Lochaber MRT. 19.

JUNE 4th-5th – Soloing at Poll Dubh, Richard Bond fell 10m, fracturing a vertebra and sustaining cuts and bruises. Companions raised alarm. Stretcher carried to ambulance by Lochaber MRT. 14.

JUNE 5th – Below the Red Burn, Michelle Shaw (16) stumbled on a large stone and tore leg ligaments. She walked down with help, till stretchered by Lochaber MRT. 16.

JUNE 20th – Norman Harland (72). Fatal slip when using binoculars, falling18m. He had been accompanying his wife on Nevis Gorge path. Body stretchered out by Lochaber MRT. 17.

JULY 1st – Joan Powell (57) broke an ankle on opposite side of river from Glen Nevis road near caravan site. Airlifted by RAF Sea King. 17.

JULY 19th – James Campbell (15) and Neil Murray (12) cragfast on the west-facing slopes of Carn Dearg NW. They shouted for help and could be seen from the Ben path. RAF Sea King lifted six Lochaber MRT on to the hill. Meanwhile, the mist level lowered and the boys extricated themselves safely. They had seen the helicopter so they phoned in. 32.

JULY 29th – David Podd (42) severely disabled, with artificial legs, had tried to ascend Ben Nevis. ('93 Challenge). Doctor advised him to abandon the attempt as his spine was suffering from continual jolting. Helicoptered from West Flank Zig-Zags. Lochaber. 38.

JULY 30th – Three disabled men helicoptered from Ben path. They became exhausted in bad weather during '93 Challenge. Neil Howard (26), Graeme Stewart (26) and David Donaldson (20).

AUGUST 9th – Andrew MacFarlane (10) got separated from his father and three others just above Halfway Lochan on the Ben path. Three Lochaber MRT were alerted but Andrew got down safe aided by others. 1.

AUGUST 13th – Just above Halfway Lochan on the Ben path, Natasha Groot (21) stumbled while descending injuring her knee. Nine Lochaber MRT members stretchered her to hospital where she was released after treatment. 39.

AUGUST 21st – Christine Sanderson (40) slipped descending Ben path, near second aluminium bridge, with ankle injuries. Splinted and stretchered by Kinloss and Lochaber MRTs. 37. (KMRT used private Vodaphone in marginal Cellnet cover area).

AUGUST 27th – Robert Atchison (75) exhausted on Ben path. Stretchered by Lochaber MRT. 20.

AUGUST 28th – At the second zig-zag on the Ben path (300m) James Green (42) took ill. His sister contacted police from the Youth Hostel. Lochaber MRT stretchered him to hospital for treatment. 12.

AUGUST 29th – Descending Ben path from the summit Muriel Tourneur (27) stumbled and fell on her knees, tearing two leg ligaments and bruising shoulder. Due to mist, Sea King could not reach incident (above West Flank Zig-Zags) so Lochaber MRT stretchered her down to winch point. 40.

SEPTEMBER 2nd – The wife of James Kerr (63) got worried about his tiredness at second aluminium bridge, descending the Ben, so she got a passing walker to alert Lochaber MRT. However, they met him when they were less than 1km above Achintee, and he got down OK. 10.

SEPTEMBER 22nd – Loretta Bailey (35) used mobile phone. Her party of four had missed the Ben path in the dark and were unable to find the way down. A Lochaber team member escorted them to Glen Nevis YH. 4.

SEPTEMBER 26th – Leonard Cook (44) died of a heart attack only half-an-hour after starting to walk up Ben path with his daughter and niece. Lochaber team, Ambulance Service, RN Sea King. 56.

OCTOBER 23rd-24th – Poorly equipped to climb Tower Ridge in icy conditions, and starting at midday, Robert Bennison (45), Brian Allman (29), Karl Price (26) and Andrew Slater (24) got cragfast at Tower Gap. Winched off by RAF Sea King at 07.00 on 24th. Lochaber MRT. 20.

DECEMBER 30th – Climbing roped with three companions on Castle Ridge, John Tingay (21) lost balance and fell 15m, sustaining broken femur. Winched off by RAF Sea King. 22.

GLENCOE

(Including Buachaille Etive Mor)

JANUARY 5th – Three men climbed Boomerang Gully, Stob Coire nan Lochan, finishing near the summit. Two were hit by a massive gust of wind. Both were blown into Coire nam Beithe – a long fall down an ill-defined couloir. Ian Lancaster (25) had minor injuries and was airlifted by RAF Sea King. Ian Freegard (25) fatal, stretchered down by Glencoe and Lochaber MRTs. 274.

JANUARY 24th-26th – Nicholas Simpson (32) was found 700m up Buachaille Etive Beag on an easy snow slope. Face injuries suggested he had fallen. He had a rucksack and was wearing crampons and holding an ice-axe; he probably died of hypothermia. Glencoe, Kinloss and Leuchars MRTs, SARDA, RAF Sea King and Wessex helicopters. 800.

JANUARY 23rd-24th – Jonathan Shepherd (26) and Henrietta Shepherd (24) got be-nighted climbing Cleft Weave (II/III) on Stob Coire nam Beithe. They got moving at 08.00 after a night in bivvy bags. Found walking down Fionn Ghleann, cold, but uninjured. Glencoe, Lomond and Kinloss MRTs, SARDA, RAF Wessex. 155.

JANUARY 30th-31st – Steven Roberts and Brian Munday (both 23) climbed Summit Gully, Stob Coire nam Beith, then went down into Glen Etive and bivouacked. Walked wrong way down the glen, passed a phone kiosk (not working) and walked back to Glencoe, passing houses, while a search was on. Glencoe and Leuchars MRTs, RAF Wessex. 113.

JANUARY 31st – Elizabeth Taylor (31), Ian Brown (23) and Colin Wylie (26) were going up Stob Coire nan Lochan from the Lost Valley, wearing crampons (slope was hard névé). Wylie slipped and fell 25m, self-arresting with his ice-axe – minor injuries). Taylor slipped and fell 45m before going over a 5m waterfall, sustaining severe head injuries from which she died on February 7th. Going to help them, Brown slipped with minor injuries. Rescue and first aid by Glencoe and Leuchars MRTs was very difficult in the waterfall. RAF Wessex helicopter, essential for this rescue, winched all three aboard. 60.

JANUARY 31st – Descending hard névé, at night, without crampons, from Stob Coire nan Lochan into Coire nan Lochan, James Jedrzejewski (43) slipped and broke an ankle. Glencoe MRT and RAF Sea King. 33.

FEBRUARY 1st-2nd – Andrew Caren (32), Angela Murray (22) and Joseph Duffy (19) were overdue on Curved Ridge, but before full search started they were seen near top of Stob Dearg walking down Coire Cloiche Finne next morning. Glencoe MRT. 43.

FEBRUARY 1st – Karen Paton (18), with friends, descending Coire nam Beithe, slipped on hard névé and slid 10m. Crampon caught and twisted her ankle. She walked part way and was then airlifted by RAF Sea King. Glencoe MRT. 40.

FEBRUARY 2nd – Stob Coire nan Lochan. Elizabeth Jones (22) was trying to climb a very small ice face unroped when she slipped and fell 6m, catching a crampon in the ice and breaking an ankle. Walked down part way, then stretchered by Glencoe MRT, then winched by RAF Wessex. 40.

FEBRUARY 6th – With four others, climbing Curved Ridge (II/III) roped, Vincent Mitchen (62) was hit by a rockfall not far up the climb. His arm was broken but, unable to descend for some reason, he completed the climb and walked down Lagangarbh Coire in darkness. Glencoe and Kinloss MRTs. 51.

FEBRUARY 6th-7th – Robert Burdett (36) with two friends, found Aonach Eagach (rock and névé) was too hard for him. He got cragfast, refusing to move, so all bivouacked. One got down at 10.55 next day. Glencoe MRT brought Burdett down below full cloud base at 600m and he was winched by RAF Wessex. 28.

FEBRUARY 13th – Descending Coire nam Beith without crampons, Lionel Fretz (31) stumbled and injured an ankle, but was still able to walk. He got painkillers and strapping from other walkers. GMRT helped him off the hill but he refused medical treatment in glen. RAF Wessex unable to reach Glencoe due to poor weather. 39.

FEBRUARY 20th – Patrick Gray (45) Stob Coire nam Beith. Fatal. Gray was cramponing down Summit Gully (I/II) unroped, with a companion. They met two who were climbing up and traversed to allow free passage. At start of traverse Gray slipped and fell the length of the gully. Stretchered down by GMRT and Lochaber. RN Sea King went to Glencoe but was used on Black Mount rescue. 86.

MARCH 6th-7th – Gerard Beard (52), Joanna Girvan (21), Stefano Cappaccio (21) and Ruth Sullivan (20) climbed Agag's Groove and then went to the summit of Stob Dearg. Attempting to get down the hard névé headwall of Coire na Tulaich they got cragfast and bivouacked because they had no ice-axes or crampons. Helped down next day by Glencoe MRT. 33.

MARCH 13th – Buachaille Etive Mor, near Crowberry Ridge. Four started to walk up to their intended route, Easy Gully, but strayed up the wrong side of Crowberry Ridge. Noting the mistake, two tried to traverse left on steep snow with no ice-axe or crampons. Martin Smith (22) fell into a bergschrund; a waterfall broke his fall, but he was bruised, grazed and had slight hypothermia when double stroplifted by RAF Wessex. Glencoe MRT. 36.

MARCH 20th-21st – Six females missing overnight on north slopes Stob Coire nam Beith. They turned up safe. RAF Wessex recalled.

MARCH 22nd – Alison Pitts (30) sprained her ankle from a slip descending Coire na Tulaich, Buachaille Etive Mor, wearing crampons. Party of six. Stretchered down by GMRT because RAF Wessex could not hover safely due to strong wind. Heavy snow showers during rescue.

MARCH 24th – SC Gully (Grade III), Stob Coire nan Lochan. Peter Andrew Law (45), despite wearing a helmet, died instantly from head injuries, and his friend, Mark Baxter (41) had cuts and bruises, when they fell roped to the foot of the climb. A belay had failed. Glencoe MRT, RAF Wessex. 37.

MARCH 27th-28th – After traverse of Aonach Eagach (east to west) two men separated descending SE Face of Sgor nam Fiannaidh. Mike Smith (32) had been very ill sometime before and he was moving very slowly. Benighted, he had lost a crampon and had no torch. Companion alerted GMRT who roped him and escorted him off the hill. Glencoe MRT and SARDA. 56.

APRIL 3rd – Patricia Chisholm (36) was glissading inside a polythene bag with no ice-axe for braking, high on Stob an Fhuarain (Sgor na h-Ulaidh). She sustained a crush fracture of 3L vertebrae with no lasting damage. GMRT walked up and used a vacuum stretcher for airlift by RAF Sea King. Air Ambulance on 4th to Glasgow. 57.

APRIL 6th – Coire na Tulaich, Buachaille Etive Mor. Without helmet, crampons or ice-axe, Frederick Wright (38) scrambled on rocks above a long snow slope when heading for the top of the Buachaille. He slipped and fell 45m. on to the snow with broken elbow, cuts and teeth knocked out. Glencoe MRT put him on a stretcher and he was winched on to an RAF Sea King. 28.

MAY 17th – One of a group descending below Ossian's Cave, Aonach Dubh, Anthony Graham (26) slipped (wearing Army boots) and fell 20m. grazing his legs and breaking a collar bone. His four friend slowered him down the the crag. Glencoe MRT took over and walked him down. A Sea King was recalled en route. 38.

MAY 17th-18th – Solo walking on Buachaille Etive Beag, Paul Waghorn (30) strayed on to a loose, steep face (NE Face of Stob nan Cabar). He probably slipped on wet rock or scree and fell a long way, dying from head injuries. Found and winched off by RAF Sea King. Glencoe, Kinloss and Leuchars MRTs, SARDA. 65.

MAY 21st - Anthony McMahon (23), Gerard Frolongo (23) and Anthony Carroll (22) walking on Stob Coire nam Beith in thick mist, started climbing dangerous ground near The Pyramid and got cragfast in Summit Gully. One managed to go and raise the alarm. He had no clue where the others were. Glencoe MRT carried out a long search and a very technical cliff lower that lasted more than seven hours. RAF Sea King flew for three hours, but could not take part because of thick mist. One of the three had very slight injuries from a 10m fall. 132.

MAY 22nd – Fraser Leslie (29) got cragfast on wet rock after wandering from Pleasant Terrace into the Shadbolt Chimney area (above Ossian's Cave). One of his two companions raised alarm. RN Sea King flew three of Glencoe MRT to a point above him, then tried to winch him, but decided he might fall. GMRT hoisted him on a rope, hoisting a 'barrow boy' on another rope. All were winched off the top of Aonach Dubh. 45.

MAY 22nd – In a party of four climbing out of a gully west of Clachaig Gully West, Robert Fleming (37) had his upper arm speared by a sharp rock dislodged by a member of a separate hillwalking party. He also got a head injury, not serious. Winched by RN Sea King. Glencoe MRT. 21.

JUNE 8th – Descending Meall Mor, Elise Vandenberg (39) slipped on grass beside a stream, injuring her ankle. Companion went for help. Stretchered by Glencoe MRT to a good place for winching by RAF Sea King. 40.

JULY 23rd – Myra Reid (36) got separated from her brother in thick mist just below the top of Buachaille Etive Mor. He walked down Coire na Tulaich and raised alarm. She walked out safe to Glen Etive. Glencoe MRT. 49.

JULY 24th – Descending just below Bidean nam Bian summit eastwards, Louis Mullen (27) slipped on wet slabs, dislocating a shoulder. Assisted by three companions he got down to Bealach Dearg (head of Lost Valley) but then Glencoe MRT had to help. He was winched out by RN Sea King. 50.

AUGUST 2nd – Solo traversing Aonach Eagach west to east in mist, Susan Paton (31) descended too soon and fell on wet rock above Piper's lay-by with arm and leg injuries. Her calls for help were heard by people in the lay-by. Glencoe MRT climbed dangerous, loose ground and lowered her off. She then walked down but was detained in hospital overnight. 30.

AUGUST 23rd – Ines Hernandez (72) slipped on stones and damp grass near a stream and sprained her ankle. She had been descending the coire east of Am Bodach, Aonach Eagach. Stretcher carry by Glencoe MRT. 43.

AUGUST 25th – Stewart Wilson (60), who ran a hillwalking company, was guiding seven people traversing Aonach Eagach, with a fellow instructor. He was killed at the Pinnacles when he slipped on dry rock and fell 100m north into Coire Cam. A doctor went to him. Glencoe MRT guided the group down and also accompanied RAF Sea King for a difficult winch out. 56.

SEPTEMBER 18th-19th – In a party of two men and two women (aged 26-40) traversing Aonach Eagach east to west, one woman was very slow. Descending Clachaig Gully path they wandered off and got cragfast. They flashed torches for help and were roped down by Glencoe MRT, then walked off. 61.

OCTOBER 11th – Without torches and overdue from Aonach Eagach traverse, three Frenchwomen had only reached Meall Dearg when it got dark. Glencoe MRT called out, but they escaped unaided down the large scree gully south to Achtriochtan Farm. 9.

OCTOBER 16th – Traversing Aonach Eagach east to west, David Hudspith (44) and Paul Watson (38) ran out of daylight, and also got cragfast on Sgornam Fiannaidh (Clachaig Gully West area). GMRT members climbed to them with difficulty and roped them to easier ground then escorted them to the road. 53.

NOVEMBER 7th-8th – RAF Leuchars MRT and SARDA found three male hillwalkers benighted near the summit of Am Bodach, Aonach Eagach. Safe but wet, cold and embarrassed, they had been unsure of position and bivouacked. 346.

NOVEMBER 20th – Mark Wilson (21) was leading a pitch on Plumbline (VS), Central Buttress, Buachaille Etive Mor, when he slipped. His runners ripped out, and he fell 18m and hit a rib of rock as he fell. Fatal with severe facial injuries. No helmet. His second went down to his rucksack and summoned help with a mobile phone. GMRT stretchered Wilson to a suitable winching point for RAF Sea King. 58.

NOVEMBER 27th – Buachaille Etive Mor. There were freezing hard sheets of verglas on the mountain some 6m wide. Mike Dennison (41) and a companion went to climb Curved Ridge, but decided against it. Retreating to the traverse path across a slippery grass/rock slope from the base of the ridge they both wore crampons but no helmets. Mike slipped about 110m above the Waterslide. He fell about 80m into a shallow gully with very bad injuries: skull, spine, ribs, tibia and hypothermia. Unconscious, he was given advanced paramedic treatment by GMRT, put on a stretcher and winched off by RN Sea King. First to Belford Hospital, transferred to Glasgow, then Newcastle. 50.

DECEMBER 2nd – Partial false alarm, partial rescue. Motorists on A82 reported slow moving lights in Coire na Tulaich, Buachaille Etive Mor. Two men had chosen a very bad day; rain low down, snow on tops, so they climbed North Buttress very slowly and came down in the dark, failing to find the bridge over the swollen River Coupall. GMRT escorted them last few hundred metres at 23.00. 4.

DECEMBER 10th-15th – Two Paratroopers were killed in Summit Gully (Grade II) of Stob Coire nam Beith, perhaps by both falling roped together, or by being swept down by an avalanche. Paul Callaghan (26), David Read (24). They left Clachaig at 11.15 Friday 10th to climb at Stob Coire nam Beith and were reported missing by their friends, after their own searches, at 14.20 on Monday 13th. Searches commenced immediately. On Tuesday 14th rope, karabiners and ice-axe were found. Both bodies, roped, were found under 4.5m avalanche debris at the foot of Summit Gully at 13.20 on Wednesday 15th. Glencoe, Kinloss, Leuchars Lochaber, Strathclyde Police MRTs, SARDA, RAF Sea King. 2705.

OTHER CENTRAL HIGHLANDS

JANUARY 24th – On West Highland Way, 2km west of Kinlochleven, Heather Frame (30) was troubled by an old ankle injury. Delay and bad weather caused hypothermia. Rescued by Glencoe MRT vehicle and recovered. 5.

FEBRUARY 12th – John McSorley (30), Matilda Mooney (30) and Clare Potter (26) were overdue on Geal Charn, Drumochter. Found by RAF Sea King 3km SW of the peak. Lost, they had descended wrong side and were spending night at Loch Ericht. Kinloss MRT. 36.

FEBRUARY 20th – Roger Gemmell (46) slipped on a narrow snow band descending NW side of Sron na Creise, Black Mount. Unable to brake with axe he struck a boulder, sliding 45m on snow into scree causing serious head injury. Airlift RN Sea King. Glencoe and Lochaber MRTs. 34.

MARCH 10th – Sean Campbell (12) Fatal. Skiing Snow Goose Gully, Aonach Mor.

APRIL 3rd – Leiterchullin, Loch Duntelchaig, Inverness. Campbell got cragfast descending Stac na Cathaig. He was persuaded to climb up again, but lost his footing and fell 11m with serious spine, head and leg injuries. RAF Sea King, Police, Ambulance Service.

APRIL 12th – Solo and wearing crampons, Peter Bate (39) got lost in mist and snow between Aonach Beag and Aonach Mor and descended a snowfield into Coire Giubhsachan. He slipped and tumbled 200m into rocks, breaking a foot, with cuts and bruises. After less than two hours he was lucky to be found by another walker. Winched by RAF Sea King. Lochaber MRT. 20.

JUNE 22th – Catherine Laird (59) slipped descending NE Ridge, Mullach nan Coirean, Mamores. She was stretchered down with a broken ankle by Lochaber MRT. 27.

JUNE 27th – Pilot of an American F16 jet fighter reported a man waving frantically on Meall na Duibhe, 4km east of Kinlochleven. It was a false alarm as Police found nothing. Glencoe MRT standby. 2.

JULY 17th – Descending between Carn Mor Dearg and Aonach Mor, Adrienne Redhead (30) slipped and broke a tibia and fibula. Leuchars and Lochaber MRTs, RAF Sea King. 27.

AUGUST 8th – With her husband, a teacher was descending steep, wet grass on the NE Face of Beinn Bhan. Just above Ballachulish village she slipped and twisted her ankle, breaking it. She was vacuum splinted and stretchered down by Glencoe MRT. 13.

AUGUST 9th – Maria van Mergroot (51) was walking with a tour party from Glen Nevis to Corrour. She tripped on a stone near Tom an Eite and broke an ankle. Lochaber MRT stretcher carried her. 57.

OCTOBER 31st – Descending Ben Starav, Glen Etive, but low down (less than 150m) Patricia Clay (60) stumbled on the rocky path, breaking an ankle. Stretchered down by Glencoe MRT. 57.

NOVEMBER 28th – One of 17 walkers on Geal Charn, Drumochter, separated from the party despite group decision and attempts to call him back. Cairngorm MRT stood down when he walked out along shore of Loch Ericht.

NOVEMBER 28th – John Neave (57), an experienced hillwalker, was descending NNW Face of Creise, Black Mount, into Fionn Gleann with nine companions. Wearing crampons down névé interspersed with boulders, he slipped and fell 70m sustaining a severe head injury. He stood up, walked a few steps and fell again. This happened three times. Glencoe MRT paramedics tried to keep him alive to no avail. Resuscitation was also attempted in hospital after airlift by RAF Sea King. 82.

NOVEMBER 28th-29th – Alexander Gordon Gow (40). Probably gully (NNW facing) between Stob Coire Easain and Stob a' Choire Mheadhoin. Killed after slip or being blown over, or possibly walked through cornice. Found on iced scree/vegetation. Lochaber MRT. RAF Sea King. 124.

CAIRNGORMS

DECEMBER 26th, 1992 – Neil Culpan (28) and Andrew Brown (26) were overdue because of a broken crampon on the penultimate pitch of Polyphemus Gully, Lochnagar. Grampian Police MRT. 3.

JANUARY 10th, 1993 – Male skier with major head and back injuries airlifted from Lecht by RAF Wessex.

JANUARY 11th – Craigowl Hill, Sidlaws. Man who saw two people walking in poor weather and then found an empty tent alerted Tayside Police SRU. Tent had been abandoned by local youngsters because of bad weather. 24.

JANUARY 12th – Searches by Aberdeen, Braemar and Grampian Police MRTs for man thought to be lost in drifts. Taxi refused to take him to cottage because of drifts so he spent night in Inverbervie. 84.

JANUARY 23rd-24th – Three skiers got lost and benighted from Glenshee Ski Complex.

JANUARY 31st – Adrian Scott (24) fell 20m climbing The Vent, Coire an Lochain, Cairngorm, then fell 15m when colleagues lowered him (waist knot untied). Ankle injury, cuts and bruises. Cairngorm MRT happened to be in area and helped carry to winch point for RAF Wessex lift.

FEBRUARY 4th – Gregory Hall, mountain instructor (41) was instructing two others in winter climbing when he was struck on the head by a falling rock, receiving fatal injuries. Red Gully, Coire an-t'Sneachda, Cairngorm. Evacuated by RAF Sea King. 4.

FEBRUARY 5th – Kevin Brown (30) had been going to help another climber on Forty Thieves Gully, who had taken ill, when a cornice collapsed and he fell 180m. Serious arm, leg and facial injuries. Aladdin's Couloir, Coire an-t'Sneachda, Cairngorm.

FEBRUARY 6th – RAF Wessex lifted a skier from The Cairnwell, Glenshee with serious internal, pelvis and leg injuries. Male (25).

FEBRUARY 6th-7th – Grampian Police and Braemar MRTs were called out because Susanne Davies (37) was overdue walking between Loch Morlich and Braemar Youth Hostels. She was found at Derry Lodge, safe and well, just after midnight, having had to divert to avoid uncrossable meltwater burns in the Lairig Ghru. 4.

FEBRUARY 7th – Leading Coffin Corner at Craigie Barns, Dunkeld, Nicholas Dunne (32) was 18m up. He had one piece of protection which came out at a tricky stage. He fell when attempting to place another runner, landing on the path at the bottom, dislocating a shoulder and spraining an ankle. Tayside Police SRU and RAF Wessex.

FEBRUARY 9th – Burn o' Vat, Dinnet, Deeside. Frightened by the noise of rushing water at the Vat, an eight-month Border Collie bitch broke free of her lead and ran off. She was spotted on a ledge 5m down from the cliff edge. The teams were called out, and one member climbed down to the ledge. The dog became very aggressive and backed off towards the edge of the ledge. A few minutes later she had still not calmed down and suddenly leapt from the ledge 16m on to rocks below. She died from internal injuries 15 minutes before the vet arrived. Grampian Police and Braemar MRTs. 6.

FEBRUARY 11th or 12th – Woman (52) suicide. Crags of Kinnoull Hill, Perth. Recovered by Tayside Police SRU. 20.

FEBRUARY 14th – Anne Siobhan Shuker was practising ice-axe braking in Coire an-t'Sneachda. She lost control and twisted a leg which broke at an old injury. Evacuated by her own party of 17 Scout leaders using MR stretcher held at Coire Cas.

FEBRUARY 18th-21st – Dr Christopher Mayo (45), Michael Mayo (40), Matthew Mayo (15). Youth Hostel warden reported party of three, who had pre-paid accommodation, had failed to return on Thursday 18th. At 11.15 on Friday 19th, body of Dr Christopher Mayo (father 45) was found 75m from the foot of the Great Slab, Coire an Lochain. It was initially assumed he had fallen over the Coire rim. At 11.51 on Saturday 20th, body of Matthew Mayo (son 15) was found in a bivvy bag buried in snow, apart from the tip of one gloved hand, near the start of the route, Oesophagus, about 180m (height) above his father. This was the first firm evidence that the party had intended to climb Y Gully. At 10.58 on Sunday 21st, a 15cm square of red cagoule was spotted at 982033 and body of Michael Mayo (uncle 40) was uncovered. No route card was left. They started from Coire Cas at midday. The group was ascending Y Gully (Grade 2), without helmets, one axe each. Only one had crampons, the other two had bendy boots. They were unroped.

The following is a theory based on the evidence from John Allen:– It is thought the group intended to climb The Couloir (Grade 1) and went into Y Gully by mistake. The visibility was reasonable lower down and we are certain they did intend to be in Coire an Lochan. The mist level on the day of the incident was coming up and down over the crag tops. A climbing guide was found on the person of Christopher Mayo. We believe that somewhere just below the Grade 2 final pitch of the climb Michael fell.

He was injured but managed to carry on past the lochan where he died in the boulderfield. Christopher meanwhile dug a shelf in the gully. As he was wearing crampons he would be able to do this. He gave Michael his bivvy bag, left him in the little 'cave' and descended to try and find his brother. He then fell and was killed. Matthew, left uninjured in his high bivouac died later of hypothermia. Rescue groups involved were Aberdeen, Braemar/Grampian Police, Cairngorm, Glenmore Lodge, Kinloss, Leuchars, Mountain Guides of Ogwen Valley, RAF Wessex and Sea King helicopters, SARDA, Scottish Avalanche Project. Person hours: 2900 (figures of four groups only).

FEBRUARY 19th – Patricia Furneaux (54) was blown over on névé descending Braeriach East Ridge. Fell 30m cutting her head and breaking a wrist. She was with two men, one of whom attracted the attention of an RAF Wessex on the Mayo search. Kinloss MRT. 12.

FEBRUARY 23rd – In a party of nine, Ian Sanders (16) tripped over his crampons descending the Goat Track, Coire an-t'Sneachda. He slid 120m. Serious leg injury. RAF Sea King. 9.

FEBRUARY 28th – Male (35) suicide. Sea cliffs at Stonehaven. RAF Wessex. 8.

MARCH 11th – Three Grampian Police MRT were climbing Parallel Gully A (Grade III), Lochnagar. Two soloists climbed through them. One of the soloists, Anthony Cockram (40), got cragfast below a large cornice on the Grade IV/V direct exit of the climb. Top-roped out by the Grampian Police MRT. 5.

MARCH 13th – Party of four climbing Hell's Lum, Loch Avon. Dr Angus McInnes (47) consultant neurologist was hit on head by falling ice. No helmet. Resuscitation failed. Lowered to manual transfer point for RAF Sea King. Leuchars and Cairngorm MRTs. 110.

MARCH 14th – Bruin Cove, Aberdeen. Karen Darke (21) fell 8m with head and very serious back injuries, when rock climbing with four friends. HMCG, Aberdeen Lifeboat, Ambulance paramedics, Police, RAF Sea King.

MARCH 17th – Skier (20) fell on Carn an Tuirc, Glenshee, dislocating a hip. Airlifted by RAF Wessex.

MARCH 20th – Timothy Heales (37) had finished a rock climb with two friends at Logie Head, Cullen. He slipped descending to the foreshore at the east end of the promontory, falling more than15m, sustaining serious back, head and wrist injuries.

MARCH 21st – Playing at Bruin Cove, Aberdeen, Steven Milne (15) lay conscious in cold weather for two hours after a cliff fall, with fractured limbs. His cousin, Jamie (11), alerted rescuers. Airlift by RAF Wessex. HMCG.

APRIL 3rd-4th – Arnoud Ten Haaft (28) slipped on snow between Cairngorm and Ben Macdui, breaking an ankle. He managed to crawl into Tailors' Burn (Allt Clach nan Taillear) where he pitched a tent. At 17.30 next day he alerted three walkers in Lairig Ghru using a whistle. Winched out by RAF Sea King. Braemar/Grampian Police MRTs. 33.

APRIL 6th – James Sinclair (28) leader of a party of six Scouts aged between 10 and 15 further damaged an old ankle injury, which slowed down a walk from Auchallater to Glen Doll by Jock's Road. Found near Crow Craigies and airlifted by RAF Sea King. Kinloss, Leuchars and both Tayside teams. 407.

APRIL 11th – Elaine Onyiuke (45) slipped on the wet path descending Brown Cow Hill, Strathdon, breaking a leg. Carried to Land-Rover path. Grampian Police MRT. 1.

APRIL 12th-13th – Kenneth Webster (68), Michael Wilson (47), Andrew Wilson (20) and Matthew Wilson (15) got lost in mist and soft snow near Capel Mounth trying to find Loch Brandy, so they sheltered overnight. Found next day at Corrie of Bonhard making their way back to the road. Both Tayside teams and Leuchars. RAF Boulmer Rescue (131) unable to complete task due to weather. 685.

APRIL 14th-16th – John Raymond Ellis, botanist (36) found dead from hypothermia 300m south of cairn of Fiacaill a' Choire Chais, Cairngorm. Found on April 16th. He may have been studying alpine flora. It is unlikely he lay there long because it is a busy area. Recovery by Cairngorm and Glenmore Lodge MRTs transported by Chairlift Co. ATV to near Fiacaill cairn. 29.

APRIL 22th-23rd – Angus Aagaard (29) and Michael Holdsworth (27) suffered gastric infection and viral flu at Corrour Bothy. They walked out to Bob Scott's Bothy helped by other walkers. Grampian Police MRT. 2.

MAY 1st – Alastair Wilkinson (41) fell off his bike descending track from Loch Callater, fracturing ribs. Grampian Police/Braemar MRTs. 4.

JUNE 5th-6th – Returning from a rock-climbing camp on Beinn a' Bhuird with a companion, John Hare (36) slipped descending to a path, breaking an ankle. Hobbling to path took three hours so they camped and companion went for help on 6th. Rescue from Glen Quoich by Grampian Police/Braemar MRTs and RAF Sea King. 11.

JUNE 6th – Party of three deliberately split on plateau leaving a woman (50) as she was tired and did not want to go to Ben Macdui summit. She was later found safe in Larig Ghru by RAF Sea King. Cairngorm MRT. 12. Rule broken: Do not split party leaving weakest alone.

JULY 1st – Male (23) lifted by RAF Sea King after an epileptic fit at Loch Etchachan. 12

JULY 4th – Walking from Linn of Dee to Corrour by White Bridge, Lynn Porter (36) twisted her knee. Grampian Police MRT, RAF Sea King. 7.

JULY 10th – David Hollands (17) and Andrew Bunning (14) went for a 3km walk in Glen Tanar. They got lost in the forest and walked to Feughside Inn. A straight-line distance of 16km from their target. Grampian Police MRT. 4.

JULY 14th-25th – James Walker (84) a keen hillwalker, but latterly with a short memory span, was last seen in grounds of Mealmore Nursing Home, Daviot, on 14th. Found dead during a sweep search by 75 people on 25th. Assynt, Cairngorm, Dundonnell, Kinloss, Kintail, Leuchars, Torridon MRTs, Police, RAF Sea King, SARDA. 1000-2000.

JULY 24th-25th – Steven Best (18) crossed Ben Macdui then entered an area not covered by his map. Trying to get from Fords of Avon to Derry Lodge he walked via Faindouran Lodge, over high ground to Gairnshiel Lodge, to Crathie. Search by Grampian Police MRT. 18.

JULY 27th – Climbing Clean Sweep at Hell's Lum Crag, Loch Avon, Simon Goring (26) slipped. A runner failed so he fell 8m, with arm and chest injuries. Airlift by RAF Sea King. 10.

AUGUST 1st – Woman (42) developed severe migraine SE of Carn a' Mhaim summit. Picked up by Police near Derry Lodge. 2.

AUGUST 6th-7th – Party of three on Angels Peak split in thick mist. Two crossed Great Moss to Glen Feshie and phoned Police. James Galbraith (19) reached Ruigh Aiteachain Bothy and stayed overnight till noon before going to find a phone. Found safe at 12.30. Aberdeen, Cairngorm and Kinloss MRTs, SARDA, RAF Sea King. 60.

AUGUST 15th – Gary Smith (25) leapt 28m from a cliff arch into the sea at Bullers of Buchan. Chest and neck injuries. HMCG and Peterhead Lifeboat.

AUGUST 29th – Walkers on Craig Coillich Hill, Ballater found four empty drug containers and a man (26) ill and crawling. Grampian Police/Braemar MRTs and dog handler found him in a tent and took him to hospital. 70.

SEPTEMBER 3rd – With her husband, Alison Garfield (63) had walked Lairig Ghru from Rothiemurchus. She tripped over a boulder five miles north of Derry Lodge, bruising an arthritic hip. Managing to get to Derry Lodge she was rescued by Grampian Police MRT. 2.

SEPTEMBER 4th – Searches in Angus, including search by RAF Sea King, for man (70). He was found dead in a field.

SEPTEMBER 12th-13th – Wearing sandals and instructing eight students in river-crossing technique at the head of Loch Avon, an instructor (26) dislocated her toes. Next day, unable to get boots on due to swelling, she was airlifted by RAF Sea King. 12.

SEPTEMBER 19th – Successful rescue of four cragfast sheep, near waterfall in Coire Kander, Glen Callater by lowering team member on to ledge. Grampian Police/Braemar MRTs. 8.

SEPTEMBER 24th – Roy Henderson (26) stumbled and sprained an ankle at Loch Etchachan. Used mobile phone. RAF Sea King. 12.

OCTOBER 3rd – Two sheep cragfast in main Coire Kander. On arrival of Braemar MRT one had fallen to its death. Second sheep removed from ledge by lowering team member on to ledge, but sheep lost its footing on ascent and also fell to death. 6.

OCTOBER 16th – Euan Ferguson (15) fell off his bike on Culardoch track 4km north of Invercauld House, Braemar. Other Scouts alerted Police and Ambulance Service who rescued him. Treated for bruises and scalp cut stitched. 8.

OCTOBER 18th-19th – Cairngorm MRT searching for overdue Terence Magee (45) heard an aid cry from above them at 01.00. After a hillwalk, Terence had bummed a ride down on Cairngorm chairlift. It was soon stopped by technicians as they were only testing it. He was trapped for 10 cold hours. Unfortunately, he had thrown down his rucksack, containing gear and waterproofs, to check the height involved. Rescued by special ladder. 117.

OCTOBER 21st-22nd – Night searches by Cairngorm MRT and SARDA. Henry Begg (23) did well to survive. Wearing tourist clothes and boots he had reached Cairngorm summit in snow by walking from the top station. Lost in mist he followed Coire Raibert down to Loch Avon. Following the north shore of the loch to its head, he crossed Feith Buidhe, down the south shore, missing Fords of Avon Bothy, and crossed River Avon to get to Faindouran Lodge where he was succoured by three climbers. Evacuated by Land-Rover from Tomintoul. 189.

NOVEMBER 27th – False alarm. Search in vain by Cairngorm MRT and RAF Sea King of Hells Lum Crag, Loch Avon. Six torch flashes, repeated three or four times had been reported as seen coming from the route, Escalator.

DECEMBER 4th – Practising ice-axe braking on NW slopes of Carn an Tuirc, Gunnar Olason (28) got a foot caught under névé and broke an ankle. A companion stayed with him. Both lifted by RN Sea King. Grampian Police/Braemar MRTs. 34.

DECEMBER 11th-12th – Timothy Larradd (33) and Leslie Beaumont (30), on skis, split from pair of walkers near Cairngorm summit, got lost in poor visibility, but reached Shelter Stone and spent the night there. It may be that they had intended to ski to Shelter Stone. They were found wading through deep snow in Coire Domhain next morning. Cairngorm MRT, RAF Sea King. Aberdeen MRT on standby. 48.

DECEMBER 12th – Two of a party of six separated and were reported missing on Ben Macdui by the others. Found by Aberdeen MRT wandering down in darkness. Road lift to Linn of Dee. Conditions very poor, drifting snow. 4.

DECEMBER 12th-13th – After completing Mess of Pottage, Coire an-t'Sneachda, Cairngorm, Jane Thomas (33) and companion went too far south on the plateau in desperate weather. He went for help, but she died of hypothermia. At 12.15 on 13th Jane's body found by SARDA dog in Coire Cas 300m from the tow. At 12.16 on 13th companion's knife and compass were found on the south side of Cairngorm at 005035. Cairngorm, Kinloss, Leuchars MRTs, SARDA, RAF Sea King. 900.

DECEMBER 19th – William Sutherland (30), descending from Lochnagar to Glen Muick, was blown over at Meikle Pap col and injured a leg. Rescued by Grampian Police/Braemar MRTs with some help from a tracked vehicle. RAF Sea King unable to help due to severe weather. 80.

SOUTHERN HIGHLANDS

JANUARY 23rd – Descent of NE Ridge of Cruach Ardrain. James McAlpine (35) and Scott Williamson (24), unroped, both slipped on hard snow and ice, falling 120m, both were injured. Williamson's eye was struck by ice-axe adze causing cuts and bruises above and below the eye. Despite other injuries they got down to Crianlarich Police with the help of a companion.

JANUARY 30th – Clive Mitchener (39) slipped descending névé on the NW Ridge, Ben Challum with two others. Resuscitation was attempted for a long time, but failed. Killin and Leuchars MRTs. RAF Sea King. 135.

JANUARY 30th – Simon West (40) slipped descending névé on SW Ridge, Ben Lui and broke his leg. Leuchars, Killin and Strathclyde MRTs stretchered casualty below cloud for airlift by RAF Sea King. 155.

JANUARY 31st – Party of six on Beinn Tulaichean without crampons. Elaine Seawright (37) fell 30m on icy névé slope then another 15m over buttress. Arm injury, cuts and bruises. Other five helped down by Killin MRT. RN Sea King, Leuchars MRT. 60.

FEBRUARY 1st – James Heggie (49), Malcolm Ronaldson (47) both killed on West Ridge of Ben Lui. Descending with another they entered steep crags due to a navigation error. Two slipped 65m down hard ice/névé with fatal head injuries. Killin, Strathclyde and Tayside Police MRTs, RAF Wessex. 333.

FEBRUARY 1st – Ardvorlich. Andrew Stacey (75) caused concern after he separated from his party and was overdue. Walked out to Glen Artney and contacted police. Tayside Police SRU, Central Scotland Police, RAF Wessex.

FEBRUARY 6th – German student slipped on ice, Beinn Achaladair. Leg injuries.

FEBRUARY 14th – In a party of five descending wet rock and grass on NE side Ben Oss, Neil Cocker (53) slipped and slid 50m with head, neck, chest and ankle injuries. Stretchered out by Killin MRT as helicopter was unavailable due to adverse weather. 124.

FEBRUARY 15th – Party of three on Beinn Achaladair. Ian Rose-Smith (43) died and David Stevenson (52) was injured from falls while descending.

FEBRUARY 28th – German male walker on West Highland Way slipped with muscular injury to leg. Lomond MRT searched from Inversnaid and Inverarnan. Found and evacuated by Luss Rescue Boat. 73.

FEBRUARY 28th – Further to the above incident, one man and two children, overdue going south from Inversnaid to Inverarnan were found and evacuated by Luss Rescue Boat. Lomond MRT.

MARCH 1st – Joan Taylor (66) with her husband, Harry (70), had crossed Beinn a' Chreachain and Meall Buidhe. Going to Beinn Achaladair, Joan slipped and injured an eye socket falling on to her ice-axe. Oban and Dumbarton MRTs found them walking down slowly .

MARCH 6th – Oban and Dumbarton MRTs on standby for two men (aged 31 and 32) who turned up safe from being overdue on Beinn Achaladair.

MARCH 23rd – Leuchars team called to assist Arrochar, Dumbarton Police and SARDA in a search for a missing German walker in the Arrochar area, but he turned up safe. 54.

MARCH 26th-28th – Vain searches by Arrochar, Leuchars, Kinloss and Oban Police MRTs, RN Sea King, SARDA and HMCG for Andrew Campbell (43) missing from a camp 4km SW of Portsonachan, Loch Awe. He had gone for a walk and disappeared. Found on June 12th. Post mortem stated he had been drowned. 574.

APRIL 4th – Christine Davidson (48) descending Ben Ledi tourist path slipped on wet grass and broke an ankle. Killin MRT stretcher carry. 27.

APRIL 10th – Sarah Crompton (44) slipped descending Ben A'an path and fractured radius and ulna. Killin MRT helped Ambulance Service. 20.

APRIL 10th – Betty Brazier (52) slipped on grass on The Law, Ochil Hills, injuring a leg. Police and Ambulance. 2.

APRIL 11th-12th – Samuel McClements (53) slipped descending steep snow and rock face on north side Stuc a' Chroin with a companion. Fatal. Disappeared in mist. Killin MRT had no success searching in 5m visibility. Found by SARDA. Lomond MRT called in. 176.

APRIL 15th – Paul Inns (16) was killed mountain biking on a steep hill track north of Loch Katrine.

APRIL 18th – Lomond MRT and SARDA alerted from exercise for Ian Trotter (56) overdue from a forest walk around visitor centre. He had got lost and turned up in Aberfoyle village. 12.

APRIL 21st – Janet Menzies (55) collapsed with a viral infection descending King's Seat Hill, Ochil Hills. Police and Ambulance. 2.

MAY 1st – One of 147 competitors in Stuc a' Chroin Hill Race, Ronald McIntosh (43) became ill and collapsed on Ben Each ridge. Treated with glucose and airlifted to Stirling. Killin MRT, RN Sea King. 20.

MAY 3rd – Climbing Coriander on Ben A'an, Andrew Faulk (27) fell. Piton failed to hold fall. Fell 3m with serious back injury. Airlift by RN Sea King. Killin MRT. 8.

MAY 21st – Graeme Brady (28) recovering sheep was swept away in River Dochart, Killin. Fatal.

MAY 16th – False alarm. Walker on summit of Ben Lomond heard cries for help in cloud and strong wind. Searches in bad conditions by two RAF Sea Kings, Lomond MRT and SARDA. 190.

MAY 21st – Frederick Flecken (34) weight 18st (114kg) slipped on dry rock descending Conic Hill, Balmaha, fracturing ankle bones. Stretchered by Lomond MRT, Police and Ambulance Service. 32.

MAY 21st-22nd – Very poorly equipped, Rober Chumley (50) went on after his wife turned back, in an attempt to walk up Schiehallion. Spotted by Tayside Police SRU next morning making his way down. Night and first light searches failed. RN Sea King, Leuchars and Tayside MRTs. 163.

JUNE 5th – Rita Bachli (51) slipped 100m from summit of Ben Venue descending a steep path, spraining an ankle. Killin MRT, RN Sea King. 26.

JUNE 27th – Mrs van Daalen (54) sustained leg injuries, hillwalking at Gallanach, 4km SW of Oban. To Western Infirmary, Glasgow.

JUNE 28th – A Lomond MRT and SARDA assembly was sparked by a separation. A man with no navigation aids or equipment separated from his friend on Beinn Uird, Rowardennan, Loch Lomond. He got down himself.

JULY 12th – Illness cause a male to collapse on Ben Lomond path. Evacuated by RN Sea King to hospital. Lomond MRT.

JULY 12th – Lomond MRT made an exhaustive search of Devil's Pulpit, Finnich Glen, for a dog reported to have fallen into the gorge. Nothing found.

JULY 12th – Losing his way down Ben Venue, James Campbell (44) got cragfast. A fisherman went for help. Killin MRT were taken by boat on Loch Katrine to rescue him. 27.

JULY 19th – Donald Reid (26) separated from his friend when climbing the north side of Stob a' Choin, Inverlochlarig, Balquhidder. He was found dead in a steep, craggy gully 500m NE of the summit. Killin and Leuchars MRTs. RAF Sea King. 219.

JULY 31st – One of a party of 13 ascending Ben Ledi, Edward McDonald (49) slipped and broke his ankle when 200m from summit. Sea King from HMS Gannet lifted him to ambulance. Killin MRT. 15.

AUGUST 15th – Meall nan Tarmachan. Anke Klatte (21) was in a party of five trying to descend a precarious path down Allt na Ceardaich after they had lost their way in woods. She slipped and fell 25m into gorse sustaining a serious liver injury and a head wound. Winched 40m through gorse and trees by RN Sea King. Killin MRT. 30.

AUGUST 20th – Landslip on Balnaguard Burn, near Ballinluig. The burn had eroded a landslip of clay and loose rock 36m high. Two girls tried to climb it and got cragfast at 24m where it was vertical. Marek Olersowicz (43) managed to reach the girls in failing light and got one to safety. He climbed back up to Marta Kaszubska(13), but by then it was dark, and having no torch, he also got cragfast. Tayside Police SRU escorted them safely down using a fixed rope and a harness. 16.

SEPTEMBER 8th – Search by Ochils and Leuchars MRTs, SARDA, Police and RAF helicopter for woman (21) in hill forest north of Dollar. She had left a suicide note. She was found by the aircraft having taken tablets and alcohol and attempted to injure her wrists. 138.

SEPTEMBER 18th – In a party of 14 and descending grass from the summit of Beinn Chabhair, Anthony Hamilton (13) stumbled and fell 12m, breaking a femur. Wearing summer boots. Killin MRT, HMS Gannet helicopter. 47.

SEPTEMBER 22nd – Bracklinn Falls, Keltie Water, Callander. Taking part in a cableway exercise, Stephen Learmouth (36) unclipped from rope while standing on a rock ledge. He stepped back falling into a 6m gorge, breaking his nose and sustaining concussion. Treated with a neck splint and oxygen he was evacuated by back-roped stretcher. Killin MRT. 14.

SEPTEMBER 22nd – Agnes Smith (53) broke a leg when walking down Schiehallion with a companion. She fell just 1m on path. Airlift by RAF Sea King. 8.

SEPTEMBER 26th – Descending steep grass NE of Beinn Tulaichean in a party of four, Susan Isherwood (46) slipped and sustained a lower leg fracture. Stretchered out by Killin and Leuchars MRTs. 20.

OCTOBER 3rd-4th – Doreen Paton (29) and Stephen Dillon (25) separated from two others at Meall Dhamh, going on to climb Cruach Ardrain in mist with no navigation aids. They walked all night through the wrong glens, reaching Loch Katrine. Leuchars, Killin, Ochils MRTs, SARDA, RN Sea King. 516.

OCTOBER 3rd – A girl of 18, with Down's Syndrome, became distressed when benighted without a torch on Ben Ledi. From a group of 13 she had turned back with two co-workers before they reached the summit. The three were found on a path in the wet forest by Killin MRT and helped down. 42.

OCTOBER 6th – On a school project, walking above Kendrum Burn, Lochearnhead, Ina Westwood (57) slipped on wet grass and injured her ankle. Granddaughter went for help. Stretcher carried by Killin MRT. 8.

OCTOBER 12th – Search of Mill Glen, Tillicoultry for Neil Osborne (15). Ochils MRT, SARDA. 32.

OCTOBER 16th – Killin MRT found Catriona Lorans (23) walking back to Inverararnan in darkness, after she had separated from her two companions on West Highland Way and walked past the destination. Lomond MRT called out. 12.

OCTOBER 24th – Walking with a club party on Meall Ghaordie, a man (34) took an epileptic fit. Airlift by RN Sea King. Killin MRT. 22.

OCTOBER 24th – Climbing near the summit of Ben Lui with two companions, Richard Davey (21) took hold of a large rock to pull himself up. He dislodged the rock and fell 3m with the rock landing on top of him. Airlift by RN Sea King to hospital where he had subluxation of cervical 5/6 vertebrae, fractured transverse process of lumbar 3/4 vertebra and cut leg. Killin MRT. 64.

OCTOBER 24th – Luis Vidal (34) and Caroline Vidal (33) were overdue walking through Glen Quey from Dollar to Glendevon. Ochils MRT. 5.

NOVEMBER 20th-21st – In snowy weather David Stell (30) and Caroline Brown (24) became separated descending Schiehallion to Braes of Foss car park (NE side of mountain). David had the map, compass and torch, so Caroline was left without. Man descended to car park, found woman had not returned, so went back up to search for her. When it got dark, he got lost and descended to Glen Goulandie (SE side). Search continued for female who was found (on S side) cold, wet and weak. Tayside Police SRU, Leuchars and Tayside MRTs, RAF Boulmer Sea King. 238.

NOVEMBER 27th-28th – Without ice-axe and crampons, Duncan McEwan (56) attempted Ben Lawers Horseshoe, but decided to descend from bealach NW of Lochan na Cat when he saw mist closing in and snow starting. On steep, snow-covered, grass with rocks protruding he slipped, fell 45m and was very seriously injured. He was lucky that he was found by two climbers only 10 minutes later. He told them he had broken both arms and they went for help. As well as two broken wrists, he had compression spinal fracture, four broken ribs, fracture of knee, and thigh damage. Stretcher lowered to west end of Lochan na Cat. Tayside Police SRU, Leuchars and Tayside MRTs. RAF Sea King attended, but could not be used because of mist. 348.

NOVEMBER 27th – Lomond MRT called out for R. Ralston overdue in Queen Elizabeth Forest, Aberfoyle. He turned up safe. 5.

NOVEMBER 27th – Lomond MRT called out for lights seen on south shore of Loch Katrine. Boat investigating found two students (male and female) safe but overdue from three-day expedition. 5.

DECEMBER 5th – Ian MacGregor (63) ascending steep footpath (Stank Glen route to Ben Ledi) tripped over tree root on muddy section, fracturing a leg. Stretchered to ambulance by Killin MRT. 9.

DECEMBER 12th – In a party of 24, in easterly gales and heavy snow, Catherine Wright (59) slipped descending Dumbreck, Campsie Fells. Stretchered down with leg injuries by Central Scotland Police and Scottish Ambulance Service. 3.

SKYE

MARCH 23rd-24th – Six male and two female students (20s) climbed Sgurr nan Gillean by the Tourist Route. They had intended a traverse and descent of the West Ridge, but they belayed back down the Tourist Route. They then bivouacked. Snow and sleet were forecast. Found and winched off by RAF Sea King using night vision goggles at 02.30. Kinloss and Skye MRTs. 400.

APRIL 12th – In a party of six descending Sgurr na Stri, Yai Hui Lak (20) stumbled and fell 50m then stopped by a member of his party ahead, sustaining serious head and pelvic injuries. Winched by HMCG helicopter. 10.

APRIL 20th – Braes Peninsula, near Loch Sligachan. Woman walker (70s) airlifted by HMCG helicopter after breaking her leg in a fall.

APRIL 21th-22nd – Although he managed to hobble to Coruisk Hut after a slip on a rock slab on Sgurr Coir an Lochain, Gwyn Davies (45) was winched by RN Sea King next day, with a fractured ankle. Skye MRT. 22.

MAY 25th – Thearlaich Dubh Gap. Robert Healey (40) slipped and fell 10m. Serious spine, pelvic and chest injuries. Stretchered by Skye MRT to winch point by RAF Sea King. 14.

MAY 29th – Bealach Mor (between B. Dearg and the Storr). Aisling Morris (29) climbed three-quarters of a scree slope and got cragfast. Helped down by Skye MRT. 8.

JUNE 8th – Descending to Lochan Coire a' Ghrunnda near Caisteal a' Garbh Choire, with a companion, Philip Ramsbottom (44) was struck by a rock which fell and knocked him down 10m. RAF Sea King flew him to hospital on June 9th. Broken knee cap and 17 stitches for scalp cut. Skye MRT. 125.

JULY 4th – Bristow helicopter winched Timothy Noble (21) who was in a party of six from Coire a' Ghrunnda suffering facial cuts from a slip on a muddy path. Skye MRT. 16.

JULY 4th – Peter Sykes (47) suffered a heart attack in Coire a' Ghrunnda and was airlifted by RAF Sea King. Suffered mild hypothermia due to wet ground and anti-coagulant medication for a previous heart attack. Kinloss and Skye MRTs. 47.

JULY 9th – Winched at about 200m from Coire Riabhach, Sgurr nan Gillean by Bristow helicopter, William Shields (64) injured his leg by a slip on the path, accompanied by his wife. Skye MRT. 13.

JULY 14th – Calls of shepherds gathering sheep on Cleat Hill, Staffin, were mistaken for cries for help. Skye MRT and Police alerted. 9.

JULY 19th – Michelle Maunder (29) slipped in Coire Lagan when in a party of four walkers. She fell 5m, coming to rest on her back with arm injured underneath her. Winched from the head of Sgumain Stone Shoot by Bristow helicopter. Skye MRT and Police. 13.

AUGUST 10th-11th – Sron na Ciche. Thinking that they were on Cioch Buttress, and adapting a guidebook description of a (VD) to fit the route they were actually climbing, three men and one woman, got cragfast and benighted about 140m up Median Route, Western Buttress. During the afternoon of the 11th there were shouts for help. They abseiled one pitch and were then helped down by a passing climber and the brother of the woman. Skye MRT. HMCG helicopter. 10.

SEPTEMBER 8th – Bealach na Leacaich, Craig a' Lain, Trotternish. German couple, Linda Bohlen (25) and Stefan Mohr (24) were hillwalking. It is thought Linda fell up to 100m down a narrow gully, and Stefan died trying to save her. Information received on October 20th led to a search by Skye MRT and RAF Sea King on October 21st which found them in 20 minutes. The bodies were about 15m apart. Stretchered, winched and airlifted. 22.

SEPTEMBER 10th – Two members of Leuchars MRT climbing on Sron na Ciche observed a rockfall strike David Cowell (25) on Cioch Grooves. He was lowered 20m to ground by other climbers. Walked down with arm in sling and was then taken to hospital by MRT suffering chest injuries. 5.

SEPTEMBER 15th-16th – Descending Coire a' Ghreadaidh with a companion, from somewhere near Sgurr Thormaid (they were not sure of their position on the Main Ridge) H. Michael Curry slipped on wet rock falling more than 100m. His companion found him and attempted to provide shelter before going for help, but he died of chest and pelvic injuries before being found by RAF Sea King next morning, with Skye MRT on board. 208.

SEPTEMBER 22nd – David Smith (20), Colin Evans (19) and Paul Marsland (19) got cragfast and benighted on Sgurr Alasdair due to poor navigation. Winched off at night by RAF Sea King. Skye MRT and Police. 39

SEPTEMBER 22nd – Oban CG and Portree Lifeboat searched Black Rock, Portree for a girl (15). Found safe at 21.00.

SEPTEMBER 25th – 60m below the summit of Sgurr nan Gillean on the Tourist Route, Steven Skelton (37) was fatally injured by a fall of 45m when rocks gave way beneath his feet. Party of nine. Skye MRT and RAF Sea King. 43.

OCTOBER 14th – Michael Williams (24) and Angus Matheson (22) on coast walk, trapped by tide on beach below The Old Gun Point, Duntulm. Found by HMCG helicopter which could not lift them because of poor weather, so they were rescued by Auxiliary Coastguard.

OCTOBER 28th – Skye MRT called out for a crofter, Donald Graham (21), cragfast attempting to rescue a sheepdog from the Old Man of Storr. He got down safely before the team arrived. 17.

OCTOBER 28th – Skye MRT carried out a night recovery of the cragfast sheepdog (above incident). Bill Logan of Skye MRT received minor head cut. 17.

NOVEMBER 20th – Eastern Gully, Sron na Ciche. Scrambling up a small rock face, Aaron Schuer (20) gripped a loose hold and fell 5m landing on rocks, causing facial cuts and limb bruising. Winched by RAF Sea King. Skye MRT. 53.

ISLANDS
(Other than Skye)

MARCH 4th – Two nurses (30s) got lost in mist on south end of Iona. When mist cleared they got back in darkness. HMCG.

MARCH 16th-17th – Trying to get to Carsaig from Lochbuie, Mull, William Docherty (51) spent a cold night wandering lost in low cloud on hills north-west of Loch Buie. Kinloss MRT, Oban Coastguard and Lifeboat. 648.

APRIL 12th – Woman (27) got separated from a friend in mist in Coire nan Larach, Mullach Buidhe (above Corrie village), Arran. Arran MRT. 13.

APRIL 12th – Kinloss MRT treated a male walker suffering from exhaustion and dehydration at The Saddle, Glen Rosa, Arran. 8.

MAY 8th – A'Chir, Arran. Mark McGuigan (21) slipped on scree and badly sprained an ankle. Arran MRT. 12.

MAY 13th – Search for man (29) who had wandered off on Isle of Coll. Police helicopter and air-sea rescue helicopter.

JUNE 1st – Gleann Easain Biorach, Loch na Davie, Arran. In a party of 20, Christopher Holmes (12) suffered a groin strain from a slip and was evacuated by RN Sea King. David Clegg (11) had neckstrain and fatigue but walked down the hill. Arran MRT. 28.

JUNE 9th-10th – Karl Kay (37). Fatal 20m fall. Night stroll on path around Tobermory Harbour, Mull. Fell over cliffs in dark.

JULY 9th – Two walkers turned up safe from Isle of Vallay, North Uist. Full scale alert when they were overdue.

JULY 26th-27th – Jane Liston (37) left her car on Ross Road to walk to Loch Urie, near Lamlash, Arran. She was benighted in mist and rain. Found by Police before Arran MRT and SARDA searched. 8.

JULY 27th – Woman suffered ankle injury from fall on Isle of Scalpay, near Harris, when walking with her husband. HMCG helicopter.

AUGUST 1st – Hillwalking at Kame of Hoy, Orkney, Armin Gojan (34) fell. Minor leg injuries. HMCG.

AUGUST 15th – Walking in a party of three on Ben Mhor, South Uist. T. Minelly (15) slipped on rock, suffering cuts and chest injuries. The accident was on the north side of the east ridge above Glen Hellisdale. Winched off by Bristow helicopter. 7.

AUGUST 17th – David Barclay (37) and boy (16) fishing a hill lochan, descended the wrong side of Cruach Scarba (conical peak which forms the Isle of Scarba). Benighted, but well clad they spent the night in a cave and were able to cook some fish. Found and rescued by Oban Lifeboat. RN Sea King ferried HMCG searchers.

SOUTHERN UPLANDS

JANUARY 17th – Andrew Lithgow (58) suffered chest pains and cold trauma on Lowther Hill, Wanlockhead. Stretchered by Moffat MRT down to Enterkin Burn, then airlifted by RN Sea King of 819 Sqdn. flying through mountains at night in heavy snow showers, guided by Police car from Carronbridge.

JANUARY 31st – Search by Galloway MRT of wooded area near New Galloway for a forestry worker (40) who had committed suicide. 32.

MARCH 10th – D.E. Hastings (69) rescued by Drummore Auxiliary Cliff Team, HMCG. He suffered leg and arm injuries from a fall. RN Sea King. 14.

MARCH 17th – Thomas MacKay (21) was killed by a 45m fall from a cliff at Pease Bay, Cockburnspath, Berwickshire, when climbing with a friend. He was only 3m from top of cliff when he fell.

APRIL 11th – Tweed Valley MRT called out to search for a missing female walker at Pow Burn, Northumberland. She turned up safe.

APRIL 11th-12th – Michael Henderson (19) and Paul Henderson (16) were benighted and spent night out near Hopes Water, Lammermuirs and Tweed Valley MRTs. 115.

APRIL 14th – Victor Pitcher overdue on Cairnsmore of Fleet. Galloway MRT. 115.

MAY 10th – Margaret Liddle (84). Fatal. Slipped and fell into River Tweed. It may have been the result of a heart attack. Tweed Valley MRT and SARDA. 54.

MAY 15th – Five schoolgirls on award hike overdue in Yair Forest, Selkirk. Found safe by forest ranger. Tweed Valley MRT. 12.

JUNE 3rd – Simon Vallantyne (38) overdue crossing Rhinns of Kells to Loch Trool. Turned up safe. Galloway and Moffat teams alerted.

JUNE 22nd – German tourists, male (65) and female (35) separated from a guided group on the Southern Uplands Way 4km south of Innerleithen. Police suspected heart attack, but found them safe. Tweed Valley MRT and SARDA. 20.

JULY 20th – Southern Uplands Way. Path on Hare Law, NW of Broadmeadows Youth Hostel. Paul Wiggan (16) slipped when on an award hike, breaking a leg and sustaining mild hypothermia. Tweed Valley MRT, SARDA. 30.

JULY 27th-28th – Two parties of German Scouts left Loch Doon for Loch Dee, Galloway Hills. Four exhausted lads were left at Dry Loch, near Dungeon Hill while two went for help, but only one messenger arrived. Galloway MRT were called out and SARDA dog found exhausted boys 2km north of where they had been left, one 10-year-old very cold. The other party of nine Scouts was found on road to Forrest Lodge. 120.

AUGUST 6th-7th – Alastair Ratcliffe (18) not equipped for a bivouac, was found by Tweed Valley MRT on a damp, misty night on the Southern Upland Way west of Galashiels. 86.

AUGUST 20th-SEPTEMBER 4th – Searches of forest by Tweed Valley MRT, Lothian and Borders Police and SARDA for a hospital patient found with his wrists slashed in suicide attempts. 55.

SEPTEMBER 17th – Mario Namburg (20), wearing shoes, broke his leg when scrambling down a very steep, wet slope of forest, rock and scree, exploring Scott's View, River Tweed after dark. Also wearing shoes, Holger Bartschat (21) went down to help his companion. He fell 60m farther and was more seriously injured (skull, spine, leg and fractured arm with hypothermia and blood loss). Tweed Valley MRT, Border SARU, Police, Fire, Ambulance, RAF helicopter. 280.

SEPTEMBER 24th – Search by Tweed Valley MRT and RAF helicopter for patient suffering depression near Penicuik. Found with hypothermia by Police. 15.

SEPTEMBER 27th – Paraglider, Eiki Mittelbach (31) found conditions unsuitable at Loch Skeen, so headed back to Moffat on foot. Caught out by darkness he waited for moonrise, but wife reported him missing. Found by Moffat HRT on route search. 21.

OCTOBER 8th-14th – Large scale searches by Borders SAR, Tweed Valley MRT, SARDA, and RAF helicopters for Bill Thomson (78) walking at Galashiels. Suffering Parkinson's Disease, he had slipped on a path in wet forest and fallen into the River Tweed leaving a shoe in river at assumed point of entry. His body was found on the 14th, 25 miles downstream with severe fractures. 967.

OCTOBER 28th – Tail Burn below Loch Skeen. Barbara Johnson (63) slipped on scree breaking her ankle. Found by Moffat HRT. Winched by RN Sea King. Air Ambulance attended.

NOVEMBER 1st – Tweed Valley MRT called out to search for a missing man later found dead by Police. Kelso area. 3.

NOVEMBER 17th-19th – Moffat HRT sweep-searched Stell Knowe, a wooded hill in Eskdalemuir Forest and found a woman (30) who had hanged herself. A suicide note had been left in an abandoned car. 38.

NOVEMBER 20th – Anne Crozier (30). Fatal. Hills in area of Eskdalemuir. Moffat HRT.

NOVEMBER 20th – Geology student (20) fell on rocks at Cove Bay, Cockburnspath. He was stretchered out with ruptured knee ligaments. RAF Boulmer Sea King, HMCG, St. Abbs Lifeboat, Ambulance Service.

DECEMBER 12th – Hart Fell, Moffat. John McCulloch (60) in a party of 17 died of a heart attack in a white-out. Trained first aiders were unable to revive him. Body was left on hill for safety reasons and stretchered out next day by Moffat HRT. Bivvy bag in tatters with the wind. 175.

DECEMBER 19th – Tweed Valley MRT called out to find 14-year-old boy who was later found dead by Police in Penicuik area. 8.

NON-MOUNTAINEERING

JANUARY 11th-13th – Leuchars MRT, Tayside MRT and RAF Wessex assisted many people, stranded in cars by blizzards in Fife, Angus and Tayside. Assistance continued for three days with aid to elderly folk trapped at home. Maternity case airlifted to hospital. Food flown to snowbound babies. 650.

JANUARY 13th – Leuchars MRT (with Stafford and Leeming) searched for missing Banderante light aircraft. Recalled when crash found near Sellafield. 165.

JANUARY 17th – Leuchars and Tayside MRTs and RAF Wessex rescued householders during floods (from Perth to Pitlochry). Helicopter rescued 24 people. Teams assisted farmers rescuing sheep. 160.

MARCH 18th – FFA AS Bravo crashed 10km south of Ayr. RAF Sea King directed services.

APRIL 18th – Visiting roadside Achray viewpoint, Aberfoyle, Florence Dischler (14) slipped on wet grass, dislocating knee cap (recurrent injury). Lomond MRT on exercise alerted ambulance and police. 9.

MAY 18th – Well-intentioned false alarm that a Hercules aircraft had crashed in Ballater area. Leuchars MRT.

MAY 27th-29th – RAF Hercules aircraft crashed at Glen Loch, Blair Athol. RN and RAF Sea Kings, Leuchars, Kinloss and Tayside Police MRTs and local Fire Service, carried out recovery, crash guard, and photography duties, and prior-impact searches. There were no survivors from crew of nine. 1500.

JULY 17th-18th – Leffnoll Point, Loch Ryan, Stranraer. Galloway MRT searched for a murder weapon and discarded clothing at Police request. From a family of four camped on July 9th father had been killed, mother and two children badly wounded. 77.

AUGUST 27th – Fallen cyclist (21) at David Marshall Lodge, Aberfoyle. Lomond MRT rendered first aid. 3.

SEPTEMBER 15th – R177 helicopter found crashed Piper Warwick light aircraft with dead pilot near Sanquhar. Leuchars MRT carried out crash guard and casualty evacuation. 498.

SEPTEMBER 16th-17th – Daylight and darkness searches in the Newton Stewart area for missing man (56) later found in South England. Galloway MRT. Police dog, RNLI boat, RAF Sea King, HMCG. 136.

OCTOBER 12th – Glider from Glen Feshie force-landed in Glen Einich. Spotted by motor glider. Subjects made their own way back to Glen Feshie. RAF Sea King and Police called out. Cairngorm MRT informed.

NOVEMBER 19th – Tweed Valley MRT and SARDA called out to search for a missing driver (47) involved in a road traffic accident. She was found by police in a village church with head injuries, bruising and hypothermia. 69.

NOVEMBER 27th – Nairn Police asked Cairngorm MRT to search a steep, narrow ravine in Cawdor Woods. Suicide note found on bridge. No one found but Police were able to close file. 50.

NOVEMBER 28th-29th – Torridon MRT called out 08.00 on 29th to search for Michael Dolan (41) missing since 16.00 on 28th. Body found washed up on the seashore. 32.

IN MEMORIAM

GEORGE LYNN GIBSON j.1976

IN MARCH 1982, I received a Youngers Tartan beer mat through the post. It had a Fijian stamp and had survived the long air journey from the South Pacific unscathed. On the back, under the logo of the white-bearded old man was printed a sketch of a climber and a short eulogy of Ben Nevis – 'A five-mile path leads to the summit, but for the true mountaineer there are still many challenges.' Around the side of the mat George had written: 'Am I still a true mountaineer or just a waster, I ask myself as I gaze into the amber liquid?'

The mode of communication was typical George. However sorely he missed his beloved Bens, while following his strenuous career as a tropical forester, his wit and personal warmth raised the spirit. He was a true character, a man imbued with the traditions of Scottish climbing, who gave to his many friends a companionship they will never forget.

Born in Hawick and brought up in Annan, George was proud of his Borders' roots. He started climbing with the Carlisle Mountaineering Club and before leaving school had already accomplished White Slab on Cloggy and most of the harder climbs on Castle Rock of Thirlmere. Coming to Edinburgh University in 1971 he very soon acquired a reputation. Arran was a favourite stamping ground, including early ascents or attempts on Bogle, Brobdingnag and Blinder. His fascination with the Forth bridges was legendary too. Perhaps not many now remember that the road bridge was put up for sale in 1973! Under George's inspiration the party had climbed two 'remarkably similar' summits, and abseiling down to a suitably-exposed level had strung a Student Charities banner across. More frequently, the rail bridge was traversed, this being an initiation test for most of his girlfriends. At the last count he had made 16 ascents, each time leaving offerings of brown ale for the Bridge police on the summits.

Weekends with George were always memorable because his energy, humour and bubbling enthusiasm for life attracted the unusual. He had a rare capacity to relate quickly to people from all walks of life and invariably got himself and his companions into unlikely encounters which later became the basis for the endless tales stored in his prodigious memory. Once in a pub in Arran he got himself into an arm-wrestling contest with a flame-haired Orcadian linesman and (to the surprise of them both) George won. As the locals queued up to take on the newcomer it seemed wiser to flee to Glen Rosa. Another time, finishing Observatory Ridge after dark with Sheila Kirkwood, they found themselves sharing the summit shelter with a retired Professor of Divinity and his apprentice, who provided amber liquid comfort in addition to the spiritual variety. On a New Year bothy trip with David Geddes and another unfortunate girlfriend, a first-footing of the station master at Corrour and the demolishing of an inordinate quantity of whisky resulted in another fund of stories about Victorian signalling equipment and the reincarnation of the Ben Alder Cottage ghost.

On our trips in the mid-1970s vile rock was frequently the goal, in perverse defiance of modern rock-climbing trends. A long-sought ascent of Beinn Nuis Chimney, surely one of the vilest, was at least partially successful, although Silo and an even viler unclimbed line to its left on the North East Face of Cir Mhor easily repulsed us. Between these writhings in slimy chimneys and grovellings up crumbling granite we would usually fit in a romp up South Ridge, while dips in the Glen Rosa pools and endless quotes from the incomparable Cir Mhor chapter of *Mountaineering in Scotland* were *de rigeur*.

George's interest in, and respect for mountaineering tradition, led him to a broader vision of mountaineering focusing not on 'gymnastic problems' but on the great classics and 'the pursuit of distant white domes'. He was a powerful influence in extending the horizons of his contemporaries at university. It was through him that many got to know W.H. Murray's *Mountaineering in Scotland,* for every foray into the hills, indeed almost every conversation about climbing was peppered with apposite quotes from 'the works'. The cult was such that he always signed himself 'Bill' and usually addressed me as 'Bill' too, though I was never sure which of us was supposed to be Murray and which McKenzie. Successive girlfriends were known as Mrs McAlpine and Mrs Malloch – the only two female characters in the book. Other favourites for quotation were J.H.B. Bell and B.H. Humble, with whom he struck up a close friendship.

In 1975, George accompanied Des Rubens, Dave Broadhead, Dave Page and myself on an expedition to the Hindu Raj in Pakistan. His mechanical skills were of great service in keeping our ailing vehicle together on the long overland journey, and the initiation into the stark contrasts of life in the Third World clearly captured his imagination, as did our stay with Buster Goodwin in Rawalpindi, a last survivor of the British Raj. Although our mountaineering achievements were modest we did reach the summit of an unclimbed 6400m peak, where it was George (naturally) who celebrated with a can of Guinness.

After a further year in Edinburgh (as EUMC President) in which he contrived some good climbs as well as a good degree, George went to Ecuador on a posting from the Overseas Development Administration, with a brief to conserve tropical forest species in the remote Oriente Province. With his natural talent for languages he was soon fluent in Spanish, and threw his phenomenal energies into work that was often frustrating. Asked to work in a 100,000-hectare reserve of virgin jungle he found that the Government had parcelled it into 50-hectare lots in which colonists were crazily cutting down everything in sight. His letters home gave vivid descriptions of life both in the jungle and on the mountains. Lago Agrio, the nearest town:

'No light in the evenings, no tap water –all rain in 40-gallon-drum stuff – no sewage. Turds float around everywhere, the smell is unbearable in the hot tropical night, drunks fall into the ditches screaming obscenities. The hotel is 50p (most expensive), with clean? sheets, mosquito nets and whore, if you want, thrown in. At night the entire town falls into a state of mosquito and God Knows What Else ridden anarchy.'

However later in the same letter:

'Tomorrow its off to the hills to a little snow peak of 5300m a little to the south of Quito. There is one really good route on it but I have a bit of a problem finding suitably adventurous persons to climb with, so will be trying an easier route. The climbing company has a tendency to be a bit punterish here – one of the keenest, M, an ex-Forestry Commission chap is who I'm going with. A friend of a friend met him in Quito and described him as a 'bit of a Bertie Wooster type'. He is certainly not a champion of 'exuberance and unconventionality'. The smallest and most boring 'adventure' seems to require space blankets, bivvy sacs, glucose sweets, toilet paper, torches, spare batteries, bulbs, Kendal Mint Cake, compass, spare compass, whistle, spare whistle. Sometimes this really bores me when I think of days of grovelling up many a slimy gully with the lads. This, in fact, inspired me to solo a hill of 5100m called Tungurhagua the other week. Starting at Baños, at 6000ft, I waddled up through orchids and weird trees to the refugio at the tree line, Mas o Menos at 12,000ft. Now being a fiesta (Easter) this rather sordid hut was full of Eccies, up to Subir the volcano. So the dour Scot lurks in a corner, while young boys surreptitiously cuddle their chicas. Reading through the log book, I find such entries as Jim Fisher, Glasgow, Dec. 21 – 'Ah'm gaun hame fur ma Hogmanay'. So George schemes to leave at 2a.m. and sets the alarm for 1.30a.m. The Eccies play a transistor till 11.30p.m. but sweet is the revenge at 1.30a.m. as the alarm splits the silence of the night. Dropping a pan or two on the floor completes the revenge, and its out into the cold night at 2.30a.m. with two young Eccies. The moon shines fitfully through ragged brown clouds and 3000ft of vertical ash (Not being M, I had neither clinometer, nor spare clinometer) led to some iron hard snow. Here, with beard white with ice, just before dawn, it was on with the crampons, 0° 30" south of the Equator, in five minutes. Now the Eccies had home made seven-league crampons and firstly had to wrap cloth and poly bags round their boots to make them big enough for the crampons. The minutes ticked by, my cold and impatience increased. Remembering what Patey did on Coire Ardair Girdle I gave the buggers my torch, and with a triumphant cry of: 'Nos vemos a la cima,' set off into the cloudy 45° slope, on iron snow. 750ft or so led to the crater lip, and in the dawn light I could see holes with smoke coming out of them – there is very little snow within the crater – it erupts every 40 years or so! Then up the curling rim of the crater, the clouds died pink with the sunrise. Still in dense cloud, and with a terrific wind blowing. I stormed up. About 10m below the summit (5150m) I burst out into intermittent sunshine as the cloud alternately was swept clear and came back. The crater was full of cloud and every blink of sun gave birth to a Brocken Spectre in the crater, with the bulk of Chimborazo behind (6100m). An amazing 40 minutes was spent on the summit, admiring the cloud sea and peaks sticking out, and trying to thaw the camera out. Then there was the 10,000ft descent to Baños, and I walked into my friend's hotel, precisely 30 hours after leaving. This time, nothing, not even a Humble mystery tour could drag me out of a quiet pipe and that eiderdown sleeping bag.'

While in South America George was deeply saddened by the death of Ben Humble and promised himself to do a memorial climb on his return to Scotland. Aaaaagh!

So it came about that a group of 10 gathered in Lagangarbh on a dreich Sunday in October, 1978. George dressed for the hill in baggy plus-fours, white socks and puttees, dress shirt with cuff-links and chain, waistcoat, cravat, tweed jacket and feathered black hat. For the purposes of ascending Crypt Route George and I shared his nailed boots – he the right and I the left, with the other feet being shod in 'modern' rubber soles. Raymond Simpson, in the lead, disappeared into the mountain as though some invisible monster had put out its maw and pulled him in. Then George followed, tricounis scraping on the greasy rock, stout tweed adhering well to the slimy walls, jaunty hat and Alpine guide's sack completing the picture.

After his stint in Ecuador, in which time he climbed a number of noteworthy Andean summits, George moved to the Oxford Forestry Institute. His first job there involved travelling to 35 tropical countries in an international collaborative research project on the tree, *Pinus Caribea*. He became an expert traveller on airlines great and small, enjoying the gin and tonics in long haul 'Club Class' as much as the uncertain excitements of smaller local airlines. Family and friends were always remembered with hilarious phone calls in the dead of night or postcards (usually of the Royal Family) from far-flung corners of the world. He revelled in anywhere with the flavour of the former Empire: cricket at the Selangor Club in Kuala Lumpur, or chauffeur-driven tours with the 'Chief Conservator of Forests' in Orissa, India. The work was stressful, lonely and at times repetitive, with no settled existence, but his sense of humour always got him through. From a letter from the heart of the Congo in 1981:

'This trip has really been hard going, and sometimes as I swayed from side to side trying to assess trees in 95°F, I began to think that tussling with turgid regressions in boring Britain was not so bad after all. Did a lot of drinking in Ivory Coast so I suppose that aggravated the swaying quite a bit. Had some laughs though in the markets with a camera and done a bit of rock climbing on some 20ft-high sea cliffs I discovered. Found a jug handle just like the one at the top of the S Crack and if I closed my eyes I could see that spindly wee bauchle, whatever he was called, on the first ascent.'

Throughout the 1980s George continued to develop his forestry career. Deeply involved in the genetics of tree breeding he became an expert in the practicalities of seed collection, conservation of genetic resources and improvement of native tree species. With his intensely practical intelligence he clearly saw the multitude of constraints on rural development in the Third World but he never became cynical. An understanding of the importance of multi-purpose tree species and a keen awareness of the need to obtain the full-hearted support of local populations for forestry development, together with his ever-widening experience made him in great demand as an adviser in projects all over the world. In the late 1980s he spent more than three years in Honduras setting up a project to conserve and cultivate species which were fast disappearing from their natural habitat. With his wife, Lucy – a highly-talented musician – and young son, Hamish, (and later Anna), he continued to live life to the full, combining the forestry with ever-ready hospitality to colleagues and friends who made their way to Central America.

In 1991, George finally returned to his beloved Scotland and after a year in the private sector joined the staff of Edinburgh University. He was an extremely conscientious and popular lecturer who always took pains to smooth the path of overseas students and visitors. While still involved in projects in China, India, Nepal, Cuba, Mexico and Latin America, he somehow found the time to do radical home improvements, and was also a convivial host and had begun to go to the hills again more frequently.

He had long cherished an ambition to do the Orion Face Direct, although he harboured some doubts about his ability to climb it. On our first attempt, the Ben shrugged us off disdainfully with winds – worse than anything we had experienced in 30 years of climbing, – that completely flattened us before we even reached Coire Leis. Our second attempt, a few weeks later, found good conditions and a safe, if slow, ascent was made, the last few pitches by torchlight. Unfortunately, there was an uncommonly violent storm on the plateau and a welter of hypotheses about George's tragic fall into Five Finger Gully came down in the end to Humble's 'simple slip'. Had fate not taken George so prematurely he would undoubtedly have made a grand old man of the SMC. With his love of tradition and wry deprecation of all things modern, his inexhaustible fund of stories and quotes, and most of all, the twinkle in his eye and the warmth of his company, he was absolutely cut out for the role. Difficult though it may be for many to find comfort in it, a consolation is that if there is a hereafter he will really be enjoying it now – in the company of Collie, Raeburn, Stott, Goggs, Bell and the rest. For those who are left there is an aching loss but a sense of gratitude for having known such a funny, gifted and warm-hearted friend.

Geoff Cohen.

J.K. ANNAND j.1947

I FIRST met Jim Annand in 1933, when, as a first-year student at Edinburgh University, I joined the JMCS which, at that time, used to meet regularly in the SMC rooms in Castle Terrace. In an assortment of old clapped-out motor-bikes and beat-up cars, a group of us, including Jim, used to travel to the hills most weekends – or so it seems in retrospect. From that time, until 1939, when most of us became embroiled in one or other of His Majesty's forces, we were wont to leave Edinburgh at around lunchtime on Saturday with tents and the crudest of equipment, have some sort of expedition in the hills on Sunday, and travel back, arriving home, tired but happy, usually well after dark. I very soon found that Jim – one of natures gentlemen – was a most rewarding companion to be on the hills with.

His interests were very wide-ranging. No mean scholar and linguist, he had become an articulate poet, and it is from these poems that one can get a clear idea of the considerable variety of his interests, and in his life in general. His particular interest in mountainous country, at a variety of locations in his beloved Scotland, comes through quite clearly in his little books, *Poems and Translations,* and *Two Voices.* In these, he recalls days shared with his many friends, in every part of Scotland, from the Borders to the North, including Arran, Skye and other islands. His love of nature and folklore shines out in every mention he makes of particular areas. I recall expeditions we made together on the closer Munros around Callander and Tyndrum, which we used to reach, there and back in a day, at weekends. I remember one outstanding day in particular, when the JMCS had booked the Killin Hotel for a New Year Meet. On December 31, 1935, as a meet, we made a mass assault on Meall nan Tarmachan in marvellous weather. The snow was down to Loch Tay, and was very hard. I recall the subsequent dinner in the hotel, which took us right through to 1936, with much reel dancing.

Sadly, these expeditions were cut short by the war, when Jim joined the Navy and served, as I recall in a variety of craft. Hence the title of his book of poems *Two Voices* – 'Two voices are there, one is of the sea, one of the mountains, each a mighty voice'.

I next met Jim when I moved to Dolphinton in 1954, and contacted the Edinburgh Section of the SMC. Again, a group of us, now sadly reduced in capability, but not in enthusiasm began to have expeditions, albeit somewhat less ambitious. Many of the same people took part in these latter-day hillwalking trips, including Jim Annand. I found that his enthusiasm for the Scottish hills had not diminished, and that he was just as rewarding a companion to be with as on the previous period. Those of us who remember Jim will miss his good fellowship and pawky wit.

C.C. Gorrie.

I ONLY knew Jimmie Annand in his later years and recognised him as that rare thing in Scotland – an unsuborned intellectual. Like MacLennan (SMCJ, xxix, 1968, 89-91) and Dick Brown (SMCJ, xxxiv, 1989, 328-329) his culture was embedded in the traditions of Scotland and Europe with none of the obligatory obeisance in other directions. In the mountains he was a competent Salvationist. He had no need of more as he was part of them, particularly among the Border hills where he could converse with shepherds, keepers and lave in his, and their, native doric.

He would have been a good companion for Hogg and might have straightened him out socially and politically. Indeed, I can see him as a worthy member of the colourful embassy that went through the Border hills to seek an audience of Michael Scot, the wizard of Aikwood, as told in Hogg's *Three Perils of Man*.

He did not use the mountains to exorcise some demon within him but as a source of inspiration for his poetry and prose which ranged from war poems and bairnsangs to translations from other European tongues. A particularly successful example of the last was a translation of Ronsard's *Elegy for Mary Stuart* of which I have an unpublished copy by me as I write.

His loss adds another verse to Dunbar's eternal poem *Lament of the Makars*, but his will be a cheerful one about a journey well made and cheerfully undertaken.

I.H.M. Smart.

DAN LIVINGSTON j. 1985

DAN LIVINGSTON died peacefully at home in Alligin on February 11, 1992. He was 82 and had been a mountain man all his life. He knew the Scottish hills better than most and, over the years, extended his climbing to the Austrian Alps, the Pyrenees, the Swiss Alps, Corsica and Nepal. In between he made walking trips to Greece, Crete, France and Southern Spain.

His great love was the Pyrenees. He first went there in 1957 with John Lowe and returned on no less than 12 occasions over the next 30 years.

Dan took great pleasure in introducing others to the hills, and throughout his long teaching career brought many of his pupils and friends to share his own joy in the mountains.

He graduated in 1931 from Glasgow University with an Honours Degree in Maths and Astronomy. He taught at only two schools – Airdrie Academy (1931-1946), and Rutherglen Academy (1946-1969), where he was principal teacher of maths and latterly depute rector. At Rutherglen he ran the school camp in Arran and the Cairngorms, where many a youngster had their first taste of the mountains. He was an instructor at Glenmore Lodge for a short time.

Dan's other main interest was in astronomy. For many years he was curator of Airdrie Observatory, where he spent much of his time instructing and encouraging youngsters. He was a founder member and former president of the Astronomical Society of Glasgow, and a Fellow of the Royal Astronomical Society.

On retirement Dan built his dream house, Creag Bhan, in Alligin, commanding a stunning view over Loch Torridon. This became a convivial venue at all times for his many friends. He quickly became involved in local activities and was the first secretary of the newly-formed Community Association – playing a key role in successfully obtaining for the area one of the first Post-Bus services in the Highlands, and also in inspiring the community to renovate its Village Hall and greatly expand the range of social and recreational activities based upon it.

He maintained his links with Rutherglen Academy after settling in Alligin, and masterminded their acquisition of the empty village school there for an outdoor pursuits centre. For many years he assisted and encouraged the enthusiastic school staff who voluntarily ran the many courses and activities based there.

He was a founder member of the Torridon and Kinlochewe Mountain Rescue Team, and unfailingly turned out under all conditions for many years – latterly assisting by manning the base wireless vehicle, often through long, cold nights.

Dan Livingston was a man of boundless enthusiasm, wit, good humour and curiosity. He had a talent for making friends, to whom he was unswervingly loyal and generous.

John Craig, Charlie Rose.

Notice has also reached us of the death of A.L. Cram.

PROCEEDINGS OF THE CLUB

New Members

The following eight new members were admitted and welcomed to the Club in the year 1993-94.

Gillian E. Irvine (33), Doctor of Medicine, Aviemore.

Alexander Keith (29), Solicitor, Edinburgh.

Iain M.G. Peter (33), Mountain Guide, Penmachno, Gwynedd.

James R. Blyth (27), Sales Assistant, Ayr.

Bruce Goodlad (22), Student, Prestwick.

Nicholas H. Harper (39), Company Director, York.

Mark Litterick (29), Electronics Engineer, Glasgow.

Graham A. Penny (33), Fire Fighter, Blairgowrie.

The One-Hundredth-and-Fifth AGM and Dinner 1993

And so we went to Fort William, as mandated by the dissatisfied customers of 1992. The Club has associations with the Alexandra Hotel going back for years, and while the hotel appeared at first glance to have changed little from the days of Ling and Glover, it now revealed an acceptable modern interior which more than suited our purposes.

Those seeking a comfortable seat for the AGM were quickly disillusioned on discovering that the meeting was in another place – no Parliamentary splendour, but rather the assembly hall of Fort William Junior School, where no doubt the austerity coupled with the absence of suitable refreshment led to one of the shortest annual meetings on record. The business proceeded initially with little incident. It was thought best to let the Ayscough bequest accrue meantime. The reports were accepted, and the Committee, despite their best efforts, were re-elected and the appointment of trustees meekly agreed. Thoughts were turning to salmon and venison when Curly Ross, abetted by Malcolm Slesser, fanned the flames of that burning ember – abandonment of the Loyal Toast. The small flame rapidly became a forest fire as argument raged and President Lang eventually tackled the blaze by calling for a vote. Never a Club for royalists, the outcome was nevertheless a close-run thing and poor Queenie was forced to abdicate in favour of the Bens and Glens.

The dining room looked too small but somehow everyone was accommodated with apparently more comfort than last year. The food was fine and the service reasonable. More tradition was abandoned by the absence of a top table which made the Dinner Secretary's job easier and the President less lonely. Splendid piping was provided by Iain McLeod, one hopes a regular feature, but the Club song in spite of an excellent delivery by Curly, found a somewhat restrained choir.

The President rambled on and long asking the company to remember those who had fallen into the last deep crevasse from which there is no escape. The Club's attitude to the increasingly competitive nature of our sport was questioned but met with apparent indifference – probably much to do with earlier excess of choux pastry. In addition to the insult of being placed with their backs to the speakers' table, our guests were mercilessly slaughtered by Colin Grant. No one escaped, with the Cairngorm Club – who like the poor are always with us – bearing the brunt. An eloquent and well-prepared reply was put up by Professor Bill Donaldson who, being unattached to any particular club, had escaped the worst of Dr Grant's bedside manner. A fine rendering of *Dark Lochnagar* sent the company to the bar.

In spite of pre-circulated recommendations to climb on Stob Ban, the weather on the Sunday was less than fair and the President took his party on his first walk in the Mamores. The writer cannot recall anyone formally thanking Robin Campbell for making the arrangments but this was an excellent Dinner and he may well have the job for some time.

John R.R. Fowler.

SMC Dinner Symposium 1993

The symposium held before the 1993 Annual Dinner in Kingussie was only alluded to in last year's Journal: so here is a summary of the four presentations given. The speakers were asked to talk about aspects of mountaineering of interest to fellow practitioners rather than give popular accounts of derring-do.

Rab Anderson presented the case for bolt climbing which he wrote up for last year's Journal. The article should be the definitive statement on the ethics and aesthetics of the Art. The talk was illustrated by some sensitive colour slides which showed that the speaker was far from indifferent to the crag environment. The sites of the battles between himself and gravity were presented in the context of the larger landscape. A distant crag viewed over a field of pastel lavender in a sunny afternoon somewhere in the warm South counterpointed the subsequent description of the moves required to ascend it.

Des Rubens gave an account of difficult decisions made on the expedition to Nanga Parbat. Specifically, he described the dilemma of whether to abandon the ascent or to allow an injured Geoff Cohen to descend alone, and of his own dilemma on whether his own incipient cerebral oedema was just temporary anoxia or a signal to turn back. He addressed the problem of whether the ascent is worth the life of yourself or your friends. It is to be hoped that the Journal will get another article from his pen one day.

Andy Tibbs presented some comments on the contemporary climbing scene at home, particularly the trend to shorter, harder new routes as the supply of longer easier ones get used up. His observations were printed in last year's Journal.

John Peden gave an account of the ski traverse of the Stauning Alps made by a combined Scottish and French party in May 1992. The former used nordic skis, the latter Alpine. Both parties believed they had made the right choice. Alpine are better downhill, Nordic better up. He also described how they got themselves and equipment up a steep col by means of a complex system of pulleys made from slings and karabiners. The illustrative slides portrayed something that looked like a spilled plate of colourful spaghetti. The account of this expedition is still being written up for the Journal.

Barely a handful of members were present for the start, but 50 or so had condescended to arrive by the end. Those who did attend had the privilege of hearing experts addressing their peers on subjects of mutual interest. We would like to record our thanks to the speakers and apologise for the absence of those members who were too busy, too preoccupied or too thrawn to attend.

I.H.M. Smart.

CIC MEETS

During the 1993-94 winter season seven weekend meets were held. Waiting lists were in force, but in reality, the hut was never full. The largest attendance was 16 on February 12-13. The most successful team was the two Als (Scott and Shand) with ascents of Mega X and Psychedelic Wall.

The mountain had the best climbing conditions for years, but the overhead conditions were abysmal on most occasions which curtailed many exploits to the lower-level routes. Climbing was rarely possible on both days on any of the meets. The best weather was on Saturday, March 26, when the mountain was assaulted on all flanks.

There were no blue skies, just piles of snow, and most infuriating, constant gale-force winds to contend with.

Inside the hut it was very gloomy indeed, as film-makers tried to recreate a 1930s atmosphere by painting half the hut a dowdy brown.

However, Colin Stead and myself cannot complain too much as we put the new Ben Nevis guide out of date before it was published by climbing four new routes.

D.F. Lang.

THE SLINGSBY SYMPOSIUM , NORWAY 1993

Early in 1993 I received an invitation via Derek Smithson of the Yorkshire Ramblers, in his capacity as vice-chairman of The Slingsby Institute, to attend and participate in the inaugural symposium of the Institute. The final details and programme were confirmed by Jan Schwarzott, chairman of the Institute.

The date was to be September 10-12, at the Klingenberg Hotel in Ardalstangen, and sponsored by the Ardal Kommune.

Bob Allen (Climbers Club) and I arrived in the black of night in Ardal after our five-and-a-half hours' trip in our jetfoil ferry from Bergen to the head of the Sognefjord. In the hotel, which fortunately was only two minutes' walk from the jetty, we were introduced to Jan. The hour was small when this fascinating little man allowed us to get to bed, having supplied us with food and drink.

Thursday, September 9, was a glorious cloudless day, the sun shone from morning till night. Bob and I had a delightfull walk up Munkenosi, to an altitude higher than Ben Nevis according to Bob's altimeter. The views to the Jostedalsbreen and the Jotunheimen were magnficent, as were the reflections in the placid waters of the Sognefjord.

With transportation provided by Rune, this young Norwegian took Derek Smithson, Ron Kenyon (FRCC) and myself on a six-hour trek via Hjelledalen, Morkaskardet, Vettismorki, Vettisfossen (the highest free fall waterfall in Norway), then finally back to the car at Hjelle. Meanwhile, Bob had set up the projection equipment, ensuring that the Symposium started on time on Friday evening.

We listened intently to Jan Schwarzott giving us a history lesson on William Cecil Slingsby, his life as a climber and naturalist and the affection the Norwegians have for this man who made more than 20 expeditions to Norway beginning in 1872. Jan's book on Slingsby is due to be published this year.

The celebrated Norwegian professor and climber, Arne Naess, whom at the age of 83 was strutting about in a body clamp with the aid of crutches due to a toboganning accident, lectured for nearly an hour-and-a-half on his theory of Deep Ecology. The evening ended with a meal, followed by social intercourse.

The sun shone all day on Saturday, but we had full programme, having started with breakfast at 08.00 and ending at 23.00 after a splendid banquet. Many speakers were involved during the sessions and the British were humbled by the fact that we spoke virtually no Norse, but the English of our hosts was excellent.

I managed to talk for 40 minutes on my given subject, 'The Privilege of Being Alone, Paradox of Scottish Wasteland Blessings'. Judging by the response it appeared to be well received.

After Tony Streather's, 'What Next?' contemplations, the Symposium ended on Sunday afternoon with the participants seated in a circle eyeing a vase of flowers in the centre. This rounding-off session, chaired by Nils Faarland, contemplated whether we were inside or outside Nature, or was there Free Nature?

After the parting farewells, Ron Kenyon and I had our gear ready to head into the Hurrungane area of the Jotunheimen National Park. I had gleaned some information from an old guide book kindly lent to me by Scott Johnston. Store Skagastolstind or Storen, at 2405m and Norway's answer to the Matterhorn, looked a good target. The fact that Slingsby had made the first ascent solo in July, 1876 was equally fitting.

Scott's map did not show a road from Ovre Ardal to Turtagro, but now there is a road of sorts and our new-found friend, Charula, dropped us off at our requested stop. At Tutagro Hotel I collected a present of a Norwegian Alpine Club Journal for our Club from the Norse Tindeklub, along with keys to their hut which we were invited to use en route to Storen. Seemingly, this hut is as exclusive as the CIC, except that we do not have pewter candlesticks, 10-foot-long oak tables, a library or an oil lamp chandelier!

Typically, on Monday – the only real climbing day – it was windy, cloudy , cold and snowing. Having left some excess baggage at the Bandet Hut, Ron and I set off into the cloud draping the mighty Storen. Unlike the easy route most people encounter, we had an enthralling climb. Very few signs of previous passage were visible on this trade route due to snow cover. The cloud cover did not help route finding either, as the head wall reared up.

The summer crux, Heftyes Chimney, bulged with ice and gave a fine pitch of grade III-IV. The summit was reached at 17.30, the final pitch being good neve.

The descent involved six 50m abseils, the abseil points having to be located from under the snow. Thereafter a long descent in snow runnels, in the dark, led back to the Bandet Hut at 21.30 to the relief of ourselves and four ladies from Oslo who thought we were spending the night on the mountain.

The morning mists lifted to reveal Storen in all its glory. Indeed it did look like a Matterhorn. All around the gabbro rock walls looked spectacular in the sunlight.

The glorious weather ensured we did not flag on our nine-hour walk out to Ovre Ardal, from where we managed to get a lift to the hotel in Ardal. Before we could get a bath, Jan ushered us to his apartment where his friends Peter and Nils joined in the celebratory drinks that Jan had ordered. We eventually got away for that welcome bath.

Jan's hospitality continued when we had an excellent meal with him in the Slingsby Room where we were further embarrassed when he produced carrier bags of cheese and cured meats for us to take home. We had prevously been presented with a tee-shirt and a signed copy of Jan's book, *Under Storen – Portrait of Utladalen and Vettisfossen*. Having arranged an alarm call for 05.00 we finally headed for bed well after midnight.

Our farewells to Jan were drowned by the noise of the ferry as it departed for Bergen at 06.10 on yet another fine day.

This was a Presidential duty I would gladly repeat.

D.F. Lang.

JMCS REPORTS

London Section:– The Club committee met rarely, but always drunkenly. Most of the committee failed to attend most of the meetings but got drunk in absentia anyway. Special thanks to Pete Whitechurch for arranging enough hut income to pay for the repair of the co-ordinated damage done to it by Nigel Charlesworth plc, at the work meet. Pete is still ensuring a regular flow of income and vomit from a range of sordidly profitable University Club block bookings. Gordon Dalgarno has religiously embezzled away all year and wished to thank Dave Edmunds for auditing away any 'accounting idiosyncrasies'.

Following repeated purges on the inactive non-paying flab in the club by Fuhrer Bashforth, the membership now looks a lot smaller and tighter, particularly Tony Buj. Inactive paying flab is, of course, as welcome and prevalent as ever. Exporting unsavoury arses to foreign countries has also considerably improved the atmosphere at Glenafon slide show nights. Will the sofa never again rebound beneath the buttocks of the Brunei-bound John Steele? The British Society for the Dyslexic shares our sadness that Peter Tibbetts is no longre porducting thi cirkuler.

As usual, climbing standards peaked in January (at the Foundry . . .) and declined rapidly through the year to a low point of garden centre visits, sailing, fish buying, fell running, canoeing and motor-cycling, in time for the unbroken spell of fine summer weather between 3.45p.m. and 5.30p.m. on Saturday, August 28.

The meets were the usual catalogue of car crashes, roadside motor-cycle mechanics, licence endorsements, burbling bikes, huge hut fires, and horrible post pub food passing games. I am sure that it is just a coincidence that this marked decline in general behaviour coincides with letting females in.

Meets: Snowdonia (4). Pembroke (1). mid-Wales (1). Scotland (3). Peak (2). Dales (1). Lakes (2).

Locations and approximate numbers attending: New Year – Glenafon, Wales (20+). January – Glenafon, Wales (30+). February – Raeburn Hut, Newtonmore (15+). March – Helwith Bridge, Dales (18+). Easter – Bosherton, Pembroke (20+). May Bank Holiday – Low Hall Garth, Lakes (12+). Whitsun – Shelter Stone, Cairngorms (4!). June – Three Stags Head. Peak – (24+) July – Alps (20+). August – Dinas Mawdyy, Wales (12+?). September – Wasdale, Lakes (9+). October – Glenafon, Wales (7). November – Bull and Thorns, Peak (50). December – Cairngorms (8). New Year – Glenafon, North Wales (30+).

The meets provided many good climbs and laughs – including bagpipes for breakfast drunks; the great Shelter Stone port disaster; cannoging in Coire Cas; the great Ryvoan fire-eating contest (additional fuel supplied by the Treasurer's down pit . . .); the 'lively' Glenafon plate dance night; the Gelder Shiel spindrift avalanche etc.

At least 20 members were in the Alps this summer, encountering perfect motor-cycling... err, oops, sorry climbing conditions. This included ascents of the South Pillar of the Ecrins, the North Face of the Ailfroide, the American Direct and the West Face of the Dru, and the North Face of the Pic Sans Nom. Two teams travelled East to Nepal and the Garwal Himalaya. Two visits were made to the Verdun Gorge and others to Fontainbleau, Costa Boltkit in Spain and the 'nouveau Suisse' resorts. Over-enthusiasm has resulted in many impulsive gatherings, including three trips to the Cairngorms in four weekends, and many mid-week Peak District escapades.

The club has experienced significant geographic emphasis away from London, with the most active trouble-makers now earning much less but climbing much more – Sheffield, Nottingham, Leeds and Manchester are the unfortunate Magis-trates Courts . . .

Officials: *President*, Hugh Jordan. *Secretary*, Andrew Walker, 1 Hancock Court, Main Road, Bamford, Derbyshire 0433 651707. *Hut Custodian* (Glenafon, Snowdonia), Peter Whitechurch, 1 Dale Cottages, Tangier Lane, Frant, Tunbridge 0892 523531. *Treasurer*, Gordon Dalgarno.

Andrew Walker.

Perth Mountaineering Club (JMCS Perth Section): – *The Saga continues.* Following the creation of Perth Mountaineering Club as a cloak for the Perth Section of the JMCS, we have flourished, membership continues to grow, and meets are well attended.

Members of the club have had an active year, mainly walking, but with growing interest in climbing – many thanks to the patient leaders who have helped out there. Ski-touring, both Alpine and Nordic, has been on the agenda this year, though strong winds have made any overweight tendencies a distinct advantage.

A recent 'How It Was' evening meet was arranged and members were encouraged to bring slides from previous club events. Apart from the development of light-weight camping, one major point of interest was the growth in the presence of C_2H_5OH at Compleations, from a bottle of Babycham to the (temporary) cairn of bottles that forced the assisted descent of a previous Section Secretary from Ben More, Mull.

The Club hasn't managed a meet abroad this year, but various members ventured to Spain, Puy des Anges, and Mount Elbrus.

Antony Lole.

Glasgow Section:– Club attendances have once more remained variable, possibly the result of numerous weather-watchers, making some meets popular and others less so.

Over the year, 21 meets were held at various venues – Torridon, Skye and Rum and Arrochar. Of the more notable meets, the President's weekend remained a firm favourite even if he did arrive late with damp squibs (bought at discount?). Likewise, a wet and windy Christmas meet at Lagangarbh saw the year's slides analysed in depth while the New Year meet at the Raeburn Hut made amends with some excellent weather and much snow. Another popular meet was our long

548   SCOTTISH MOUNTAINEERING CLUB JOURNAL

overdue return to Milehouse. Sadly, this turned out to be a black day for the Club
when our stalwart member of 24 years, Dr Angus McInnes, was killed while
climbing on Hell's Lum Crag – a fate we still find difficult to believe.

Beyond Scottish shores, Club activities were quieter than usual but a number
kept the flag flying and ventured to colder, warmer or drier climes. In the Swiss
Alps John Park, Stuart Fish and Geremy Evans made ascents on the North Face of
Mont Blanc du Tacul, Cosmique Arete, Chapelle de la Gliere and other Tacul
routes. David Ritchie – also in the Alps – climbed on the Croux and the Petite
Clocher. Later in the year Neil Marshall flew west to winter climb in Talluride, US
– Bridalveil Falls and Ames. Carl Schaschke visited Norway and Sandy Donald
went to Morocco.

The Cairndow Hotel hosted the Whole Club Dinner, while our own Section
Dinner was held at the Kingshouse where our guest speaker, Sandy Cousins, jogged
the memories and enlightened the younger members on those many graduated
JMCS characters before rounding off with a showing of 'Climbing on the Cobbler'.
The occasion was marked by a rare stay at Black Rock Cottage.

The Coruisk Hut enjoyed a successful year with hut maintenance carried out in
traditional style. Those present worked conscientiously – they tell me – to earn that
customary rest day on the Cuillin, while evening festivities were free from those
'other' moments.

Our Club membership, when finally updated, highlighted a few shock names in
default – so stands about 80, including lifers. Over the year only four members were
admitted to the ranks.

Looking ahead to a good winter and with a number of new venues arranged
together with some old faithfuls the rather lean spell will hopefully fade into the
horizon in 1994.

The AGM was held in November and the following officials were elected: *Hon.
Member,* W.H. Murray; *Hon. President,* Ian Cumming; *Hon. Vice-President,*
Benny Swan; *President,* Sandy Donald; *Secretary,* Donald Ballance, 1/2 11 Airlie
Street, Hyndland, Glasgow G12 9RJ. (Tel. 041 357 3073); *Coruisk Hut Custodian,*
Sandy Donald, 15 Smeaton Avenue, Torrance G64 4 BG. (Tel: 0360 622541).

Edinburgh Section:– This year numbers have remained steady at just under 70,
while those active showed a promising increase to about half the current membership.
New members were comparatively thin on the ground with only two new additions
– general interest in the section, however is still buoyant.

Although the weather was on occasion none too generous, enthusiasm and
activity continued unabated with many members active throughout the winter
months. The number of miles accumulated by members in pursuit of the elusive
summer sun was beginning to be alarming. Most notably this occurred over the
Skye weekend meet which saw members initially meeting at the Cluanie Inn and
then on to Jock's Spot – via an Inverness takeaway. Some climbing was eventually
achieved in Northumberland. Club meets included trips to the traditional venues –
CIC, Black Rock and our own two huts. Yorkshire gritstone and the Lakes were also
visited. There were 14 summer, and 10 winter weekend meets held during 1993.

In many small groups the members were climbing in four continents during the
year, although by the end of which the Seven Summits concept remained an elusive

endeavour. Several made the annual pilgrimage to the Alps where the more notable successes included the Mittellegi Ridge, traverse of the Monch and Jungfrau; while in Chamonix, the East Face of the Dent du Requin was completed. One member, abandoning the rain that had earlier thwarted attempts in Chamonix, visited California and climbed routes in Yosemite and Tuolomne Meadows. Asia was visited by several, with two making separate trips to Thailand. A three-month walk-about in Australasia was undertaken by one member with an ascent in the Southern New Zealand Alps. Further ski-touring excursions were made on the North Island volcanoes of Mt. Ruapehu and Mt. Ngauruhoe. While in Australia, he scaled Mt. Kosciusko, while another did her bit for the club's Seven Summits bid by climbing Mt. Elbrus in the Caucasus.

The Section was represented at the annual dinners of the Perth Section and of the Whole Club during the year. There was a good attendance at the AGM and Dinner, held at our 'local' – Newtonmore Hotel. This was possibly due to the attraction of the mountain bike meet which ran concurrently with the date and location of the AGM. Other social events in the calendar included the annual slide night and the Water of Leith Pub Crawl – both proved successful.

Office Bearers: *President,* B. Donaldson; *Hon. President,* J. Fowler; *Vice-President,* C. Stupart; *Hon. Vice-president,* M. Fleming; *Treasurer,* B. Finlayson; *Secretary,* R. Sinclair, 11b Fettes Row, Edinburgh, EH3 6SE; *Smiddy Custodian,* F. Fotheringham, Tigh na Sith, Braes, Ullapool; *Jock's Spot Custodian,* A. Borthwick, 2 Aytoun Grove, Dunfermline: *Committee,* D. Buchanan, K. Dry, S. Holden, J. Inglis, B. Leatherhead.

Lochaber Section:– Membership of the section remained much the same as 1992 – around 55 members, 30 based in Lochaber, the rest scattered around the country.

The Club held several meets during the year, the most popular venues being the Ling Hut, Glen Etive and Skye. Hillwalking and climbing are still the mainstays of the Club's activities although some members have branched out into other fields such as parapenting, mountain biking and canoeing.

The Club continues to meet socially every Thursday evening in the Nevis Bank Hotel, Fort William. During the winter months these evening sometimes incorporate a slide show or lecture.

During the summer, in addition to activity at home, several members travelled abroad, most to Chamonix and one to Alaska.

In September, the President welcomed, on behalf of the Club, Douglas Scott to the section as an Honorary Member.

In November, the Annual Dinner was held at Achnasheen where around 40 members and guests enjoyed an excellent meal and hospitality.

During the year a lot of work has been done to the Steall Hut in Glen Nevis, with more planned for the coming year. Bookings have been very steady with several dates already filled more than a year in advance.

The AGM was held in December and the following officials were elected: *Hon. Members* – Bert Bissell and Douglas Scott. *Hon. President.* Donald Watt; *President,* Willie Anderson; *Vice-President,* Ian Donaldson; *Treasurer,* Ian Walker, *Secretary,* Kenny Foggo, 19 Abrach Road, Inverlochy, Fort William. (Tel: 70 6299). *Steall Hut Custodian,* John Mathieson, 43 Drumfada Terrace, Corpach, Fort William. (Tel. 772 599).

K. Foggo.

SMC AND JMCS ABROAD

Europe

MARTIN MORAN reports:– Between June 23 and August 13, 1993, Simon Jenkins and I made what is believed to be the first continuous traverse of all 75 Alpine 4000m peaks. We climbed every peak or top with a height separation of 35m or more from its nearest neighbour. This gives as good a criterion for defining '4000ers' as any of the published lists.

Our time of 52 days was achieved with the help of high-level support teams, valley back-up from our wives, and the use of radios to co-ordinate the operation. The journey was entirely self-propelled. We used bicycles to move between the massifs, and thus made a continuous, unbroken route from the Piz Bernina in the east to the Barre des Ecrins in the west. Short touring skis were used on the Piz Bernina and in the Bernese Oberland.

The summer was the most unsettled in the last seven years, with an abnormally cold and snowy July. This gave winter conditions and absolute solitude on all the peaks of the Pennine Alps. Hot and thundery conditions developed in early August, which necessitated a good deal of night climbing on the Mont Blanc massif. The climax of the trip was a non-stop, 33-hour traverse of Mont Blanc and its 11 satellite summits on August 6 and 7.

We have so far raised £16,000 from the journey for Blythswood Relief Aid to Eastern Europe.

ROB MILNE writes:– Who says business and pleasure don't mix? During 1993 I was very successful at combining business trips with short climbing excursions. All it takes is a few business meetings in the right part of the world at the right time of year, and a climbing partner based in France with a car and the climbing gear. (All but the trip to Colorado were with Dr Louise Travé-Massuyès from Toulouse, France). The following is a short summary of my exploits.

February 20-21: After a meeting in Toulouse, we had a weekend of ice climbing near the Cirque de Garvanie in the French Pyrenees. Climbed a 1000ft Grade 4 snow gully system to the summit of Tallon, and had an afternoon of front pointing up waterfalls near there in the Cirque de Troumousse. The weather was near perfect with blue skies.

March 1-14: After a meeting in Bilbao, Spain, I took the train to Tarbes in the Central Pyrenees. I managed my first French limestone of the year at Penne Haute. The next day we did a 500ft E1 (French 6a A1) route on the Pic du Gar. This is a fine collection of rock towers in a rarely-visited area. It has enormous climbing potential and very few visitors. The weather was again, lovely warm sunshine.

April 1: A day of cross-country skiing in the high mountains of Colorado. Perfect sunshine and blue skies. We skied to a high mountain cirque above treeline at 12,000ft, and tried not to get sunburned. The descent through the trees on cross-country skis was 'interesting'.

April 4: Another day of rock climbing on French limestone near Toulouse. I was suffering from jet lag after being in Colorado, but the security of the bolts compensated. We spent most of the time practising for Half Dome, making hanging belays every three bolts.

May 22-29: After a business trip to a resort island near Seattle, we went to Yosemite for 10 days. We warmed up on the Central Pillar of Frenzie (5.9) and then climbed the North-west Face (VI 5.10 A2) of Half Dome. (see article p ???)

June 19-20: After a meeting in Barcelona, we spent the weekend climbing at Montserrat nearby. An amazing area of conglomerate rock domes and steep walls. We concentrated on 6+ pitch French 6a routes. Clear skies and warm sunshine again. Then to London for three days.

June 26-27: Back to Toulouse for another meeting and a weekend of climbing. Climbed the Spigolo Route on the Aiguille de Ansabere. An eight-pitch E2 (French 6a A2). Superb weather and great limestone climbing on the backbone of the Pyrenees.

August 26-27: Three days in Chamonix before a conference in nearby Chambery. The weather became stormy and in spite of a night at a hut, we didn't climb anything.

September 2-3: After a week of perfect weather, we left the conference early and went back to Chamonix. The weather was still good, but getting windy. We arrived in Chamonix and took the telepherique two hours later. That night and the next day, we climbed Route Major (TD) on the Italian side of Mont Blanc. We really felt the lack of acclimatisation near the summit. Breakable crust, wind slab and high winds are okay in the Cairngorms, but the lack of acclimatisation was a real killer. The next day we left, having spent three days in Chamonix.

October 9-10: Another weekend of rock climbing near Toulouse. On Saturday, we did many short limestone climbs to French 6b at an area called Le Pubis. (It looks like it sounds). On Sunday, we did a six-pitch 6b A2 route in Les Gorges de la Frau. Superb climbing with blue skies and warm sunshine on a rarely-visited crag.

By November, mixed climbing was again possible in Scotland, so I stayed home to climb, and the weather was rotten.

Morocco

HAMISH BROWN was in Morocco from February to June, 1993, with various friends and was able to visit many areas, to which he would be glad to give detailed information. SMC/JMCS members involved included Drew Sommerville, Dave Dawson and Sandy Donald.

February skiing was largely impossible as there was no base for the heavy snow falls of that month, but days at the Oukaïmeden resort gave excellent piste skiing and acclimatising. An Eagle Ski Club group then went up to the hills above Taroudant on the southern slopes of the Western Atlas, the pick-up being snow-stopped an hour below Tigouga.

A party had a marathon climb up Moulay Ali in deep snow, and rockier sport on the Mqqorn peaks south and north of the Tizi n' Ouguersiwid before leaving the

Medlawa Valley. The major objective of peak-bagging on ski in the Central High Atlas floundered, but an enjoyable trek was made through this area, far more attractive in spring blossom and snow than when most trek it in scorching summer.

A Land-Rover delivered the party (just) to Imi-n-Ouaqqa and Jbel Rhat saw an attempt from Tarbat n' Tirsal before heading over the Tizi n' Tirghiyst (superb rock carvings) to work along the Bou Willi and Bou Goumez valleys. Exit was made over the Tizi n' Aït Ourit to Sremt and Aït Mohammed, a magnificent pass, a fine village and a recommended way into/out of the region. A planned raid on Toubkal was wiped out by a storm at the Toubkal (Neltner) Hut, where the mice took delight in filling ski boots with spaghetti stalks. This hut is becoming impossibly over-crowded both in ski season and later with trekkers and Toubkal-baggers.

Ramadan (March) was spent exploring a-wheel, in the south-west – Igherm, Tata, Amtoudi, Sidi Ifni, Sidi Rbat, Immouzzer de Id Outane, before going up to Tafraoute from Tiznet to explore in the Ameln Valley and among the rock pitons an 'Blue Rocks'. Twin-topped Adrar Mkorn was climbed from Al Mouda. It gave good scrambling and huge vistas, and there was even a pilgrim route up to a shrine. The team then shifted to the Tizi n' Tichka pass and in to Telouet and Animiter, possibly the finest architectural survival of old kasbahs in Morocco. The ascent by the Oued Ounily was stopped well below Tamda Lake by a blizzard that rendered Anhromher (3609m) impossible but one pair climbed Zarzamt (3113m) before returning to base. More bad weather followed.

April however, saw excellent weather , but was mostly spent a-wheel including a visit to southern Spain, but some useful recces were made to Arghbala and the neglected country between the main chain and the middle Atlas.

May saw real summer conditions with the snow largely stripped off the peaks. An exciting Land-Rover trip deposited the party at Zawat Ahancal in the Moroccan Dolomites, an area of magnificent rock climbing strangely ignored by the British. (All its descriptions are in *La Montagne*). Taghia and the start of the gorges were visited and Jbel Timghazine (3382m) climbed from a bivouac, before returning to Zawat and Tizi Yllaz under Azourki. Walking to Agouti off-piste was a delight but the traverse over via Arous to the upper Tessaout plateau was hit by cloud and snow that almost led to an unplanned bivvy, the mules fighting through just before dark. Ighil M'Goun (4008m) and Tarkeddid (3585m) were done in various combinations and Jbel Ouqs (Jbel Tifdaniwine) (3462m) was added returning to Arous, then Aït Imi and a Land-Rover out to Aït Mohammed for shared taxis to Marrakesh. Most of the party then climbed Toubkal.

June gave very hot conditions, often over 100°F, but delighted a group partly there to see the Alpine flowers. Bus, mules and scooter brought the three parts together on the Tizi n' Test pass whence they descended to Souk Sebt and Zrit, a village in a valley west of Igdat and offering further ploys. The Tizi n' Aghbar (2648m)/Tizi n' Tiddi (2751m) led into the upper Ougdemt Valley and from a bivvy above Arg Jbel Igdat (3616m) and Idoudan (3316m) were climbed.

Camp was then shifted to the next valley north and from the Tizi n' Tighfist a good traverse made over the ridges and peaks linking Jbel Erdouz (3579m) and Jbel Gourza (3280m). The east ridge Erdouz gave Cuillin-type work and from Jbel Tameksaout (3344m) the party dropped to bivvy in the Asif Tislit (c2600m) valley. Adrar-n-Takawcht (3012m) saw the ridge resumed and Jbel Imlit (3245m) gave the toughest stretch before Gourza was done, unladen, from the col before it, Tizi n'

Imiri (2855m), whence a descent was made southwards to bivvy at the first water. (Gourza is taken as the peak climbed by Hooker and Ball a century ago and has strange shrines on top).

The walk out took in historic Tinmal Mosque, now restored, and watching the weird antics of the goat-skin clad figure seeing off the Sheep festival at Ijoukak. The party then went up to Imlil and from there or the Tazarhart (Lepiney) or Toubkal Huts made ascents to Toubkal, Tibherine, Afekoï, Ras and Timesguida Ouanoukrim and Tazarhart which are well enough known. Flowers, rather that the peaks, led to the Tizi n' Tichka and Oukaïmeden. On the way back Hamish went up into the hills from Taza and into the Gouffre Friouata, an impressive pot and tunnels.

Notes:
Several parties used Land-Rovers to enter or leave areas which, while expensive, is easy and saves precious days. Where ever possible mules were hired to carry gear which meant good food, tents and gas cylinders for cooking can be carried. Mules also ensures the cheery company of the Berber helpers and, invariably, one or two of their guides or aspirants whose expertise can often avoid many problems the Brits-only gangs face. The Hotel Ali in Marrakech is the city base for guides and much used by British parties. (Excellent local food). Hamish can give details on the many practical matters or English-speaking helpers. Motoring out proved an expensive luxury and is not worthwhile.

Asia

GRAHAM LITTLE reports:– In 1992, I made two trips to the Indian Himalaya, one pre-monsoon to the Kumaon, one post-monsoon to the Garwhal.

The former was a joint Indian-British expedition, and partnering Chris Bonington I made the first ascent of Sahdev East 5750m, and the first British ascent of Panch Chuli II 6904m, via the first ascent of the West Spur (see SMCJ 1993).

The latter expedition, with fellow SMC members, Dave Saddler, Matt Shaw and Gareth Yardley, was an attempt on the formidable South-east Ridge of Nilkanth 6596m. We reached an altitude of around 5600m at a snow col between the third and fourth pinnacles, but abandoned the route due to the worrying amount of loose rock and the committing nature of the ridge (see Himalayan Journal, Vol. 49).

In June-July, 1993, I enjoyed some excellent climbing in the Lemon Mountains of East Greenland with Chris Bonington, Jim Lowther and Rob Ferguson. Flying into a base on the Chisel Glacier, we made the first ascents of five peaks, all by technical routes (see Alpine Journal, Vol. 99). The last peak climbed (Bonington-Little) was the stunning rock monolith of Needle 1945m. This gave a 22-pitch big wall route with 10 pitches of 5a or above, and involved 24 hours of continuous climbing (see Climber & Hillwalker, October, 1993). A four-day journey out to the coast, mostly on skis, allowed a rendezvous with the pick-up plane, bringing to an end a very sociable and successful expedition.

DES RUBENS reports:– The Scottish Nanga Parbat Expedition 1992 was organised by Pete Long of Edinburgh. Other members were Ali Kellas, Geoff Cohen, Barry Owen and myself. Our plan was to attempt the first British ascent of the mountain, if possible by the still unclimbed Mummery Rib on the Diamir Face.

However, in 1991, Roger Mear and Dave Walsh made a fine ascent by the Kinshofer Route on the same face. We decided to still attempt the face in Alpine style, following in the footsteps of Collie, Mummery and Hastings whose attempt in 1895 was a courageous first attempt to climb a high mountain in the Himalaya.

After a short, but spectacular and beautiful walk in, we arrived at the base camp meadow at 13,000ft on June 11 1992. We were flanked by the great peaks of the Mazeno Ridge, culminating in the 12,000ft Diamir Face of Nanga Parbat itself.

Many avalanches were in evidence, one of which cascaded over the entire Mummery Rib just as we arrived We therefore decide to attempt the Kinshofer Route, already under siege by several Korean and European teams. It was the only unthreatened route in the entire cirque.

We were still concerned with style and determined not to attempt the mountain until we had acclimatised on surrounding peaks.

Over the next two weeks we enjoyed some fine Alpine climbing on the Mazeno and Galano peaks. Although no major peaks were ascended, we had some superb excursions in remote serious settings with wonderful views of Nanga Parbat.

Barry unfortunately, never acclimatised well and, despite our attempts to dissuade him decided to leave the expedition. The four of us then set off with 20kg sacks on July 4 to attempt the Kinshofer Route. This route takes a steep line up a spur projecting from the face. The spur then merges into an icefield. At about 23,000ft the route traverses near the top of the icefield to the Baszhin Basin where a traverse of easy-angled snowfields lead to the foot of the final steep slopes of the mountain.

During the second day of our attempt, Geoff took a long time to reach our stopping point (known as Camp 2) at about 20,000ft, probably due to not having shaken off completely a recent infection. The next day, Pete decided to descend the fixed ropes with Geoff, thus giving up his chance of the summit

This decision was taken after much heart-searching, as Pete was obviously fit and well acclimatised, and Geoff insisted that he was quite capable of descending safely on his own. However, as leader Pete felt a degree of responsibility for the rest of us which extended to seeing Geoff safely down.

Over the next two days, Ali and I made good progress to below the final Trapezoid at a camp at about 24,000ft. The weather was good and we were going so well we were daring to think of success. However, just before reaching our camp I began to feel uninterested and lethargic. The next morning, although feeling no particular discomfort, I knew I had to descend. Ali, though he must have been disappointed, was anxious to see me down to lower altitudes. (Discussion of symptoms later indicated the possible onset of a serious high altitude illness). In two days, in very bad weather which might have robbed us of the summit anyway, we returned to base.

Attempting Nanga Parbat was a great experience. I am sure that if we had sieged the mountain, we would have stood more chance of success, particularly as we would have acclimatised at higher altitude. But then, I think , we would all have been less satisfied. On a short trip one really only gets one shot at the summit and therefore to get everything right – weather, fitness, acclimatisation etc. – there is a certain degree of luck.

We acknowledge the generous assistance of the Scottish Mountaineering Trust, the mount Everest Foundation and the BMC as well as other suppliers listed in our report.

REVIEWS

The First Munroist – The Reverend A.E. Robertson; his Life, Munros and Photographs:- Peter Drummond and Ian Mitchell. (The Ernest Press, £13.95, ISBN 0-948153-19-9).

One of the consequences of the growth of interest in mountaineering has been that there are now enough climbers to support the steady production of books about our recreation, even – as this book demonstrates – biographical works about climbers of modest historical significance such as Robertson. When I heard that the Ernest Press were to publish an account of Robertson's climbing life, based on his personal diaries and collection of photographs, I hoped that those few of us who have tried to describe the early history of Scottish mountaineering would have several things to be pleased about: that Drummond and Mitchell would be two new recruits to the historical enterprise; that their book would provide a firm basis on the Salvationist side (in addition to Crocket's *Ben Nevis* and Humble's *Cuillin of Skye*) for future historical research, and that the publication of Robertson's diaries and photographs together with other contemporary material uncovered by research would provide us with fresh insights and new raw material. After all, the authors had been given every conceivable access by the Club to Robertson materials (see their Acknowledgements) as well as a gift of a set of Journals by J.D.B. Wilson's widow. These hopes have all been in vain.

In the first place, Drummond and Mitchell are worthless as historians. Errors of fact and opinion abound on every page and the sourcing of their 'facts' is capricious, unsystematic and neither collected as a bibliography, nor secured by adequate footnotes. It is, of course, particularly aggravating that neither Crocket, Humble nor I receive any acknowledgement for our painstaking efforts to get the historical record straight. It would be tedious to enumerate their errors. I will mention only a few of the grosser sort. Robertson did not 'take up rock-climbing after his Munro completion' (p.3) but was an enthusiastic climber from the moment that he joined the Club; the person charged with the murder of Edwin Rose in 1889 was called Laurie (not 'Lawrie', p.7); the alleged method of murder was bludgeoning to death with a boulder, not 'murder by pushing' and the place was Coire na Fhuaran in Glen Sannox, not 'Goatfell'; there was no 'summit cafe' on Ben Nevis in 1890 (p.7); 'Unna's ... grants' did not 'enable the (National) Trust to buy Glencoe' (p.67) nor was 'Buachaille soon to be acquired by the National Trust – due mainly to the legacy of Percy Unna' (p.119); the first ascent of the Pinnacle Ridge of Sgurr nan Gillean was not made by Robertson and the Clarks in 1898 (p.91, generous inference) nor was it (stricter inference) a 'plum of the ridge (which) had only recently been done' – it was climbed in the early 1880s; the Saddle (p.110) is not 'the only Munro with an English name' but one of many, such as Broad Cairn, Mount Keen, Cairnwell, etc.; Garbh Chioch Mhor did not 'only achieve Munro status in 1974', but in 1981 at the time of the infamous Donaldson-Brown revisions. These give a flavour only. Almost any fact which the reader takes the trouble to check will turn out to be false or misreported in some more subtle way. The errors regarding Unna are particularly reprehensible, since his 1937 letter is well-known and widely reproduced. This letter states clearly that Dalness Forest was acquired by subscriptions:- raised by the SMC from its own members and from the members of all other mountaineering clubs in Great Britain, and that the estate was handed over to NTS together with a surplus to be used as an endowment fund. How anyone who had read this letter could have come up with the fantasies quoted above is beyond me.

So, Drummond and Mitchell do not provide any sort of basis for future historical research. On the contrary, their egregious and ubiquitous errors will work to contaminate most future accounts, particularly those which will be written by busy journalists. Perhaps worse even than the factual errors and absence of scholarly apparatus are the errors of opinion. Much of the book, particularly the second part (due to Mitchell) is little more than a parade of the authors' socialist prejudices regarding wealth, occupational categories, social position, etc. We learn little from this about Robertson or his times, but only about a particular, mostly false, late 20th century view of them.

I will give only two examples. On p.32 Drummond gives his prejudiced views of the early SMC and of Robertson full rein. The club, he says, 'spanned all social classes from landowners to lawyers, doctors to divines, merchants to ministers, and professors to publishers . . . but little else'. While there is grain of truth in this sarcastic description, the failure to observe that the early Club also included a modicum of solicitors' clerks, insurance clerks, representatives and students is plainly deliberate, as is the highlighting of landowners, when only a handful of these were members. On p.93 there is a fascinating photograph of Naismith and McKenzie (I think) in Fionn Coire of Bruach na Frithe, together with two ladies, having tea in front of a tent. This is taken as an opportunity for a racy caption including unsubstantiated remarks about camping, picnics, the need for ladies to wear breeches while climbing with prurient men and some chauvinist comment about women climbers. Instead, Drummond and Mitchell might have made an effort to understand the photograph, by identifying the personnel (the ladies were, I think, the Prothero sisters, nieces of Colin Phillip who had climbed several peaks that summer, some with Hugh Munro) and seeking a better explanation for the use of the tent (Phillip used tents when painting in Skye, for shelter and to store equipment and sketchbooks). The Sligachan Hotel Climbs Book (in the National Library) would perhaps have assisted identification, since Robertson was staying there.

My final disappointment concerns the reproduction of historical materials. Robertson's Log of his traverse of the Munros is not reproduced and it might well have been (perhaps with some abbreviation) since it would have taken up only 15 pages or so. Nor is his published Journal account of the traverse included. In fact, only his Journal article on 'Old tracks, cross-country routes and coffin-roads in the North West Highlands' is reproduced. Although we are told (p.83) about Robertson's 'collection of thousands of slides' held 'on behalf of the Club' by the late Graham Tiso, there is no catalogue, only 95 of them are reproduced, and there is little effort made to identify them (particularly the people in them) properly. Besides the example discussed above from p.93, I noted that Gibbs is misidentified in the 1906 Meet picture (p.12), that Glover is misidentified on p.47, and that no one is identified in the wonderful Affric Hotel picture (p.13) except Unna and Robertson (both look dubious).

If Robertson left a description of it, this last photograph could be a valuable key to interpreting others of the period, but the reader is left only to speculate. Given this catalogue of errors and disappointments, is there anything that might be salvaged from *The First Munroist?* I enjoyed Chapter 7 – 'Transports of Delight'

– in which Mitchell makes the point that access and accommodation in the Highlands were in some ways superior to the facilities we enjoy today. This is a valid opinion, I am sure, and Mitchell makes the case reasonably well. However, the case is largely made on the basis of Robertson's own Log (so why not publish it?) and it contains the usual burden of error and overstatement. For instance, the SMC Camp (p.47) at the head of Loch Coruisk was a one-off effort (which could be repeated today with less difficulty) which did not involve a 'village of timber huts' (only three) and was not an official meet of the Club but the personal effort of a few members. Mitchell's other chapters are of little interest or value.

Those dealing with Gaelic Society in the 19th century and Access to the Hills amount to a mere two and three pages respectively! His review of Robertson's mountaineering presents a false picture of Robertson as a climber of modest competence and enthusiasm and leaves out completely his most interesting climbs (those with Raeburn on Ben Nevis in 1903 – see SMCJ viii, 86 – including the 18-minute ascent of the 18 Minute Route, the left variation of the Staircase Climb and a four-hour first descent of the Observatory Ridge in a deluge; and those with Newbigging and others on Ben Nevis in 1904 – see SMCJ viii, 220-1 – Tower Ridge by the Douglas Boulder and Recess Route, Pinnacle Arete of the Trident, Staircase Climb by the original line, another descent of Observatory Ridge.) No one reading these Journal accounts could possibly doubt Robertson's competence. It would be a pleasure to present Mitchell and Drummond with a copy of this chapter to eat (apiece) following their descent of Observatory Ridge in a deluge! However, I doubt whether their jaws would be capable of independent movement, and if they were, then saliva would be in very short supply!

Robin N. Campbell.

K2 – The 1939 Tragedy:–A.J. Kaufman and W. Putman. (1993, Diadem Books, illus., £14.99, ISBN 0-906371-69-4).

This book is the most recent, and presumably, most accurate version of the ill-fated 1939 American K2 expedition.

The account of events leading to the tragic outcome of the expedition makes a fascinating read, whether or not the reader has any mountaineering knowledge. The combination of conflicting personalities and the unfortunate accidents which beset the party from the outset would seem to have made the outcome almost inevitable.

The reader is left with the task of deciding who, if anyone, was to blame for the disaster, while the book continues with an analysis of the unanswered questions surrounding the expedition, and the blame laid on various members of the party following their return.

I found this chapter rather repetitive, and would have preferred to have been allowed to decide for myself.

After this is a chapter on a lay person's description of medical problems encountered at high altitude. The climbers' ignorance of these seemed in my opinion to have been the prime reason for the failure of the expedition.

I felt that the official reports and analysis at the end of the book merely repeated information presented earlier. Overall, however, I found the book to be an extremely interesting read which sheds light on previously unanswered questions surrounding the tragedy.

Joan Clark.

Northern Highlands – Rock & Ice Climbs – Vol. 2 Strathfarrar to Shetland:–
Roger Everett (SMC, £14.95, ISBN 0-907521-40-1).

This guide, the second Northern Highlands volume, covers perhaps the wildest and most adventurous climbing in the British Isles. It is primarily a rock climber's guide, with sandstone predominating, whether it is the Torridonian series of Stac Pollaidh, Reiff and Ardmair, or the Old Red sediments which feature in the magnificent cover photo of climbing at Rora Head, Orkney.

No guide which includes the daunting cliffs of Clo Mor and St John's Head could fail to excite the imaginative climber. Since most of the big sea-cliff routes and stacks are unrepeated, we can enjoy the unedited descriptions of the pioneers, including Mick Fowler's enigmatic gradings. In some places the vagueness of the available information itself adds to the aura of the routes. Just to know that Gog on Ben Loyal is one of Martin Boysen's 'desert island routes', is incentive enough to go and look at it, despite the absence of any concrete details on grade and line.

In contrast, the wealth of high-quality outcrop climbing in the region is documented in meticulous detail, with technical gradings and a star system to help those visitors who like to know all the numbers before launching out. The section on the outcrops of Easter Ross will be of particular service to climbers based in the Inverness district.

As series editor Roger Everett explains in his introduction, the guide does not seek to destroy the mystique of climbing in the North-west, but merely pulls together existing information which is already available in a diverse assortment of journals, magazines and other guides. There is no attempt to standardise or crudely advertise the area's climbs, and I am glad that the individuality of different cliffs and pioneers is respected.

However, the deft touch of expertise is evident in the way the guide is structured, in the detailed historical notes, and in the excellent diagrams. By assigning the writing of each section to an acknowledged 'local expert', Everett has achieved a production of remarkable quality, coupled with a distinctive personality.

The guide is a worthy tribute to the climbing in the Northern Highlands, and one of which the SMC may be proud.

Martin Moran.

On the Edge of Europe, Mountaineering in the Caucasus:– Audrey Salkeld and Jose Luis Bermudez (1993, Hodder & Stoughton, 260pp., illus., biblio., £18.99, ISBN 0-340-58547-1).

This anthology, as the authors admit, resulted from a symposium on the Caucasus organised by the Alpine Club in November 1991. It is a selection of reports from various mountaineering journals chosen to educate, inform and excite the reader, as the complimentary course selection of a gourmet meal delights the palate. This it does admirably, leaving one, as the meal should, wanting more, but with the realisation that only the mountains themselves can host the promised banquet.

Owing to 'transliterating' from the locally-used Cyrillic alphabet, basic early cartography, random name mutations and various non-English translations, the towering confusion over nomenclature of these early reports has been successfully scaled, while the addition of invaluable link passages between individual reports has allowed the authors some original input to the book, thus sidestepping claims of plagiarising the works of past generations of climbers. They accomplish their modestly stated goal of 'not adding to the confusion that already exists over nomenclature'.

The chosen passages start in 1868 with an Ultramontane Alpine Club member, D. W. Freshfield of Eton and Oxford. Privileged and rich as were all climbers of his day, they acknowledge the able Chamonix Guides who assisted them in their first ascents. Freshfield's was a M'sieur Devouassoud, poetically labeled thus: 'Knight-errant of the glacier-cleaving blade.'

Names like Dent, Donkin, Cockin, Tucker, Mummery and Raeburn delight, almost as much as the reports of their exploits do. The early exploration of these fine mountains, often compared to the Alps, though on an acknowledged grander scale, was not without incident. The deaths of Donkin, Fox and their guides subdue the reader. No doubt the Victorian newspaper reports of the day did likewise. These pioneers were bold men who travelled and climbed in these remote mountains carrying side arms as accessories. One cannot but marvel at their self-assured posture in those wild lands.

In 1913, Raeburn and Ling successfully visited the area and an extract from Raeburn's diary, first published in the SMCJ in 1955, is reproduced. The other 1962 SMCJ reprint is G. J. Ritchie's account of an epic 12-day traverse of the main ridge of Schkelda, Alpine style, followed by a large contingent of the Red Army. The insight into the Communist system of the day speaks volumes and the final piece is of Mick Fowler's ascent of Ushba in 1986, which also sadly hints at the commercialisation of these majestic peaks.

Appendix Two documents the controversy over the first ascent of Elbrus – Europe's highest mountain. The dismissive editorial comment from the Alpine Club Journal, and associated correspondence, reeks of class snobbery of the worst kind, which coincidentally established a club member as the first ascentionist.

This publication is, without doubt, essential reading for aspirants wishing to ascend the highest peaks in Europe. It is also an inspiring collection and after reading them, no mountaineer, with pulse quickening, could deny the desire to visit the Caucasus Mountains.

Colwyn M. Jones.

Mountaineering:– Catalogue of the Graham Brown and Lloyd Collections in the National Library of Scotland. (National Library of Scotland, 1994, 453pp., £15.00, Microfiche Supplement, ISBN 0-902220-98-5.)

I still quake slightly when I remember one of the guardians in the NLS; grey, cropped hair, gold-rimmed glasses, ÖberGrüppenführer of the Books as he ensured I did have a pencil, my hands were clean, and that I was not hell-bent on literary pyromania or defacement. I presume they eventually bought the book I was writing at the time so perhaps all is forgiven. (In fact, they would have had no choice, as due to legal deposit, the NLS receives copies of all current British publications). This worthy bibliography, of the collections of T. Graham Brown and Robert Wylie Lloyd – 20,000 items, and 1659 volumes respectively – will certainly make it easier to browse. The NLS prides itself in its collection of materials relating to Alpinism and mountaineering, which of course includes a few SMC-derived materials.

While the Brown name and collection is fairly well known, that of Lloyd may not be. This book, which of necessity has kept the introductory text to a minimum, does have a short note on both. We read with amusement that Lloyd, who seems to have been an obsessive collector rather than an enthusiastic reader, was energetic in raising money for the 1953 Everest Expedition (he was treasurer of the Mount Everest Committee), but that it was said that 'his assiduity in raising funds for Everest was only matched by his extreme reluctance to part with them'. Many of his books were never opened, and indeed he often collected multiple copies of the same book.

The Lloyd collection is particularly rich in Swiss material, while Brown's material is often field-worn, as he actually used the guidebooks etc. There is a microfiche copy in the end case, which can be supplemented as more cataloguing is published. The books are listed alphabetically, and the two collections are intermingled.

T. Graham Brown was astute enough, and well-heeled enough, not only to donate his collection to the NLS, but also to provide a trust fund which allows the collection to grow. This book was published using that fund, and is a publication of which the NLS and its staff should be rightly pleased.

Ken Crocket.

The High Mountains of the Alps:– Helmut Dumler and Willi P. Burkhardt (1993, Diadem Books, 223pp., £30, ISBN 0-89886-378-3)

This large format, profusely illustrated in colour, coffee-table book is a translation from the German language edition which was published about five years ago. That book was in turn descended from the classic *Die Viertausender der Alpen* by Karl Blodig, who claimed to be the first person to climb all the Alpine 4000ers when he completed the list of qualifying peaks that existed in 1911. The German language edition has been substantially re-designed by Ken Wilson, who has added a lot of new historical material, and a large number of new illustrations have been included, the major contributor being John Allen, so these two can be considered to have made almost as great a contribution to the English language edition as have Dumler and Burkhardt.

The result is a superbly illustrated celebration of the highest mountains of the Alps, for which much credit must go to Ken Wilson for his meticulous attention to quality.

Each of the mountains (or mountain groups) is described with details of the principal routes and the history of the early ascents of these routes. Ken Wilson's main contribution to the text has been to amplify the German original by adding information from English language sources about British ascents that were overlooked by the German author. The text does suffer from being a mixture of translation and original English, with some of the translated passages being rather quaint and uneven. The route descriptions add little to those already available in guidebooks such as Goedeke's recent publication, but the historical sections will be of interest to those not familiar with Alpine history.

It is the illustrations, however, that are the principal feature of this book. Many of them are reproduced in large format, and very impressive they are. The majority are the work of Willi Burkhardt using a large format camera (and often an aeroplane or helicopter). The only criticism that one can make of his illustrations concerns the tones and colour balance of some of them. The combination of chocolate-brown mountains and slate-blue skies produces some unnatural results, possibly the result of using early film stock or filters. However, where the colour balance is right, the results are superb and this must be the finest selection of Alpine photographs assembled in one book. The contributions of John Allen, Bill O'Connor and other British alpine photographers add greatly to the overall photographic coverage and quality.

There is not, as far as this reviewer knows, a generally accepted list of Alpine 4000m mountains. Many would say that this is a good thing. However, the inclusion of the Balmenhorn and Punta Giordani (two minor bumps on the southern flank of Monte Rosa) in a book entitled *The High Mountains of the Alps* seems hard to justify. Sir Hugh T. Munro would not have rated them, and the only justification for their inclusion may be the ease with which they can be ticked off. The Aiguilles du Diable and the subsidiary tops of the Grandes Jorasses and Grand Combin have more right to be included.

Please do not, on the strength of this review, rush out to buy this book within a week or two of receiving your copy of the Journal. It is out of print already. Ken Wilson's publisher, unimpressed by his optimism and enthusiasm for this book, printed only 4000 copies which sold out within a few weeks of publication last November. However, it is their intention to publish another few thousand for Christmas, so keep your eyes open for it. It is worth waiting for.

D. Bennet.

Sea, Ice and Rock – Sailing and Climbing above the Arctic Circle.:- Chris Bonington and Robin Knox-Johnston. (1993, Coronet Books, 192 pp., many illustrations in black and white and colour. £9.99, ISBN 0-340-58877-2).

This is the paperback version of the book reviewed in last year's SMCJ by our inestimable Iain Smart. The price, for a paperback, is a bit cheeky, and no doubt the reservations expressed last year remain.

Ken Crocket.

Beyond Risk – Conversations with climbers:– Nicholas O'Connell. (Diadem Books, £15.99, ISBN 0-906371-99-6).

This book is readable, possibly more to dip into rather than to read from cover to cover. The author has interviewed 17 of the world's top climbers; a group who, he suggests, have significantly shaped the history of climbing. He explores their motivation, and inspiration; why do they do it? He regards climbing as a metaphor for life and sets out with the lofty aim of exploring this larger dimension. Despite this, I was left with another impression – the personal stories of the climbers themselves.

Interviews with Reinhold Messner, Riccardo Cassin, Sir Edmund Hillary, Kurt Diemberger, Walter Bonatti, Royal Robbins, Warren Harding, Chris Bonington, Doug Scott, Voytek Kurtyka, Jean-Claude Droyer, Jeff Lowe, Wolfgang Gullich, Catherine Destivelle, Lynn Hill, Peter Croft and Tomo Cesen are reported. They were chosen as representatives of a particular style or period of climbing – Himalayan mountaineers to sport climbers, pioneering alpinists to big wall climbers. Each chapter gives a short biography and then an account of the interview. This genre can be deadly boring but I did not find it so here as it is well written. The personality of the climber came across more strongly in some interviews than in others where the questioning seemed to focus on more technical aspects.

Questions followed broadly the same themes throughout: How did you start climbing? Why? How did you survive? Relationships with climbing partners and family, ethics, risks, dangers and personal philosophy. One notable similarity between all those interviewed was that they are all still alive (with the exception of Wolfgang Gullich who died in a car accident) and I found their clear-thinking views about their capacities and reasons for survival of interest. I also enjoyed the impression of personal interactions, for example, the different viewpoints on the ethics of big wall climbing of Royal Robbins and Warren Harding.

Reasons to climb varied but tended to be nebulous: "There is no reason, If I asked you 'Why are you living?' what would you say? For me there is no difference." – Reinhold Messner.

"I just like to be in the mountains, the scenery is very impressive, it's like being in a movie, and I like the adventure; it's a very emotional game." – Catherine Destivelle.

More satisfying than these vague notions are the stories, the insights into personal emotions at the limits of human endurance and the relationships between climbing partners. The photographs are in black and white and disappointing because there are too few and of variable quality.

This a book about people and their passion. It is a good idea well presented and would be worth adding to your collection if you like this sort of thing.

Jane Naismith.

My Vertical World:– Jerzy Kukuczka – translated by Andrew Wielochowski. (Hodder & Stoughton; 189pp., £16.99, ISBN 0-340-53485-0).

If the Himalayan climbing scene can be said to go through 10-year cycles when one nationality appears to dominate, then the 1980s was the decade of the Poles. Of these, Jerzy Kukuczka, was in many ways, the greatest. The second man to climb the 8000m peaks, he climbed all 14 but Lhotse, either by new routes, or by first winter ascents. This book is the story of the eight breathtaking years he spent realising his ambition.

The characteristics which enabled Kukuczka to achieve his record performance come across early in the book and thereafter frequently. His single-minded determination and obstinacy made him the one always arguing for carrying on upwards when others were having second thoughts. Not until the 1985 attempt on Lhotse South Face does Kukuczka finally not only willingly agree to retreat, but actually propose it. However, this was while attempting his fourth 8000m peak of the year, just after his companion has been killed and with winter rapidly approaching, so this uncharacteristic behaviour may be seen in context. (Interestingly, it was this very face from which Kukuczka was to fall to his death in 1989, from a point only a few hundred metres from the top).

This psychological toughness was particularly strong in Kukuczka, but it was complemented by tremendous physical stamina, a staggering appetite for sheer hard work and, it must be said, a fair share of luck. However, it is his drive which dominates everything, including this book. While the Polish bureaucracy managed to frustrate his plans for a while (after an illegal ascent of Broad Peak, clyped on by Messner), it really was only a matter of time before it crumpled in the face of such tremendous determination.

The details of the climbing get relatively little attention, but the enormous effort involved in Himalayan climbing is made painfully clear. Additionally Kukuczka, uninterested in creating an 'image', does not flinch from exposing his less attractive character traits, such as more than a hint of ruthlessness (but not callousness), although there is little evidence of introspection of any sort. All the while the pace never relents as ascent follows ascent until, reeling, the reader is compelled to put the book down while the pulse returns to normal and the eyes cease to bulge.

Of necessity, given the scale of the enterprise chronicled in this book, much is left out. What remains may not be the greatest mountain literature, but in its own way it creates a compelling and convincing picture of a mountaineer obsessed with climbing on the world's highest mountains. No explanation for this obsession is attempted because none was required – it simply was, contradictions and all. Where it was leading does not appear to be a question Kukuczka bothered himself with, but, while it is easy to be clever with hindsight, to the reader it seems only too obvious.

Bob Duncan.

The Undiscovered Country:– Phil Bartlett (The Ernest Press, 1993, 183pp., illus., £15.95, ISBN 0-948153-24-5).

It may be either a brave man, or a fool, who attempts to answer the old question of why we climb. I feel that Mr Bartlett is not the latter, which points to the former. Information on the dust cover telling us that he teaches confirms this suspicion. The author enjoys philosophical argument, and this shows in his writing, when he sometimes chases his own tail making a point. But this is a sneaky sideswipe at what is an interesting book on the mental processes pushing, pulling and impinging on our otherwise blithely conscious climbing days.

An immense amount of reading has gone into the genesis of the book. There is (of necessity the author claims), a curtailed bibliography, and a section of notes at the end of the book, which in itself often answers in various ways, the posed question. Some good quotes may be found here by the great names in mountaineering.

The book is multipart. The broad aim is the philosophy of – why? Interspersed are brief biographies of who. It finishes with an intelligent summary. Mountains and mountaineering may be on a doomed course, destined to be overwhelmed with more and more people enjoying the increasingly rare blessing that is the quiet day in the hills. This is a depressing conclusion so easy to fall into with. Sellers of attractive photographs and alluring guidebooks are some of the guilty, organisers of tours and treks are others. We are cursed with holding the beautiful jewel we wish to share. Should we be more selfish and less greedy? Technology has pushed its glittering snout into the game. Witness, or remember, young climbers and their fascination with new gear, with shiny, expensive protection. Spot an older climber with a carefully built-up collection of crummy tat, disdainfully avoiding buying gear until well past sell dates. This may be an unspoken awareness that things should be kept simple. We climb because we are, or should be, naked against the mountain. When we have reduced a climb to a mute submission against overwhelming technology then its has been bastardised. It is this facet that makes some of us wary of sport climbing surely.

The Scottish Highlands we like because of their undeveloped state. When the likes of the Rannoch Moor is networked with Astroturf paths then we can all stay at home. When we can read in a guidebook the precise details enabling us to climb a route with nothing but the glycogen levels in our muscle tissue left to chance, why bother? We are rightly suspicious of overdetailed guidebooks, bureaucratic organisations, Olympic wall scratchings, outdoor schools, the whole shebang. 'What we have to fear,' concludes Bartlett, 'is that our passion will be . . . reduced to its lowest common denominator, that mountaineering will be turned into an Olympic sport, competition, glory, money.

Bartlett quotes the astronomer Fred Hoyle to good effect: 'The danger of technology lies not so much in the production of devices and gadgets as in trapping us into offering aims, purposes and reasons for everything we do. And so technology traps us into things that are evanescent and of no lasting satisfaction.'

A thoughtful book that will start you thinking, and one can ask for little more from any book. No solution to the problems raised, so I can only suggest step one – add this book to your library.

Ken Crocket.

Hands of a Climber – A Life of Colin Kirkus:– Steve Dean. (1993, The Ernest Press, 278pp., £15.95. IBSN 0-948153-21-0).

As an intrepid armchair climber – who has spent more than half a lifetime on first ascents in the Himalayas, in the Alps, the Andes and all over Britain – I thought I was familiar with the names of all the 'greats' in the history of mountaineering and rock climbing.

How was it then, that on being given this biography of Colin Kirkus, I had to say: 'Who?' – and I mean it? Despite being familiar with some of the names of his illustrious companions, such as Wilfred Noyce (introduced to climbing as a raw 16-year-old by his cousin, Kirkus), Frank Smythe, Jack Longland and so on, the name of this undoubtedly great pioneering rock climber of the late 1920s and 1930s had somehow escaped me.

The matter has now been completely righted as a result of reading Steve Dean's detailed and carefully-researched biography. It is a work of love and tremendous effort, having involved the author in interviews with a wide circle of Colin Kirkus's remaining climbing companions, many of them not too active after the passage of nearly 60 years. Even more time-consuming and trying must have been the task of consulting hundreds of past records from climbing club notes, journals and diaries. Collating these into a coherent and sequential whole, while constructing a believable and lifelike character from this information, has been achieved to a very high standard by the author. He must have come to feel that he knows Colin Kirkus as well, if not better, than the latter's surviving brother, despite not having been born until Kirkus's life had come to its untimely end.

Britain's plunge into the 1939-45 war and Kirkus's death in the RAF in 1942 obviously robbed the climbing fraternity of an acknowledged pioneer and leader. It also seems highly probable that, based on his one published book, we were robbed of many enjoyable and well-written books too, which would have described with considerable modesty and humour, the shared delights of this man's many climbing adventures in Britain and overseas.

Perhaps because of expertise on rock and his limited experience on snow and ice – considered a necessity in the 1930s for big expeditions such as Everest – Colin Kirkus's abilities were passed over and he failed to achieve the niche in the halls of fame achieved by some of his contemporaries. However, the analysis offered in this book of his performance on the 1933 expedition to Gangotri suggests that he would have climbed at altitude, equally as successfully as many of the top climbers who did achieve selection for these expeditions.

Northern Highlands Guide Editors – past and present – Geoff Cohen and Ian Rowe in British Columbia. Photo: Des Rubens.

Kirkus left a tremendous legacy of inaugural routes of a high standard, of striking solo routes and was instrumental in laying the pre-war foundations for the rapid development of techniques that characterised the post-war period.

Personally, I am very grateful for the extension of my knowledge of the British climbing scene in this period, gained from Steve Dean's book, and I am sure that many others, more closely involved with climbing, will find themselves echoing these sentiments.

David H. Jones.

Northeast Outcrops:– Edited by Neil Morrison. (SMC, 342pp., illus., £13.95, ISBN 0-907521-41-X).

In an area of Scotland where the climate has recently been described as 'nine months winter and three months *coorse* weather' you might be excused for thinking you had picked up a guide to Bosigran or even Les Calanques. But no; that superb cover photograph of Neil Morrison on the immaculate granite of Hole in the Wall was definitely taken on the Buchan sea cliffs. And believe it or not, good rock climbing conditions like that are not uncommon throughout the year as the coastal fringe is largely within a rain-shadow area, protected from prevailing winds by high ground to the west and south.

Since the publication of Dougie Dinwoodie's long-out-of-print 1984 edition the guide has lost the semi-subterranean, but natural, Huntly's Cave near Grantown and gained the man-made Angus quarries of Legaston, Balmashanner and Ley, plus a few crags and quarries on Upper Deeside.

The inclusion of the Angus quarries sets a precedent for SMC guides in that it is the first time that French grades have been used for wholly bolt-protected sport climbs. The reasons for, and the ethics behind treating sport and traditional climbs differently, is explained in the notes section and follows Mountaineering Council of Scotland guidelines.

Other additions to this guide include an important well-researched historical section documenting for the first time the development of climbing over the whole area, some of which dates back to the turn of the century. Also the introduction gives good hints and advice to visitors unfamiliar with the vagaries of the sea cliffs.

With more than 300 pages packed with climbs ranging in difficulty from easy to E7 6c and F8b+ this new edition has something to offer even the most jaded crag rat. A highly-commendable guide by Morrison and his band of authors and photographers.

Greg Strange.

Nothing so Simple as Climbing:– G.J.F. Dutton. (Diadem, 160pp., £12.99 hardback – also available in paperback, ISBN 0-906371-12-0).

The Doctor and his unfortunate companions, the Apprentice and the anonymous Narrator, will need no introduction to readers of the Journal, as their exploits have periodically graced these pages for many more years than I for one have been a member. This is the second collection of their stories, the first, *The Ridiculous Mountains,* having been published by Diadem in 1984 to some critical acclaim – if the review extracts on the rear of the dust-jacket are anything to go by. This collection comprises 21 stories, of which seven have appeared elsewhere, including five from the SMCJ.

Alistair Brightman and Norman Armstrong climbing 'The Wicker Man' E3 6a, Creag an Dubh Loch. Photo: Alastair Matthewson.

One does not readily criticise work which has obviously brought great pleasure to many, especially that produced by a distinguished ex-editor of the Journal, yet I confess that there is something about these stories which irritates me. Perhaps it is the Doctor's pomposity, although that exists only to be made fun of; maybe it is his companions' continued, almost insufferable restraint in the face of severe provocation; more likely, though, it is the strained extremes reached in almost every situation in which the trio find themselves. After a few stories I began to find this more than a little tedious. While faintly mocking asides or some other well-pointed barbs brought regular smiles, as the situations themselves, the centrepieces of the stories, became increasingly unlikely, so did I find them less and less funny.

Dutton's style is a slightly idiosyncratic mix of short, staccato, often single-word sentences and more complex constructions featuring an extensive, occasionally obscure vocabulary. In small quantities it reads easily and generates the intended immediacy, but in larger doses it has a contrived and slightly laboured feel, as if the author tried just a little too hard.

However, I am on dangerous ground and indeed may have already over-extended my, at most, merely modest abilities in literary criticism. Maybe, in truth, I am just not overfond of climbing fiction, especially of the humorous variety, or perhaps I have a slightly less sophisticated palate than Dutton's fare is intended for. No sexual allusions, no thinly disguised victim mercilessly lampooned? But so what if it was not completely to this reader's taste. If you are in any doubt yourself you need only look at a few back numbers of the SMCJ. Should you find that you disagree with me you will be in good and plentiful company.

Bob Duncan.

Ben Nevis – Rock and Ice Climbs:– Simon Richardson, Alastair Walker, Robin Clothier (SMC, 1994, 339pp., Illus., £13.95, IBSN 0-907521-42-8).

Well, it seems there are some advantages of NOT being in the SMC, one of them being that Donald Bennet sends you an SMC book from time to time for an impartial review!

So what's the new Ben Nevis area Rock and Ice guidebook really like? First thing to note is that it covers much more than Ben Nevis. The new winter playgrounds of Aonach Mor and Aonach Beag are right up to date, and at last, Creag Meaghaidh, so long in the wilderness, has found a home in a guidebook, though surprisingly for such a major area, there's no mention of it on the front cover.

Other areas have come of guidebook age, the wonderfully-remote routes on Meall Garbh, at Loch Treig and the rarely-visited Wee Team Gully in the Monadh Liath for instance. It seems traditional when reviewing a guidebook to try and render it out of date as soon as possible – so let's do it, and while it may be a bit unfair, an otherwise well-researched book may have been more complete had the authors taken a wee look at the most accessible gullies in the whole area – those in Glen Nevis.

Despite the spinal shiver it induces, Five Finger Gully provides wonderful sport in winter up its various digits, likewise its near neighbour, Antler Gully.

Christmas Gully continues at a steady Grade II almost to the summit of Carn Dearg SW: Surgeon's Gully is probably one of the best two-day winter routes in Scotland! All of these less than an hour from the road.

What's in the book is good though. Andrew Clarke's fine picture (p.212) of John Main on Gemini is perhaps the best of several colour pictures. The blodge of the Great Tower (facing p.116) is, if not, the worst picture, probably the least useful.

Given the time scale Donald gave me for the review, I have not had time for a word-by-word read, but what I have seen looks good and exciting. Comments I have heard, from the few others who have seen the book, vary from the sublime to the ridiculous as usual. Is Comb Gully really a IV? Did your granny actually ski the Curtain? Are the Post routes on Meaghaidh really that good? And, is Minus One Direct in summer really so brilliant, or perhaps like the Long Climb – dark, dreepy and bloody frightening? And the main question of them all – will the new winter grading system really catch on? 'Daft idea,' or 'Essential for the modern punter.' Only time will tell.

I like the book, though to be honest I have not had time to give it a thorough going over. I am worried that it will fall to pieces pretty soon, but I do love the wonderful wee quotes that are dotted about the list of first ascents. I'll leave you with these:–

MacPhee, Williams and Henderson on Glover's Chimney – 'The entire Chimney was sheeted with ice and there was no place where the leader could take a proper rest, much less to which he could bring me up. It was a thrilling experience for the second and third, straining their eyes in the darkness watching their leader's figure dimly silhouetted against the sky as he got nearer to the Tower Gap.'

Bell on Hesperides Ledge – 'It is a steeply inclined, curving shelf and is a perfect garden of mossy and lush vegetation . . . there are several exceedingly delicate corners to negotiate with a most precipitous drop on the right. The vegetation is loosely anchored, the rocks are rather loose, and there are practically no positive holds . . .'

Whillans on Patey on Crab Crawl – "A bold solo of a new route. Two weeks' earlier Patey had failed to interest Whillans in an attempt. 'Look mate,' he interrupted, 'do you know what you want to do? You want to team up with a crab. It's got claws, walks sideways and it's got a thick 'ead. This isn't a climb, it's a bloody crab-crawl!'"

Mick Tighe.

The Fife Coast:– Hamish Brown. (Mainstream Publishing, 1994, 226pp., illus., £12.99, ISBN 1-85158-608-3.)

This is a pleasant walking guide to the Fife coastline, from the Forth Bridges to Leuchars via the Castles Coast and the East Neuk. Brown divides the walk into 11 days, totalling some 131km. Amusingly enough, and we know only because Brown is honest enough to tell us, this book was accidental. On being asked for some photographs of local scenes, and despite living in Fife, the author discovered he was lacking in knowledge of his own backyard (a common enough phenomenon, I daresay). Collecting photographs, he further discovered just how interesting the ancient kingdom was, and away he went, slowly, on a voyage culminating in this book.

'It taks a lang spoon tae sup wi a Fifer,' runs a traditional saying, and true to form Brown collected firewood as he explored the coast, finding enough to heat his house over two winters. I admit to finding Fife a cold place, but then I have very little insulation.

Each suggested day is packed with descriptions of what you can see, there is a hand-drawn map, lists of where to stay including telephone numbers, and of course, photographs of what you might see en route. Brown gets in lots of bashes against the Huns and Vandals as usual, both private and Organisational, so that local councils etc. might well read the book with an eye to improving their local environment. It is interesting to see a guide to a lowland area, one steeped in history. Doocot fanciers would do well here for example. The author, in his chatty style, has avoided a dull guide. He also gives good advice as how to use it, carefully going over the relevant map the night before. The good landladies of the Fife Coast had better freshen up their paintwork; Brown's guide in hand, there should be more visitors this summer!

Ken Crocket.

Whensover – 50 years of the RAF Mountain Rescue Service 1943-1993:– Frank Card. (The Ernest Press, 1993, 342pp, illus., £17.95, ISBN 0-948153-23-7).

With a good sense of timing, given the politics of the moment, this readable book tells the history of the mountain rescue service of the Royal Air Force – manned by volunteers, men and women, of all ranks, who very often risked their lives in appalling conditions in the mountains.

Going through the index I was struck by the number of climbers' names that I knew. The RAF Mountain Rescue has obviously been a haven for a large number of climbing layabouts! One of the names cropping up in the book is that of Jack Baines – who is one half of the Ernest Press. This may in part account for the obvious affection and care with which the book has been treated. There are fine drawings – paintings and cartoons rather – by Pat Donovan, along with maps drawn by Tony Jones.

It is a book to be savoured, with many human stories. A sense of humour abounds, as might be expected in an activity as potentially gruelling as mountain rescue. Reading the book, I was struck again and again by the difference in approach from Unsworth's book (see above). If only . . .

This book is dedicated to the memory of the late George Graham, a climbing medical doctor who was responsible for the setting up of the first team. To give you a picture of just how much this was needed during the war, military crashes had accounted for 571 aircrew deaths on the mountains of Britain in 1943 alone. As mentioned above, a sense of humour is evident, just as well in a book which could have been merely a catalogue of grisly accident reports. The cartoons help too.

Next time you see a big yellow bird flying over Glen Coe, remember that it is only part of the organisation which has evolved a long way from its origins. That all-important human touch has always been present as well, as highlighted by an American veteran who remembered his own bitter experiences of returning from the Vietnam war. He was met by photographers, banged on a flight home, then left to hike on the freeways. No wonder so many minds were damaged. By contrast, during and after something as horrific as the Lockerbie Jumbo crash, counselling was quickly made available to the teams who had to go out into the fields and find the sad human remains, often collected up against a fence as though caught in a net, sometimes still strapped into a seat. The care shown by the RAF teams has often extended into local communities beyond direct involvement in rescue work. To the visiting climber the only sign of this might be a few squadron plaques on the bar wall, but it often goes deeper.

A lovingly-researched book.

Ken Crocket.

Menlove:– Jim Perrin (The Ernest Press, 1993, 290pp., illus., £9.95. ISBN 0-948153-28-8).

This is a very sympathetic view of the life of an amazing, intelligent, and fit man, John Menlove Edwards, pieced together excellently by Jim Perrin.

As a non-participant in the sport, I was surprised by my interest in this pre-war pioneer of rock climbing (not mountaineering, as Menlove stresses, this is too loose a word). His antics, mostly in Wales and Skye, along with those of his partners are quite amazing, to say the least.

Coming from a strict, church-following family, and being sent to board at Fettes in Edinburgh, contributed to Menlove's strong views and loneliness, visible in countless poems featured throughout the book.

Menlove achieved some impressive feats in his short life, a prime example of which was his canoe journey to the Isle of Man in a very basic craft, in addition to his many dangerous solo ascents.

The final sadness of his repression by society over his immoral behaviour (homosexuality), is captured perfectly in the final chapter. John Menlove Edwards certainly was a man trapped in the wrong decade, and was tortured by this thought until his predictable suicide. He should be admired and remembered for his achievements in so many different aspects of life, nonetheless.

Jennifer A. Jones.

Hold The Heights:– Walt Unsworth. (Hodder & Stoughton, 1993, 432pp., illus., £19.99, ISBN 0-340-33913-6).

This book is subtitled *The Foundations of Mountaineering,* but it is really about Unsworth's speciality, the early Alpine guides and their clients. There is the usual token mention of Collie and Tower Ridge, which is about all that Scottish mountaineering gets in this book (he said wearily, not with a chip or a grudge, but strong in the knowledge of our contributions to mountaineering.) Smith, Marshall, Patey, Lovat – none of them here. Raeburn receives a couple of lines for his Caucasus expedition, but otherwise we are on the old sepia trail again. Once more, we are presented with the *Walt Disney History of Mountaineering.*

The last two pages, summing up mountaineering since the ascent of Everest, are embarrassing. Better not to try at all, than scrape over the cracks with watered-down emulsion. The last paragraph in the book provides a handle on the style. 'Mountaineering in all its forms is more popular today than it has ever been. The challenge remains the same, of man versus mountain. It is a battle that man can never win. The best he can ever hope for is an honourable draw.' Give us a break, Walt. I could be really cruel and quote Unsworth's comment on Collie's obituary of Kellas, which is likened to building bricks without straw.

Most of the book is like the old Alpine Journal (among many other sources), dull, safe, brave batsman on a firm wicket with warm, flat beer in the club hut stuff. Like his Encyclopaedia, it must have been a long, grinding glacier plod. At least glaciers occasionally throw up something interesting in the dead guide line. Perhaps the answer might be for Unsworth to write in association with a fellow author up to speed with personalities and modern doings. Unless that happens, however, I fear we may be in for more of the same.

Ken Crocket.

Journals of Kindred Clubs

The Alpine Journal 1993 Vol. 98 No. 342:– (The Ernest Press, 363pp., £18.50).

As might be expected this edition devotes much of its space to the 40th anniversary of the first ascent of Everest. A series of reminiscences and diaries offer fresh insights into the personalities of the 1953 team, and the effect of its success on their subsequent lives. However, there is a feast of reading besides, with articles attractively batched under section titles such as New Directions and Looking Back. It is indicative of the scope of the Journal that within the same volume one can learn of the history of the Alps in Roman times and find out why committed parapenters can suddenly decide to quit the sport.

The editor, Johanna Merz, is clearly trying to break out of the reporting format that makes many journals hard to digest, and in part succeeds. However, the format of many of the expedition articles still tends towards that of the factual account rather than the gripping narrative. One might guess that some authors have already published their accounts with greater length, drama and remuneration elsewhere. Personal and lively styles of writing are needed for a journal to entertain as well as inform. In this respect, contributors to the Alpine Journal have something to learn from the SMCJ.

Martin Moran.

The Himalayan Journal, Vol. 49, 1991-92.

As ever, the Himalayan Journal is full of variety and information. This volume has also some very good writing. For historians there is an excellent article on the Americans, Hunter and Fanny Bullock Workman (who explored the Karakoram in the early years of this century), and a lengthy resume of the fascinating contents of HJ Vol. II (1930), reminding us of the atmosphere of the British Empire still in its heyday, and the formidable achievements of scholarship and exploration that it produced. For explorers of the mind there are essays on the psychological utility of mountaineering (proposing over compensation against fear as the driving force) and on the 'paranormal' experience of imaginary companions, as so often reported by solo climbers at high altitudes.

Inevitably, Everest makes its appearance several times, including an account of a solo attempt by Johnathon Pratt in 1991 (he succeeded the following year). Well known British climbers feature prominently, both in climbing and in accidents, with the touch-and-go escapes of Stephen Venables from Panch Chuli and Lindsay Griffin from Huiten in Mongolia being gripping stories well told.

The Panch Chuli expedition, which has a special resonance for the SMC since the 1950 attempt by Bill Murray and his companions, was a highly successful achievement in which our own member, Graham Little, put up a fine route on the highest peak of the group (see SMCJ 1993). The Panch Chuli also features in an attractive watercolour reproduced on the Journal cover, a nice change from more conventional photographic covers.

Two articles had a special personal interest for me: the tense story of a solo ascent of Dorje Lalpa by American, Carlos Buhler, which brought back memories of my ascent of this peak with Dave Broadhead and Dick Isherwood; and a note of a happy Indian girls' training trek to Sahastra Tal, near Uttarkashi, where 14 years ago Dave and I had an epic struggle through thick jungle in the Pilgun Gad. What was refreshing was the sense that these places remained little visited and 'unspoilt', although the article darkly mentions plans for a ski resort.

Harish Kapadia, the immensely well-travelled and scholarly editor of the HJ makes, as usual, notable contributions of photographs and articles, including a nice note on treks in the Kedarnath region of Garhwal. We must thank him yet again for producing an excellent journal which is a pleasure to read.

Geoff Cohen.

BERG '94.

The Alpenverein's year book, is a remarkable achievement, especially when considered as part of an annual series. It is published by the German and Austrian clubs, along with those of South Tyrol, Munich, Innsbruck and Bolzano, and many hands have contributed to a wide-ranging and beautifully-illustrated production. Accounts of expeditions and climbs, far and near, are expanded and illuminated by social comment and description of local customs and ways of life. Several articles touch on the history of mountaineering, attitudes to climbing, and there are interesting sidelights on, for instance, the mountaineering activities of the English occult writer, Aleister Crowley.

It begins close to home with three articles on the Lechtal which, appropriately for this book, runs through the Tyrol close to the German Border. The joys of climbing and walking in the area are well described and illustrated, with warning of the difficulty of some of the terrain. Environmental problems are brought to crisis point in the area, both by industry and by the pressures of modern tourism. And not only the landscape and its flora and fauna are at risk: tourism also threatens local customs and dialects. Ancestors of the modern 'Walser' made intrepid journeys in the Middle Ages over high passes from the Wallis in southern Switzerland (without the help of modern climbing aids) and efforts are now being made to preserve their traditions in the face of the creeping global village.

The greatest leap, geographically, is to Alaska, with a description of an expedition to Mt. McKinley – and how to survive it. Climbing world-wide stretches from Jamaica, with an amusing account of a day on Blue Mountain Peak, to a transasia expedition in 1992. Long straight roads there –measured 'not in kilometres, but in days') are contrasted, photographically, with the snow chaos nearer home of a lorry cavalcade on the Brenner Pass. There are further contrasts in skiing in the midnight sun in Spitzbergen, as against walking through the rain forest and other rich vegetation on the way to the heights of the Ruwenzori.

Women play a considerable role in this book: they describe climbing far and wide, in Jamaica and the Ruwenzori, as noted above, arranging expeditions in the Himalayas, or mountain biking in Corsica. Notes from the diary of a 'Bergführerin' range equally widely, remarking *en passant* on the necessity for the guide on long trips to be doctor, nurse, psychologist, tour guide, and so on. Two articles take a close look at women in climbing. One outlines in some detail the strengths and weakness of women *and* men in the mountains, and also gives a brief history of climbing from a female angle. The conclusion is that women's lesser participation in climbing is due less to physical factors than to psychological ones, themselves most probably springing from society's attitudes. This is just a taste of the 288 pages of this impressive book. Is it too much to hope that there might one day be an English translation, for sale world-wide? Or why not learn German? Useful for next Alpine tour.

Iseabail Macleod.

American Alpine Journal 1993.

The AAJ is regarded by many as the flagship of journals, both in terms of the comprehensive nature of its expedition reports, and in the literary merit of its articles. So how well does it live up to its reputation?

H. Adams Carter, the Journal's long-time editor, has over the years, established an effective network of international contacts, ensuring that activities in the greater ranges are fully reported and also avoiding a bias towards reporting only the exploits of American activists. In fact, the reports constitute almost 50% of the Journal's total content, and include some useful maps and topos.

The articles also have an international flavour, with contributions from a number of 'big names', including Bonington, Rowell and Ridgeway. They are largely well written, gripping, and describe big mountain experiences ranging from Himalayan and Patagonian epics to the esoteric delights of Venezuelan jungle-bashing.

I suspect that many people collect mountaineering journals but never actually read their contents. The contents of the AAJ are well worth dipping into, whether to enjoy some vicarious thrills, to research a forthcoming expedition, or to develop a wider awareness of world mountaineering. The AAJ has its competitors, but still hangs in there as a well-illustrated, near-definitive record of international mountaineering and as a source of inspirational mountain writing.

Graham Little.

La Revista del Club Alpino Italiano.

It is not always appreciated that there are more mountains in Italy than in the whole of the Alps. For the mountaineer seeking new pastures, the Revista has much to offer.

Being able to read Italian is not important, for this bi-annual publication is lavishly filled with photographs, sketch maps and diagrams of the routes. Of course, there are all the usual expedition accounts – CAI seems to have a lot of money to support expeditions but plenty about Italian mountains from Sicily to Monte Rosa.

Some issues carry the telephone numbers of all the Italian huts, and most of the other alpine huts, as well as the regional weather and avalanche warning numbers, which incidentally, you can phone from here for less money than it costs to find out the Scottish prospects! Good browsing for a wet Sunday, when you're are planning your next sortie.

Malcolm Slesser.

The Climbers' Club Journal 1992.

This production has many short articles recording various exploits from a variety of global locations, along with some good photographs. All in all, a worthwhile read.

D.F. Lang.

Also received: La Montagne, Appalachian Mountain Club, Deutscher Alpenverein, Journal of the Mountain Club of South Africa, Appalachia, Climbers' Club Journal.

OFFICE BEARERS 1993-94

Honorary President: W.H. Murray, O.B.E.

Honorary Vice-President: James C. Donaldson, M.B.E.

President: D.F. Lang

Vice-Presidents: Robin N. Campbell, James A. Crawford

Honorary Secretary: John R.R. Fowler, 4 Doune Terrace, Edinburgh, EH3 6DY. **Honorary Treasurer:** T.B. Fleming, West Lynn, Dalry, Ayrshire, KA24 4LJ. **Honorary Editor:** K.V. Crocket, Glenisla, Long Row, Menstrie, Clackmannanshire, FK11 7EA. **Assistant Editor:** I.H.M. Smart, Auchenleish, Bridge of Cally, by Blairgowrie, Perthshire. **Convener of the Publications Sub-Committee:** D.C. Anderson, 17 Hugh Miller Place, Edinburgh, EH3 5JG. **Honorary Librarian:** R.D.M. Chalmers, 14 Garrioch Drive, Glasgow, G20 8RS. **Honorary Archivist:** D.B. McIntyre, Luachmhor, Church Road, Kinfauns, Perth, PH2 7LD. **Honorary Custodian of Slides:** D.G. Pyper, 3 Keir Circle, Westhill, Skene, Aberdeenshire, AB32 6RE. **Convener of the Huts Sub-Committee:** G.S. Peet, 6 Roman Way, Dunblane, Perthshire. **Custodian of the CIC Hut:** R.T. Richardson, 2 Inchlonaig Drive, Balloch, Dunbartonshire. **Custodian of Lagangarbh Hut:** R.G. Ross, 16 Milton Road, Dunbartonshire. **Custodian of the Ling Hut:** D.J. Broadhead, 11 Cradlehall Park, Westhill, Inverness, IV1 2BZ. **Custodian of the Raeburn Hut:** W.H. Duncan, Kirktoun, East End, Lochwinnoch, Renfrewshire, PA12 4ER. **Committee:** B.S. Findlay; H.C. Irvine; D. Snadden; P.V. Brian; R.D. Carchrie; A. Tibbs; D.A. Bearhop; A. Jane Naismith; R.G. Ross.

Journal Information

Editor:	K.V. Crocket, Glenisla, Long Row, Menstrie, Clacks. FK11 7EA.
New Routes Editor:	A.D. Nisbet, 20 Craigie Ave., Boat of Garten, Inverness-shire PH24 3BL.
Advertisements:	Tim Pettifer, 35 Irvine Road, Largs KA30 8LS.
Distribution:	D.F. Lang, Hillfoot Hey, 580 Perth Road, Dundee DD2 1PZ.
Editor of Photographs:	Niall Ritchie, 37 Lawsondale Terrace, Westhill, Skene, Aberdeen AB32 6SE.

INSTRUCTIONS TO CONTRIBUTORS

Articles for the Journal should be submitted before the end of January for publication in the following issue. Lengthy contributions are preferably typed, double-spaced, on one side only, and with ample margins (minimum 30mm). Articles may be accepted on floppy disk, IBM compatible (contact Editor beforehand). The Editor welcomes material from both members and non-members, with priority being given to articles of Scottish mountaineering content. Photographs are also welcome, and should be good quality colour slides and sent to the Editor of Photographs, Niall Ritchie – address as above. Other material should be sent to the Editor – address as above.

Copyright. Textual matter appearing in the Miscellaneous section of the Journal, including New Climbs, is copyright of the publishers. Copyright of articles in the main section of the Journal is retained by individual authors.

MEMBERS

are asked to support the Advertisers
in the Journal and to mention the
Journal in any communications with

ADVERTISERS

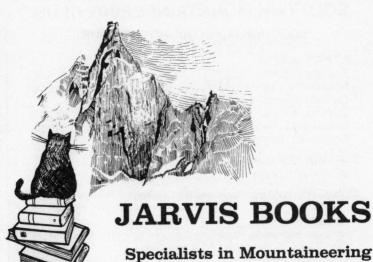

SCOTTISH MOUNTAINEERING CLUB
SCOTTISH MOUNTAINEERING TRUST

DISTRICT GUIDES
Southern Uplands	£16.95
Southern Highlands	£16.95
Central Highlands (new edition 1994)	
The Cairngorms	£17.95
Islands of Scotland (including Skye)	£18.95
North-west Highlands	£17.95

SCRAMBLERS GUIDE
Black Cuillin Ridge	£4.95

CLIMBERS GUIDES (Rock and Ice Guides)
Ben Nevis	£14.95
Northern Highlands Vol. 1	£13.95
Northern Highlands Vol. 2	£14.95
Glen Coe (including Glen Etive and Ardgour)	£13.95
The Cairngorms	£9.95
Rock and Ice Climbs in Skye	£6.95
Arran, Arrochar and Southern Highlands	£9.95

Outcrop Guides
Northeast Outcrops	£13.95
Lowland Outcrops	£14.95

OTHER PUBLICATIONS
The Munros	£14.95
Munro's Tables	£9.95
The Corbetts and Other Scottish Hills	£14.95
A Chance in a Million – Scottish Avalanches	£4.95
A Century of Scottish Mountaineering	£15.95
Ski Mountaineering in Scotland	£12.95
Ben Nevis – Britain's Highest Mountain	£14.95
Scotland's Mountains	£17.95
The Cairngorms Scene – And Unseen	£6.95
Heading for the Scottish Hills (1993 Edition)	£5.95
Scottish Hill and Mountain Names	£9.95

MAPS
Black Cuillin of Skye (double-sided)	£3.95
Glen Coe	£2.95

Distributed by:

Cordee, 3a De Montfort Street, Leicester LE1 7HD
Telephone: Leicester 543579

These books and maps are available from many bookshops and mountain equipment suppliers

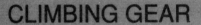